AF837408

Becoming Alive

Human beings are uniquely concerned with the question and marvel of what it means to feel alive and real, as well as the lifelong struggle of being alive together. *Becoming Alive* proffers a psychoanalytic theory of experiences of being alive, acknowledging that analyst and patient – indeed, each of us – are caught up in the larger drama and mystery of being alive.

Focusing on the challenge in any psychoanalytic theory to demonstrate the relation between culture, community, and the individual, LaMothe's theory provides a bridge between the three, arguing that organizations of experiences of being alive are inextricably yoked to cultural stories, rituals, and practices.

Enlivened by clinical illustrations and examples drawn from wider culture, *Becoming Alive* brings together psychoanalytic developmental perspectives, infant–parent research, semiotics, and philosophy to provide a comprehensive and systematic description of subjective and intersubjective experiences of being alive.

Ryan LaMothe is a Professor of Pastoral Counseling at St. Meinrad School of Theology, a Diplomate in the American Psychotherapy Association, a fellow in the American Association of Pastoral Counselors, and a member of the American Psychological Association (Divisions 36 and 39). He has published in the areas of religion and psychology, counseling, and psychoanalysis.

Becoming Alive

Psychoanalysis and vitality

Ryan LaMothe

Routledge
Taylor & Francis Group
LONDON AND NEW YORK

First published 2005 by Routledge
27 Church Road, Hove, East Sussex, BN3 2FA

Simultaneously published in the USA and Canada
by Routledge
270 Madison Avenue, New York, NY 10016

Routledge is an imprint of the Taylor & Francis Group

© 2005 Ryan LaMothe

Typeset in Times by Garfield Morgan, Rhayader, Powys
Printed and bound in Great Britain by MPG Books Ltd, Bodmin, Cornwall
Paperback cover design by Sandra Heath

All rights reserved. No part of this book may be reprinted or reproduced or utilized in any form or by any electronic, mechanical, or other means, now known or hereafter invented, including photocopying and recording, or in any information storage or retrieval system, without permission in writing from the publishers.

This publication has been produced with paper manufactured to strict environmental standards and with pulp derived from sustainable forests.

British Library Cataloguing in Publication Data
A catalogue record for this book is available from the British Library

Library of Congress Cataloging in Publication Data
LaMothe, Ryan, 1955–
Becoming alive : psychoanalysis and vitality / by Ryan LaMothe. – 1st ed.
p. cm.
Includes bibliographical references and index.
ISBN 1-58391-930-9 (hardcover : alk. paper) – ISBN 1-58391-931-7 (pbk. : alk. paper)
1. Transitional objects (Psychology) I. Title.

BF175.5.T73L36 2005
150.19'5–dc22

2004021575

ISBN 1-58391-930-9 (hbk)
ISBN 1-58391-931-7 (pbk)

Para
Cyn
mi vida,
y
Marcos
mi compadre

Contents

Preface

> For man, the vast marvel is to be alive. For man, as for flower and beast and bird, the supreme triumph is to be most vividly, most perfectly alive. Whatever the unborn may know, they cannot know the beauty, the marvel of being alive in the flesh. The dead may look after the afterwards. But the magnificent here and now of life in the flesh is ours, and ours alone, and ours only for a time.
>
> (D. H. Lawrence, 1980, p. 149)

> "Knowledge for knowledge's sake" or "art for art's sake" are claims that hide a grain of truth in a bushel of error. All human activity is for life's sake – Lengthen your cords & strengthen your stakes – life more abundant, copious, spreading out, clutching the very gate-ways to the stars.
>
> (John Macmurray, quoted in Costello, 2002, p. 94)

> Find out what makes you most alive and do that, for what the world needs more than anything else is people who are fully alive.
>
> (Howard Thurman, personal communication from Dr. Jeanne Stevenson-Moessner)

In Jeremy Leven's comedic movie, *Don Juan De Marco* (1995), Marlon Brando, as Dr. Jack Mickler, a highly skilled psychiatrist nearing retirement, desires to help a young man, Johnny Depp, who believes he is Don Juan. To Don Juan, the psychiatric hospital is Don Octavio's (Dr. Mickler's) villa. To the staff, Don Juan is simply another delusional patient, yet his passion and vitality are real. Over the course of a week, Brando listens closely to the stories Don Juan tells of his early life in Mexico, his first of many sexual adventures, his father's tragic death and avenging this death, and his exotic travels abroad. While listening, the psychiatrist is confronted with a strange fact – the putative delusional patient is more alive than the ostensibly sane staff. Don Octavio struggles between the medical system's preoccupation with diagnoses and treatment plans, which aim patients – via drugs and therapy – toward accommodation to "reality," and the very real passion of this young man and his illusions. In the end, it is the patient who helps the world-weary psychiatrist risk becoming more alive and more passionate and, ultimately, both escape the confines of the physical and ideological institution.

Before the escape, let the camera pan to this psychiatric facility and eavesdrop on an imaginery conversation between Dr. Mickler and his colleagues over lunch in the doctors' lounge.

"Listen, Jack, I know you like this kid, but he is delusional and needs to be on medication," Dr. Janet Hill remarks, as she takes a sip of her Diet Pepsi.

"Janet, you may be head of the department, but I am the one working with this kid, and right now it would be a mistake to drug him up," Jack fires back.

"Mistake?"

"Damn right. I know he has problems, but he is more alive than some of the people working around here, including me."

Dave, a young psychiatrist, stops chewing and asks, "You are saying this guy is psychotic and he's more alive than some of us? Now that sounds crazy."

"I did not say psychotic and it is not inconceivable, at least to me, to understand that someone may experience being alive and at the same time have a cherished illusion or delusion. Don't you believe in Jesus Christ – isn't that an illusion, or maybe a delusion?"

"Wait a minute. There is a huge difference between my belief and believing I am Don Juan. Your patient believes he is Don Juan and even calls you Don Octavio, for Christ's sake. I do not pretend to be Jesus Christ. More importantly, my belief in Christ is shared by many others. Regardless, to say my belief is an illusion would suggest that you actually know it is mistaken. I hardly think you would be in a position to do so."

"Okay, okay, I'm getting crotchety in my old age. Let me ask you this. Does this belief contribute to your sense of being alive?"

"Yes, but . . ."

"No, why can't his belief in being Don Juan be an expression of his experience of being alive? Or why can't his belief be connected to a self-state that represents either his desire or experience of being alive?"

"Well, for one thing, he is a patient in a psychiatric hospital," Dave responds laughingly.

"So, in some sense, are we," Jack said. "Have you noticed that the staff who have been around this kid seem lighter and more playful since he has been around? You can see them connect with this young man. Look, I am not saying he does not have some psychological struggles. I just think it is too simplistic to categorize him or to say that, because someone is neurotic or has a delusion, she or he is incapable of experiences of being alive. Hell, you and I know many so-called sane people who are pretty lifeless."

Janet sets down her fork and says, "Jack, I am not sure I even know what you mean by an experience of being alive. It seems to me that we should stick to measurable or routine diagnoses."

"Janet, you believe that our diagnoses are facts and not themselves convenient illusions? Personally, reading the DSM or case reports of patients can be quite deadening, which leaves me wondering if the reports are not examples of countertransference."

Dave sees an opening. "Let's say you are correct. How do you fit this idea of yours into the DSM-IV or your precious Freudian theories?"

"You dare mock me, you young Turk! Thank goodness crotchetiness is not the bane of old age," Jack laughs before continuing. "I concede. It would be challenging, as it would be with the cognitive-behavioral approaches you adore, but perhaps these theories point to aspects of human vitality. I guess, as I face the end of my time here, I wonder if we haven't become so focused on diagnoses, pathology, treatment plans, medication, and statistical outcomes that we overlook those moments of vitality or aliveness that our patients express. Do our theories have room for and make sense of these experiences? Do we tend to see our patients as terribly one-sided, instead of being complex, possessing and moving in and out of various self-states?"

"Ah, I hear a postmodernist sneaking into the conversation," Dave grinned.

"Jack, you aren't suggesting we get rid of all this," Janet queries.

"No, no. Theories, diagnoses, and treatment plans are important, but when I am working with this young man, I find that he does not easily fit our theories. When I remember other patients, I wonder if I have not made a Procrustean bed for them. No, theories are necessary. We all have them, but at this late stage of my life I seem to see the gaps and hear the questions."

Wiping her mouth with a napkin, Janet smiles gently at Jack, saying, "I've known you for over twenty years and, while you can be quite maddening, I have always appreciated your verve and questions. Maybe in your retirement you can take time to write your theory of aliveness."

"If I do, I won't let it get in the way of living. Now give me two more weeks to work with this kid."

While I am not yet near retirement, I am going to take up Dr. Hill's challenge. This book offers a theory about experiences of being alive and their organizations in human life. To be comprehensive, the theory and model proffered relies on and integrates psychoanalytic theories, infant–parent research, semiotics, philosophy, and recent neurological perspectives on the brain. My intent in bringing together different disciplines is to hold in dynamic tension the particularity of the mind–body, parent–child interactions in human development, and cultural rituals and stories. That is, experiences of being alive and their organizations are embodied, relational, and culturally conditioned, representing multiple layers of semiotic processes (see Bucci, 1997, 2001). As many psychoanalysts have long known, couch and culture are inextricably connected, which means that the patient and therapist's aliveness (or deadness), while shaped by the peculiarities of past family romances, are also formed by the narratives and rituals of their respective cultures.

Since I maintain that experiences of being alive link the mind–body, other, and culture in an intricate dance, I use a variety of examples from clinical settings, culture, literature, and religion to illustrate (not prove) my claims. In so doing, I hope to appeal to clinicians interested in theory and intrigued by the question of being alive, as well as teachers and scholars, in related disciplines, who are interested in psychoanalysis and culture.

The first chapter addresses the questions of vitality in psychoanalysis. I claim that the topics of passion and aliveness, while more common in some analytic circles today, have been present, albeit latently, since the early days of psychoanalysis. In this brief overview, I identify various attributes of being alive that I use in the succeeding chapters. This chapter also lays the foundation for the rest of the book, outlining fundamental claims, salient features of human development and potential space, and four modes of organizing experience. I wish to note that the title of each mode is comprised of two terms. The first signifies the most distinctive feature of the organization (e.g., corporeal, taxonomic, symbolic, and narrative) and the second points to the type of relation, which is a part of the experience (e.g., contiguous, object, subjective, communal).

The following four chapters address each of these modes of organizing experience and the dynamic characteristics of potential space as they pertain to experiences of being alive. In writing these chapters, I have tried to show both the developmental continuity and discontinuity of experiences of being alive by holding to the idea that the ingredients that make up experiences of vitality are present in each mode. Let me clarify this further. When reading different theories of development, one notes that each stage possesses particular crises, obstacles, and achievements, though these achievements (or failures) are carried forward. This is to show that there is continuity in the midst of significant cognitive and relational transformations. For example, Erikson's (1952) first stage of trust–mistrust is a developmental challenge that parent and child must handle. Yet, issues of trust and mistrust continue throughout one's life. In this way, Erikson was trying to show continuity even as new capacities, challenges, and virtues emerge. My perspective is slightly different. I argue that the necessary, interrelated ingredients for a sense of aliveness (agency, emotional regulation, continuity, cohesion, and validation) are part of each phase of development, though how we experience and understand each component is very different. For instance, I argue that agency, which is joined to a sense of freedom and spontaneity, is a necessary facet of being alive. While many people define agency in terms of I-ness, I have a broader position. The infant has a rudimentary, somatic agency, which becomes dynamically part of the later aspects of more traditional depictions of agency – subjective and intersubjective. Thus, agency, emotional regulation, continuity, cohesion, and validation have significantly different meanings given the mode of organizing experience.

The final chapter comprises some concluding thoughts on how this model of human experience alters traditional psychoanalytic views of trauma and its relation to the repetition compulsion and regression. Because a sense of deadness in human life is not simply the result of trauma, I also explore how culture plays a role in the diminution of experiences of being alive. And, I offer some thoughts on how this theory and model shape one's understanding of psychoanalytic goals and process. This final chapter marks the end of the book, but not the end of further thoughts and questions. I leave for a later work how this theory alters how we understand the unconscious – a semiotic view of the unconscious – as well as the all-important ideas of transference and countertransference.

Before proceeding, I wish to make two acknowledgments. Kristeva (1969) once commented, "Any text is the absorption and transformation of another" (p. 37). In absorbing, playing with, and making use of psychoanalysts such as Freud, Winnicott, Ogden, Lacan, Mitchell, Fonagy, and Target and philosophers such as Arendt, Heidegger, Hegel, Peirce, and Macmurray, I have, no doubt, emended them. The lively use of the insights and perspectives of others is, in my view, the highest form of flattery and respect. It is also a necessary path toward arriving at new perspectives and practices.

The transformation of texts is not unlike what occurs, we hope, when patient and therapist, at times playfully and at times gravely, grapple with each other's stories and experiences in the hope of being more alive together. The story of therapy usually begins when a patient seeks help and the person's suffering and the ways that he has devised to survive confront the therapist. The most common impulse is for therapists to develop or use theories that help account for the patient's neurosis or pathology, much like Dr. Mickler's colleagues when discussing his delusional patient. What is wrong, what has gone wrong in this person's life? How has he managed and been helped to become so miserable? Of course, Don Juan's misery is not divorced from his aliveness and passion. Over the years, listening to patients and colleagues alike, I have become more interested in how we become alive, how we create ways to experience being alive together, and, naturally, how we find ways to avoid being alive together. So, my second admission is that I have been privileged to work with and learn from people who bravely survive incredibly difficult and painful experiences and, yet, who have the courage to give voice to their longing to be alive. Like Dr. Mickler, patients teach me not simply about the tremendous resiliency of human beings, but the mystery of the human longing to experience being alive with others. This book, then, proffers a psychoanalytic theory of experiences of being alive, acknowledging that analyst and patient, indeed, each of us, are caught up in the larger drama and mystery of being alive.

Acknowledgments

To write a book requires a community of people who sustain the author's vitality, especially during periods when the computer's blinking cursor incessantly and loudly taunts one to write. I have been fortunate to have people who have directly or indirectly sustained me over the months. I am very grateful for Joanne Forshaw, editor at Routledge. Without her initial interest in this book and her encouragement, I would not be writing this acknowledgment. A special thank you to the late Dr. Paul Adams. Paul was a brilliant, iconoclastic, and creative child psychiatrist and analyst who, over the decades, contributed to the education of many. As mentor and colleague, he read and critiqued the first four chapters. Sadly, another mentor, Dr. Liston Mills, died while I was writing this book. Liston, over the years, was interested in and encouraged this and other writing projects. I also wish to thank Dr. Tom Robbins, Dr. Randall Sorenson, Mary Jeanne Schumacher, and Cindy Geisen for their willingness to read, edit, and discuss drafts. Mary Jeanne went above and beyond the call of duty. I am grateful for Carol Heeke's secretarial help. Thanks to Dr. Tom Walters and Dr. Clayton Jefford for their editorial suggestions and counsel, and Dr. James Hyde, whose interest, questions, support, and insatiable curiosity have been a needed pleasure and boost. I have also appreciated my colleagues at the Louisville Psychoanalytic Society and the Kentucky Psychoanalytic Institute – may we remember that psychoanalysis is a tool that can either be wielded for the sake of healing and life or division and exclusion. Finally, thanks to Cyn and Marcos, for whom this book is dedicated.

Chapter 1

Vitality in human life and psychoanalysis

> People say that what we're all seeking is the meaning for life. I don't think that's what we're really seeking. I think that what we're seeking is an experience of being alive, so that our life experiences on the purely physical plane will have resonances within our inner most being and reality, so that we actually feel the rapture of being alive.
>
> (Joseph Campbell, 1991, p. 3)

> Oh God! May I be alive when I die.
>
> (Winnicott, quoted in Kahr, 1996, p. 125)

Pause and recall a moment when you felt the simple, though intricate, pleasure, awe, and wonder of being alive. An early morning sun, burning off the mountain's sweaty haze, may have seized your attention and offered a fleeting instance of rapture. A silently shared sense of gratitude and affection that passes between lovers as one of them faces death may be an occasion for being alive in the midst of suffering and loss. Being swept up in raucous laughter or intense play can create a sense of vitality. A bar mitzvah, baptism, wedding, communal prayer, a conference or gathering, a graduation are all possible moments for personal and communal experiences of being alive. And, of course, there are those who carry a preconscious, background presence of being alive and real, which may come to mind quietly and sporadically.

When we listen to ourselves and remember experiences of being alive, we recognize that these experiences are not necessarily confined to peak moments. They exist on a continuum of intensity, from the seemingly mundane to moments of ecstasy, and they are limited only by our imagination and our willingness to risk. In our ruminations, we might also realize that being alive appears to coexist with suffering and loss. Indeed, the poignant joy one experiences watching the surf swallow the evening sun takes place against the background of loss, revealing the non-static nature of experience, in general, and experiences of being alive, in particular.

Diane Ackerman (1999), after marveling at the sight of the Hale-Bopp comet, said, "When I realize that I won't be around for the comet's next passage, so many sadnesses fill my heart, fill it with grief both ontological and particular" (p. 209). On a different, though similar tack, Andrew Solomon (2001) wrote, "I can see the beauty of glass objects fully at the moment when they slip from my hand toward the floor" (p. 24). It appears, then, that suffering and loss are somehow inextricably bound to the possibility of one's experience of being alive. Solomon understood this as well when he said, "Through chemical manipulation, we might locate, control, and eliminate the brain's circuitry of suffering. I hope we will never do it. To take it away would be to flatten out experience" (p. 38). And yet, as Solomon well knew, experiences of being alive are diminished or annihilated by agony, misery, and trauma. When this occurs, we are reduced to mere survival, at which point memories of once being alive only seem to increase our despair. Winnicott's brief prayer in the epigraph to this chapter portrays an old man's hope that the vicissitudes of dying do not extinguish the possibility of his being alive. We know, of course, that aliveness is not always contingent on whether natural events overwhelm our capacity to be alive. Human beings are paradoxically capable of generating vitality and also annihilating it.

Surely, as a species, we fall under the classification *homo paradoxum* and our essential contradictoriness is bound up with the fact that we are also questioning animals (*homo quaere*). What does it mean to be alive? What are the attributes of experiences of being alive and real? What contributes to or diminishes these experiences? How do we become alive and real and how do we maintain an ethos that fosters these experiences? These are existential questions that implicitly concern every human being. Are they not embedded in philosophical musings from Plato to Derrida and are they not found in the teachings of such diverse religious teachers as Buddha and Jesus? Indeed, social, religious, economic rituals and philosophical ruminations stand for human attempts to create and express subjective and intersubjective experiences of being alive.

Queries about being alive and their innumerable replies do not fall solely within the province of philosophy and religion. In 1902, prominent American psychologist William James, who struggled with depression, made sure to include Professor Leuba's remark, "Not God, but life, more life, a larger, richer, more satisfying life is, in the last analysis, the end of religion. The love of life, at any and every level of development, is the religious impulse" (James, 1958, p. 382). In a similar vein, Erich Fromm (1966, p. 132) noted that the Christian notion of sin represents a sense of deadness and the active destruction of being alive. Whether we believe it is a religious or philosophical impulse, the desire for human vitality in all its guises may be studied and understood from psychological and, more specifically, psychoanalytic frameworks. To be sure, as long as psychoanalysis does not divorce itself from the incredibly diverse social, cultural, and religious discourses about being alive, it can continue to offer its own unique contributions to understanding what it means to be alive and how human beings tragically impede and destroy a sense of vitality. This is the aim of this book.

Psychoanalysts, like philosophers, construct theories, which are usually connected to deeply personal interests and questions (Scharfstein, 1980). Professional interests are usually personal. My fascination, dread, and delight about what it means to become and experience being alive and real began when I was in my twenties. Like many young people, I blithely sought to adhere to the stated and unstated directives and interests of my parents and other elders, which purchased me a sense of safety and acceptance. Compliance screened a low-grade depression, an agitating sense of emptiness, and a pseudo sense of being good-enough. Slowly, a modicum of self-awareness lifted the veil to my own desires and passions, though it was as if seeing through a glass darkly. Guided by this foggy recognition, I made the decision to leave the Army and pursue graduate studies in a subject that intrigued me. In retrospect, this decision was distinctly different from previous ones. I did not feel as if I was choosing between equally viable pathways. Rather, there were two paths, yet at some level I realized that there was no choice. To fail to act would have meant choosing to survive in the safety of the familiar. I felt a sense of deadness when I imagined traveling that road. The other path, however, was filled with uncertainty, anxiety, and risk. I could fail. What if I was wrong? What if my desire to leave the Army and attend graduate school was a mistake? How many of my earlier decisions had been made to please others and how do I know if I am not indeed doing that same thing? Even with these questions and anxiety, I noticed a sense of energy and vitality on this path. This was the first of many stumbling steps toward deeper experiences of being alive, which were supported by friends, mentors, colleagues, therapists, family, and a fiercely loyal and loving wife.

This growing awareness and curiosity gradually expanded to include professional questions and interests. I became enamored with psychoanalysis or that part of psychoanalysis that provided tools to explore the limitless complexity and plasticity of human communication and experience. A psychoanalytic ethos provided me with the framework and concepts to struggle with and draw conclusions about a dominant question that both intrigues and hounds me. In this chapter and those that follow, I offer a psychoanalytic perspective to the questions and problems that captivate me: how do we become alive and real and "to what extent can we survive, enjoy, tolerate, and use each other's aliveness?" (Eigen, 1996, p. xxiii). Or how much variation of aliveness can we accept?

Focal questions such as these typically serve to reframe psychoanalytic issues, concepts, and concerns and, at the same time, give rise to their own set of related questions. For instance, how are experiences of being alive organized in relation to one's own body, to objects, and to other subjects? How, in other words, are experiences of being alive organized and represented during different phases of development and how are earlier phases related to subsequent ones? What role do cultural and religious rituals and narratives play in facilitating, shaping, and obstructing experiences of being alive? How are these rituals themselves signifiers and organizers of subjective and intersubjective experiences of being alive? How do analyst and patient alike construct and thwart experiences of being alive as well as repair moments of disruption? What does the analyst listen for in the session given this perspective? Put another way, how does the idea of being alive shape the analyst's understanding of the process and goals of the psychoanalytic ritual? And how does this idea alter our view of defenses and psychopathology?

It is important to acknowledge that, just as experiences of being alive are partial, perspectival, variable, and mediated by a particular tradition and time, so too are the theories, knowledge, and psychoanalytic versions of reality that claim to view and explain these experiences (cf. Marcus and Rosenberg, 1998). Since this work is also historically and contextually limited, there are two initial tasks to complete. First, it is necessary to position this book within the diachronic discourse in psychoanalysis on human motivation and cure. Both motivation and cure, regardless of how they are conceptualized, point to socially constructed values, beliefs, and rituals that implicitly answer questions about what it means to be alive.

It becomes readily apparent, then, that while I place the idea and question of vitality in the foreground, interest in persons' experiences of being alive and its corollary, deadness, has been present, in various forms and degrees, within psychoanalysis from the beginning. Thus, I use the question and problem of being alive as a lens to interpret other psychoanalytic perspectives. Of course, this should not be understood to be a comprehensive representation of other theories. Rather, it is more of an eisegetical exercise that relies on the metaphor of vitality and the problem and question of being alive to frame interpretations of analytic versions of human experience. This brief and incomplete survey also provides a way to identify differences and similarities between this book and previous analytic views. A final task of this chapter is to identify and amend the specific psychoanalytic perspectives I rely upon in answering the questions above.

Vitality in psychoanalysis: motivations and cure

Despite the variety of models and definitions of psychoanalysis,[1] a common thread has run through it since its inception. Psychoanalysis began as, and continues to be, a study of human suffering. Psychoanalytic versions of the human condition typically start by addressing what goes awry in human life. Neurosis and psychopathology became modern categories that represented the price people paid to survive overwhelming events or deal with troubling fantasies. Attempts to understand and explain neurosis and its origins also addressed fundamental human needs and motivations and, at the same time, required analysts to consider techniques and processes to effect a cure. That is, trying to understand and explain suffering invariably led to efforts to articulate the motivations for and attributes of a good life. Thus, psychoanalysis is a science of the origins and experience of human suffering as well as a science of health, wholeness, authenticity, and vitality, and each is entwined with culture and religion. For instance, even though Freud and other psychoanalytic theorists attempted to explain how motivations become twisted intrapsychically and interpersonally, ending in neurotic suffering, their work can be reframed in terms of how one comes to experience being alive and how these experiences of being alive are fostered or inhibited by cultural activities. So, I begin with Freud.

Freud, motivation, and vitality

Freud, like other keen observers of human nature, made numerous additions and revisions to his theories. And yet a constant theme throughout his writings is the idea that human life is one of conflict and tragic compromise. Human beings are poised between pleasure and unpleasure, wishes and reality, Eros and Thanatos, love and work, and nature and civilization. In his early works, Freud addressed the quantitative aspects of pleasure. Years later Freud shifted to the qualitative characteristics of pleasure and experience (1924a, p. 160), believing that a person is fundamentally motivated to seek pleasure and avoid pain while adapting to the dictates of reality. If the demands of reality and civilization required one to renounce pleasure, then a wish represented the motivation for the pleasure that was repressed or sublimated.

An Aristotelian continuum exists whereby too much repression by society leads to reduced pleasure and freedom, while too much narcissistic involvement in seeking to satisfy one's wishes and fantasies leads to an inability to live in a civilized community. To obtain the security of living in society, Freud claimed, a person had to renounce some pleasure and freedom – some measure of aliveness. Later, Freud conceived of the ego as an arbiter between instinctual demands – the unformulated desires of the id – and the super-ego, representing the negotiations of the Oedipal complex and related demands of civilization. The ego's successful acceptance of the reality principle and sublimation of id impulses results in a person experiencing a degree of freedom and pleasure.

The importance of freedom and pleasure in human life was also manifested in Freud's theories of symptom formation, which not only explained how human development and motivations were derailed, but also pointed to what was needed to effect a cure. Initially Freud, along with Breuer, argued that neurotic symptoms and, in particular, hysteria were the result of a traumatic experience (Breuer and Freud, 1895). Symptoms were signifiers of unspoken suffering, the inhibition of freedom, an anxiety-driven distortion of the motivation to seek pleasure, and a concomitant reduction and distortion of pleasure. While he never entirely gave up this idea of trauma, Freud went on to suggest that neurosis results from disturbing, anxiety-laden fantasies that are repressed, though latently present in the manifest symptom. The analyst's task was to facilitate the movement from unconsciousness to consciousness, from primary to secondary process, from id to ego, from symptom to speech. The analytic method offered the hope of freedom from the bondage of one's symptoms.

I hasten to add that Freud was less than sanguine about the goals of therapy, which signified his ambivalence about freedom and joy in human life. He wrote, "Much will be gained if we succeed in transforming your hysterical misery into common unhappiness. With a mental life that has been restored to health you will be better armed against unhappiness" (1895, p. 305). The cure – achieving happiness or common unhappiness, whether through analysis or some other strategy – was not, however, simply a matter of a correct interpretation or movement from symptoms to speech. Psychoanalysis, Freud also wrote in a letter to Jung, is a cure through love (McGuire, 1974, pp. 12–13). And years later he said, "in the last resort we must begin to love in order not to fall ill" (Freud, 1914, p. 85). It could thus be posited that the development of neurotic symptoms resulted from a lack of love and the analytic ritual of transforming silent symptoms to speech was a labor of love. We love people into freedom and pleasure, into being alive.[2]

Pleasure and freedom represented in Freud's conflict model and his depictions of the formation of symptoms were connected to his views regarding nature and civilization. According to Freud, pleasure and freedom are constrained by the limits imposed by reality and the necessity of human survival. Nature demands a death, though civilization keeps this juggernaut at bay, for a time, and provides members enough safety and security to experience a degree of pleasure and freedom. It seems that the instinct to survive, which is manifested in the formation of symptoms, has precedence over the motivation for pleasure and freedom. This explains why a person sacrifices *some* measure of pleasure and freedom when accommodating to harsh reality and the limits of civilization. Symptoms likewise represent the sacrifice of happiness and freedom for the sake of survival. Of course, survival is also a matter of perception and fantasy, all of which could be distorted by an individual's anxiety and guilt. Creating societal taboos and rituals, for example, is meant to organize communal behavior for the sake of group survival (Freud, 1950), though Freud believed that much of this creation is fraught with illusion. Sometimes the precedence of real or imagined survival results in attenuating and distorting (e.g., perversions) pleasure and freedom, which reflects a reduction in one's experience of being alive.

Religion, for Freud, represented a clear obstacle to genuine experiences of being alive, though it offered people tools for psychological survival, not unlike the formation of neurotic symptoms (Freud, 1907). Despite Freud's unconscious motivations for his attacks on religion (Rizzuto, 1998; LaMothe, 2004), he viewed religion as a refuge for those feebler creatures who could not endure the harshness of reality. Religious folk were satisfied to renounce pleasure and freedom for the safety of illusions: they refused to risk the adult pleasure and freedom that depends on having the courage to face human life's exigencies. Put differently, religious people sacrificed freedom and pleasure to obtain an omnipotent sense of security and avoid confronting the ruthless and impersonal forces of nature. Religion was mired in and focused on survival – it kept people in bondage in the dark depths of a Platonic cave.

Mere survival, however, was not Freud's (1927b, 1930) hope for humanity. Paradoxically, one could both survive – by renouncing some pleasure and freedom – and at the same time risk sublimating and expressing one's desires. The person who stood the chance of healthy pleasure and freedom was someone who rationally and bravely faced the anxiety and hardships of reality as well as his/her own fantasies and needs. And though Freud did not stress love and tenderness in attaining freedom, there are instances when he seemed to consider realistic love to be a crucial factor for human health. Freud's hope for humanity was embodied in science and the psychoanalytic ritual. Psychoanalysis became a ritual wherein the analyst heroically entered the cavern of the patient's unconscious for the sake of freeing him/her from the bondage of symptoms, anxieties, and from the excessive constraints and superstitious taboos of religion and civilization. The patient, thus freed, would travel to the surface where s/he was no longer captivated by the illusions flickering on the walls of the cave, but instead saw clearly real objects illuminated by the sun. Here on the surface of the world, though less safe than the cave, the patient's sense of pleasure and freedom was more real and lively, though this liveliness was tied to the limits of human relationships and death (cf. Eigen, 1995; Hoffman, 1998).

Freud would have understood Diane Ackerman's (1999) depictions of deep play or a person's intense pleasure and sense of peace while watching a sunset as experiences that, while ephemeral, resulted from the successful navigation of earlier developmental phases. The relative absence of emotional conflicts creates a space for a person to feel free enough to experience these simple joys. And yet, Freud did not make much allowance for illusion, tenderness, surrender, and mystery (not knowing – cf. Lear, 1998), all of which are indispensable for play and the aliveness one feels when the last rays of light are extinguished by the veil of darkness. In the final analysis, I wonder if Freud's creative renderings of human existence and his labor in creating a community of disciples were ways to articulate and experience being alive with others.

From England to America: variations on motivation and cure

Whereas Freud emphasized the idea of human motivation dominated by the pleasure–unpleasure principle, early critics like Adler, Jung, and Reich challenged Freud's views by offering other motivational perspectives. Given the numerous psychoanalysts who have made their own contributions, I wish to narrow the field and concentrate on theoretical shifts that took place in England and later in the United States, which altered and extended the meanings and characteristics of being alive. For instance, Ronald Fairbairn, while continuing to use and value Freudian concepts, rejected Freud's theory regarding the death instinct and his conflict model of psychopathology. Instead, Fairbairn "focused his disagreement with the drive theory on two basic principles: libido is not pleasure-seeking but object-seeking; and impulse is inseparable from structure" (Mitchell and Greenberg, 1983, p. 154).

According to Fairbairn, aggression was not endogenous, as Freud believed, but a reaction to deprivation (Kernberg, 2000). Fairbairn argued (Mitchell, 2000b) that the infant's motivation for gaining the object is based in his/her need to be "treated as a person in his [the infant's] own right" (Grotstein and Rinsley, 2000, p. 10). And when this did not occur, one would expect to see aggression, splitting, and de-emotionalization (Kernberg, 2000, p. 47). Thus the experience of pleasure was a derivative of a type of relationship wherein the child experiences a sense of importance and worth. Guntrip (1969), one of Fairbairn's disciples, remarked,

> Meaningful relationships are those which enable the infant to find himself as a person though experiencing his own significance for other people and their significance for him, thus endowing his existence with those values of human relationship which make life purposeful and worth living.
>
> (Guntrip, 1969, p. 243)

The unfortunate child who does not have this kind of relationship may survive, but s/he suffers, not from an intrapsychic conflict based in fantasy, but from a real and fundamental deficit (Grotstein, 2000). Both Fairbairn and Guntrip emphasized the importance of meaningful activity and experiences of being valued, which are motivations and aspects of a person's feeling alive.

South of Edinburgh, a contemporary of Fairbairn was also altering Freud's ideas about human development. Donald Winnicott (1971, 1989), like Fairbairn, emphasized the necessity of good-enough parenting for psychological health. The environmental mother, non-intrusive holding, parental containment of the infant's aggression, and mirroring are all ways of demonstrating the importance of a parent's responses to the infant's assertions. If all goes well between parent and infant, the infant would initially obtain a belief in and experience of his/her own omnipotence (Winnicott, 1956), which is necessary for his or her ability to organize experience and to obtain a sense of efficacy or agency. Eventually, the infant will be disillusioned, gradually and non-traumatically, with regard to his/her omnipotence as the mother moves from maternal preoccupation with her child to other concerns. The baby's transition from absolute dependence and merger to relative dependence and object use coincides with the parent's recognition and acceptance of the baby's emerging capacities and his/her libidinal and aggressive expressions.

Winnicott (1971) recognized that the child's internal sense of aliveness depended "on the existence, aliveness and behavior of the external object" (p. 9). The result of all of this is the formation and consolidation of a true self, capable of spontaneity and playfulness in relation to other people. A child who possesses a true self would be able to use and contain aggression and love in the service of creating meaning. The true self represents vitality, which is an interpersonal achievement. Parental failures – impingement and deprivation – lead inevitably to the construction of a false self – overly compliant (Winnicott, 1989, p. 43), delinquent, or excessively isolated (Winnicott, 1990, 1971). Put differently, cumulative parental misattunement leads to "a failure to represent and display actual emotional experience adequately [and] also to the construction of an experience of self around this false internalization" (Fonagy, Gergely, Jurist, and Target, 2002, pp. 43–44).

A false self is not necessarily pathological or neurotic. However, it represents a person's attempt to survive in the face of the real loss of a mirroring object and his/her attempt to retain, in fantasy, the desired object. Human beings are fundamentally social creatures and the false self stands for the sacrifice of spontaneity, freedom, creativity, and pleasure for the sake of surviving in relationships marred by distrust and painful disillusionment. A sense of unreality and deadness surrounds false self-organizations. In sum, psychoanalysis concerns itself with "why it is that creative living can be lost and why the individual's feeling that life is real or meaningful can disappear" (Winnicott, 1971, p. 69).

Freud was antagonistic toward religion, viewing it as a distortion of reality that accompanied a consequent reduction of human freedom and pleasure. Winnicott (1971), however, viewed religion, art, and science as cultural activities that can contribute to spontaneity and freedom of creative living. Illusion is necessary, not for the sake of survival but for the sake of playing in cultural space. The question shifted from explaining the neurotic origins of religion to understanding how religion (and other cultural objects and activities) contributed to or inhibited creativity, imagination, and subjective and socially shared experiences of being alive.

Another contemporary of Winnicott and Fairbairn, Melanie Klein (1949a, 1949b), who made her way to England from Nazi Germany, also added to the shift by addressing the importance of the mother–infant relationship with regard to human emotional development. Unlike Fairbairn, Klein accepted Freud's drive theory, though she believed that the drives "are inherently and inseparably directed toward objects" (Greenberg and Mitchell, 1983, p. 136). Like Fairbairn, Klein argued that the infant is motivated to seek the object and it is the object (or parent) that is the linchpin for emotional development (Klein, 1952). She noted that "it appears in retrospect that when emotions were lacking, relations were vague and uncertain and parts of the personality were felt to be lost, everything seemed to be dead" (1946, p. 108). The parental object was not sought merely for gratification of the instincts, but was needed for experiences of love, gratitude, and a sense of being cared for, all of which contributes to a sense of aliveness (Klein, 1964). With this said, Klein tended to focus on what was taking place within the infant's mind (fantasies) and less on the parent's "real" responses to the infant. For example, Klein recognized that there are times when "external circumstances" (e.g., a depriving mother) "increase greed and persecutory anxiety" in the child (Klein, 1957, p. 11), exacerbating the child's envious impulse. Greed and persecutory anxiety are endogenous and are increased when there is deprivation or decreased when there is parental love. The challenge and hope of human development is not the eradication of greed and envious impulses. Rather, it is the cultivation of enough love, gratitude, and ego-strength to keep destructive impulses at bay.

While there are important theoretical differences among Fairbairn, Winnicott, and Klein, their emphasis on the importance of infant–parent relationship for the emotional development of both infant and parent, and a stable sense of self represented significant alterations of Freud's views on motivation and cure and, naturally, the meaning of being alive. The child needs to experience him/herself as significant in the eyes of the parent, needs to possess a sense of efficacy, and requires the care and interest of the parent to experience being loved and validated as a subject in his/her own right. Each of these is integral to developing a true and vital self. Parental failures do not destroy the child's motivation to seek satisfying objects, but impingement and deprivation, which are relational deficits, contribute to an intrapsychic deficit, false self, or the schizoid position. Cure is not viewed as mere adaptation to reality, because adaptation may be a sign of a compliant sacrifice of one's authentic desires and experiences. Nor is health viewed as the mere absence of neurosis. As Winnicott (1971) stated, "It is of first importance for us to acknowledge openly that the absence of psychoneurotic illness may be health, but it is not life" (p. 100).[3]

This was an important shift in that object relation theorists were realizing, along with socialist theorists (e.g., Fromm, 1941), that large social, economic, and political systems often demanded conformity, resulting in the loss of personal significance, spontaneity, and pleasure, leaving persons with a sense of depersonalization, unreality, and deadness. A person may be highly functional in the social realm, but not experience him/herself as being fully alive. Cure, then, is best understood in terms of *self and relationships* characterized by freedom, spontaneity, pleasure, zest, imagination, significance, efficacy, and a sense of continuity. Analysis was both a ritual and a relationship that fostered potential space whereby patient and analyst work to repair the deficit and make way for the emergence of a true and vital self (Winnicott, 1989, p. 75).[4]

The shifts taking place during the mid-twentieth century in psychoanalysis and in other fields were dramatic. Winnicott and others advertently and inadvertently challenged the hegemony of Western preoccupation with reason or rationality in relation to "reality," character, mental health, and by implication, vitality. Traditional views of sanity and madness were deconstructed or turned on their heads, which was a step toward the growing acceptance of the paradoxical nature of human living. For instance, Winnicott (1945, p. 140) remarked, "We are indeed poor if we are only sane." Winnicott also valued psychoanalysis for its role in his achieving some level of insanity. "I was sane and through analysis and self-analysis I achieved some measure of insanity" (1964, p. 450). Too much rationality makes life insipid and, in some cases, leads to violent madness that is socially sanctioned (Laing, 1959). Whether in the hallowed halls of government or in the analyst's office, too much reason is a form of madness, which conceals emptiness, despair, and fear and is accompanied by the loss of individual and social experience of life as real and meaningful.

These changes also radically altered Freud's view of pleasure and freedom in human life. Illusion, imagination, fantasy, and some level of chaos were increasingly recognized as necessary ingredients in a person's sense of being alive and real. To possess some measure of freedom and pleasure, one must be a little crazy, at least with regard to previous renderings of that term. Understanding Ackerman's (1999) deep play or a couple's enjoyment of a setting sun entails the paradoxical nature of human experience – sanity in madness and madness in sanity, illusion in reality and reality in illusion, freedom and spontaneity in the face of ineluctable attributes of human life.

Across the pond: American variations on motivation and cure

More recently, and on the other side of the pond, numerous relational theorists have increasingly relied on the metaphors of deadness and aliveness when addressing various aspects of child development and issues regarding transference and countertransference dynamics in analytic sessions.[5]

Thomas Ogden, a Kleinian of sorts, believed that "Coming alive as a human being involves the act of being held by and within the matrix of the physical and psychological aliveness of the mother" (1994, pp. 176–177). This echoes Winnicott's work as well as Edith Balint's assertion that "the first imaginative perception can only arise out of a state of eager aliveness in two people, the infant with the potential for life and the mother alive inside herself and tuning into the emerging infant" (1993, p. 102; see also Green, 1999). This "quality of experience," Daniel Stern posited, "arise[s] directly from encounters with people, a quality that involves vitality affects" (1985, p. 55). These are not categorical affects, but kinetic qualities such as surging, fading away, fleeting, and bursting. They operate inconspicuously within the background of one's experiences throughout life. Furthermore, Stern argued that vitality affects are not simply endogenous. Rather, the "infant experiences these qualities from within as well as in the behaviors of the other person" (p. 55).

From a different theoretical position, Fosshage used "the term, relational selfobject experience, to refer to vitalizing attachment experiences" (1998, p. 122n). In other words, it is the mutual "vigorous engagement of creative activity [that] can evoke integration and vitalizing self-experience" (Bacal, 1998b, p. 149). Stolorow, Brandchaft, and Atwood (1987) likewise argued that one of the struggles in human life was between preserving a vitalizing connection to oneself and an emotional bond to one's parents. Chodorow (1999), affirming the connection between emotional life and vitality, moved toward a description of "an alive I" (p. 271). Each of these writers recognized that an infant's preverbal experience of being alive depends to a large degree on the expressive, non-intrusive vitality of his/her parent.

These early, preverbal vitalizing attachment experiences and vitality affects eventually become yoked to language, to the word. Loewald (1978) wrote that the "emotional relationship to the person from whom the word is learned plays a significant, in fact, crucial part in how *alive* the link between thing and words turns out to be" (p. 197; emphasis mine). Language, which for Loewald comprises primary and secondary processes, is more than simply a conveyor of meaning. Language is also used "to evoke states of mind, to generate and link domains of experience" (Mitchell, 2000a, p. 15). The analyst and patient's journey, for instance, involves "transforming a mode of survival into a living experience" (Green, 1972, p. 212). When it comes to language and communication, in general, I would like to think that Ogden's (2001) poetic rendition of the task of an analytic writer refers also to the routine interactions between parent and child, between analyst and patient, and between friends. Earlier, he said that the "work of the analytic writer, like the writer of poetry or fiction, begins and ends with his effort to create in language the experience of human aliveness" (Ogden, 1997, p. 6). Hence, verbal and non-verbal communications carry, educe, and reveal subjective and intersubjective experiences of being alive.

Analytic authors who focus on the emergence of experiences of being alive in human development also understandably consider those experiences that arise as a result of relational failures or failures of personalization (Khan, 1963, p. 185). For instance, Goldberg (1995) noted that lifelessness, deadness, and meaninglessness are related to successful dissociation wherein the mind is "abstracted from the body and the instincts are starved of sources of aliveness" (p. 496). The consequences of defensive dissociation, Goldberg argued, is a pseudointegration that is linked to pseudovitality or lack of an authentic sense of self. Similarly, Strenger (1998) said there is a desire of self-creation that arises when the parent acknowledges the child's assertions, which leads to the child's sense of authorship and vitality. When this desire is not expressed or recognized, the "result is a sense of not being alive" (p. 627). From Safran and Muran's (2000) perspective, over accommodation to "objective reality" and therapeutic impasses reflect a loss of a sense of aliveness and realness. Ongoing impasses in early life represent significant and unmended disappointment and disillusionment, which may move the child to depend on and use his/her mind as an object (Corrigan and Gordon, 1995). This defensive retreat is a strategy for psychological survival, though the cost is a sense of deadness, depersonalization, and an air of unreality. Indeed, all forms of psychopathology "represent a specific limitation of the individual's capacity to be fully alive as a human being" (Ogden, 1997, p. 26).

The metaphors associated with vitality refer primarily to a person's experience and indirectly to his/her motivations. For example, Lichtenberg, Lachmann, and Fosshage (1992) put forward the idea that five motivational systems are present throughout the life span: the need for physiological and emotional regulation; the need for attachment and affiliation; exploratory and assertive needs; the need to react aversively; and the need for sensual and sexual pleasure. The experience of vitality develops when there are

> appropriate responses to the need for sleep, nutrient, elimination, and exercise, by involvement in and successful accomplishment of exploration and assertion in play and work, by aversive responses removing obstacles or assuring safety, and by sensual soothing and sexual orgastic excitement.
>
> (Lichtenberg et al., 1992, p. 138)

The child, then, is not *motivated* to experience being alive, yet these motivational systems are inextricably joined to vitalizing experience. The experience, one could say, is discovered in interactions in which motivations are expressed and realized. Thus, the desires for self-creation, authorship, mastery, etc. are aspects of the phenomenology of being alive. This may explain why vitality must be pursued obliquely.

Use of the metaphor aliveness or vitality, along with other philosophical changes (Aron, 1996), has shaped notions of analytic process and cure.

Ogden became increasingly aware that "the sense of aliveness and deadness of the transference-countertransference is, for me, perhaps the single most important measure of the moment-to-moment status of the analytic process" (Ogden, 1997, p. 23; see also Ogden, 1999). The analytic process and goal, Mitchell (1993) argued, "is not a rational re-working of unconscious infantile fantasies: what the patient needs is a revitalization and expansion of his own capacity to generate experience that feels real, meaningful, and valuable" (p. 24). This means, for Mitchell, "not a renunciation of infantile experience but a reconciliation of different organizations of experience throughout the life-cycle" (p. 35). Because of the emphasis on infant–parent interactions, a number of analysts (e.g., Mitchell, 1988; Bromberg, 1998; Hoffman, 1998) believe that the patient and analyst co-construct experiences that feel real. Momentary experiences of being fully alive and real are created and destroyed in each session.

This is a far cry from Freud's more tragic vision of a powerful analyst-healer transforming hysterical misery into common unhappiness. Relational analysts are a bit more ambitious and may be viewed as realistic Romantics (Schafer, 1976). Healing neuroses or other psychic wounds is only part of the task for both patient and analyst. Eigen (1996), for instance, mentioned an analyst who sought his help. Eigen eventually realized that this analyst "had used psychoanalysis to close wounds, not to open his heart" (1996, p. 111). To heal is necessary for survival, yet one can survive and not feel alive. It is my contention that Eigen and other relational analysts consider the telos of psychoanalysis to be healing accompanied by opening one's heart to experiences of *being alive with others*. In the analytic adventure, both analyst and patient are engaged in a more dangerous and riskier task of creating and letting go of experiences of being alive.

In summary, early analysts did not mention patients' experiences of being alive, though the metaphor certainly began to make its way into analytic discourse during the 1960s. Since then, it has become more directly linked to conceptualizations of human motivation and analytic cure. Freedom, spontaneity, self-creation, authenticity, agency, subjective desires, and other human attributes such as emotional regulation, continuity, cohesion, and validation have become part of the web of vitality. While the metaphors associated with vitality have been implicitly or explicitly present in many renderings of psychoanalytic thought regarding suffering and healing, *the question and problem of being alive has not been in the foreground of analytic theorizing about human development.*

An outline of human development: models and attributes

The ephemeral sense of aliveness (or deadness) one derives from playing, sharing a meal with a friend, or reading a sonnet is deeply complex, calling into play intricate, mutually interacting webs of physiological, cognitive-emotional, memorial, and social processes. This complexity is daunting and I, for one, do not wish to assert that my attempt to describe these processes, in answering the developmental problem and question of becoming and being alive, is definitive or that it approximates the very experience of being alive. My answer to the question about being alive is, to be sure, a theory and I think of theories as maps that give people directions and topographical depictions of geographical locations. We would be a bit mad if we were to mistake the map for the rich experiences of taking the journey and arriving at the destination. The following chapters serve as a linguistic map that charts the experiences of being alive in human development. Most maps have legends – explanations of the symbols on a map – and below I briefly identify the developmental model used and salient features present in each phase of development as depicted in the following chapters.

Developmental models

Psychological theories of development have often been depicted as linear, sequential, and hierarchical. Many psychoanalytic developmental perspectives have relied on a linear-hierarchical model, wherein each stage of development is self-enclosed, which comes "to its ascendance, meets its crisis, and finds its lasting solution during the stage indicated" (Erikson, 1952, p. 271).[6] Early stages are viewed as foundational, or primary and primitive, and later stages as mature. One of the problems with this model is that "each phase becomes a sensitive, almost critical period for the development of a single phase-specific clinical issue or personality feature" (Stern, 1985, p. 20). As Daniel Stern points out, there is no evidence that psychological trauma during a specific phase results in "predictably specific types of clinical problems" (1985, p. 23). In a similar vein, Fonagy et al. (2002, pp. 61–62) argued that it is overly simplistic and reductionistic to view adult pathology in terms of deficit, regression, or developmental delay. Another difficulty is that therapists make assumptions about their own "stage" of development, which, not surprisingly, is "higher" than their patients. A cursory glance at the history of psychoanalysis and how analysts have treated other analysts (e.g., Ferenczi, Reich, Rank, and Bowlby, to name a few) who introduced new ideas should demolish any claims about arriving at a higher stage of development as a result of being "fully" analyzed. Fully human is a better goal than fully analyzed.

Other analytic writers (Stern, 1985; Ogden, 1989; Benjamin, 1995; Shane, Shane, and Gales, 1997; Mitchell, 2000a) have challenged this model of development. Mitchell (2000a) and Ogden (1986), for example, suggested that even if phases of development emerge sequentially, these phases are not exclusive or discrete geological layers. Rather, the mode of organizing experience of one stage is transformed by a succeeding stage and continues to operate dialectically with later stages. The developmental perspective used in this book relies on these recent insights regarding development and, in particular, on a non-linear, dynamic systems theory and model for depicting how experiences of being alive are organized during sequential phases of development (Benjamin, 1995). A transformational and non-linear model of development comprises independent and interdependent modes of organizing experience that "mutually and persistently influence one another in a fashion that is relatively unpredictable" (Shane et al., 1997, p. 30). Each phase of development, then, may be seen as a system comprising particular constitutional and social processes for organizing experience, which interacts with and is transformed by subsequent systems and their processes. Every succeeding system operates in conjunction with other systems, resulting in more complex and dynamic organizations of experience. These systems include social interactions with others as well as associated cultural expectations and rituals.

Diane Ackerman's (1999) experience of poignant pleasure watching the Hale-Bopp comet with friends, for instance, represents a deeply complex and dynamic interaction of multiple systems and their processes. A sense of deadness or pathology, on the other hand, represents a dominant activation of one system even as it continues to interact with other systems. For example, a patient described how she enjoyed, for the first time in many years, the sensual pleasure of rubbing lotion on her legs and arms after an evening bath. Previously, a bath was purely functional and habitual, leaving in the background processes associated with organizing and integrating sensual experiences. The result was a flattening of her experience. The relative absence of a sense of being alive not only was due to physical and sexual abuse, but also was the result of a social milieu and religious ethos that was quietly misogynistic and wary of sensual pleasures.

The mind, sociality, and vitality

Alterations in models of development have often been accompanied by debates about one, or two, person psychologies (Aron, 1996; Maroda, 1999). These debates may eventually lapse into silence as evidence from the neurosciences demonstrates the interrelation between mind, brain, and relationships (Damasio, 1994; Siegel, 1999). The relation between the mind and body that Freud and many others struggled to address is too narrow, remaining bound to problems and questions related to Descartes' illusions (Macmurray, 1957). More accurately, what is the relationship between the mind, brain/body, and social interactions? As Luria (1980, p. 33) put it, functional brain systems do not arise autonomously "but are formed in the process of social contact" (cited in Sroufe, 1955, p. 155). Vygotsky (1978) and, lately, Aron (1996, p. x) asserted the "notion that the mind is inherently dyadic, social, interactional, and interpersonal." In this book, I emphasize persons' developmental experiences of being and becoming alive, yet I understand experiences of being alive to be individual (mind–body), social, and communal. A person, in other words, is able to organize and own his/her experience of being alive – like Ackerman observing the Hale-Bopp comet. However, Ackerman's capacity to organize and share her experience of being alive was contingent upon her past and present relationships and concomitant constitutional capacities. Likewise, the patient who felt a sense of pleasure when putting on lotion was connected to relationships of care and trust that served as foundations for her enjoyment. Her experience of aliveness cannot be separated from the relational realm, even though it was in the privacy of her own home. An experience of being alive, whether at the age of 2 months or 80 years, is both an individual and social achievement; it is indeed a mind, body, relational event. Psychopathology (or mental health) is not, from this perspective, merely an individual phenomenon. Madness is a property of the individual and of society. Thus healing is a function of relationships and community.[7]

Four attributes of developmental phases

Linear, hierarchical models of development frequently depict stage-related features that a child must successfully navigate if s/he is to move on and handle the discrete tasks of the succeeding stage. The specific attributes and dynamics of one stage are left behind as the child develops. Instead of this line of thinking, I focus on four salient features of human life that are present in each phase of development. Each of these characteristics, briefly outlined below, is handled and organized differently in each phase, with earlier modes and processes of organizing experiences of being alive continuing to operate dynamically as the child grows. Additionally, I do not see these attributes as something simply within the child. Rather, each attribute is part of and within the child–parent system (and the larger social ethos) throughout childhood. For example, during the first phase of life, these four features are integral to the infant's preverbal and embodied experience of being alive and her organization of trust. This "intrapsychic" experience and organization are linked to and dependent on infant–parent interactions as well as the parent's own patterns of organizing trust bodily. These four attributes, which are not part of any one phase of development, comprise the dynamics of potential space.[8] Hence, the potential space of each phase reveals the particular budding aliveness associated with each mode.

Generating and surrendering to experience

The first feature of each phase of development is the dialectical tension between generating and surrendering to an experience, event or other person. A key aspect of human existence, according to Hegel, is that we do not "*receive* contents of the world [so much] as we *take up* our experience in a kind of spontaneous activity" (Pinkard, 2000, p. 164, original emphasis). To take up our experience means one is willing to be moved by the objects of the world. Heidegger (1971) also argued that part of human experience involves one's readiness to undergo it.

> To undergo an experience with something – be it a thing, a person, or a god – means that this something befalls us, strikes us, comes over us, overwhelms and transforms us. When we talk of "undergoing" an experience, we mean specifically that the experience is not of our own making; to undergo here means that we endure it, suffer it, receive it as it strikes us and submit to it. It is something itself that comes about, comes to pass, happens.
>
> (Heidegger, 1971, p. 57)

These two philosophers suggested that in the moment of taking up or surrendering we encounter something that moves us and is outside our control. Each, in his own way, said that that taking up or surrendering to the limits of reality, to language, to others, to one's own experience was inextricably yoked to human freedom and creativity.

Psychoanalysts have addressed the idea of surrender. Ferenczi (1931) encouraged his patients toward a deeper relaxation and surrender to his/her experiences. Later, Angyal (1965) made a similar claim when arguing that there is a drive for autonomy (assertion) and a drive for homonony (surrendering to something greater). More recently, Ghent (1990) proposed that masochism involved a pseudo surrender; submission that had the appearance of surrender.[9] Surrender, for Ghent, is not voluntary and is an experience of being "totally present," which is connected to a sense of aliveness and "the discovery of one's identity, one's sense of self, even one's sense of unity with other living beings" (1990, p. 111). Unlike surrender, though often confused with it, submission implies domination, compliance (Winnicott, 1971, p. 28), the presence of a false self (p. 34), the perversion of object use, lack of self-integration, and "losing oneself in the power of the other" (Ghent, 1990, p. 115).[10] Ghent, like Angyal and, implicitly, Winnicott, viewed surrender as necessary for the achievement of a true self and a sense of aliveness.[11]

To surrender, to be moved by thc other, is not mere passivity. It does not mean that one is absolutely constructed by the other, by language or culture. In the moment of surrendering to language, for example, one also constructs or generates experience by using the signifying functions of language. The poet, Heidegger (1971) argued, generates meaning in his/her use of language in constructing verse and, at the same time, the poet surrenders to the word, experience, and the other. The disruption of this paradoxical tension between surrendering to and generating experience is revealed in the "habit of always hearing only what we already understand" (p. 58). In those moments, we use language to construct experience, while refusing to be open to being moved or surprised by the other's meaning, needs, and desires. To surrender is to be moved, while also constructing experience through signifying functions.

There is a paradoxical aspect to this feature of human life. To undergo an experience involves openness to being moved and transformed by the other, all the while generating meaning and value. Ideally, a person who surrenders to an experience or to the other is actively constructing it. She is not a mere passive instrument of the event or the other person. The mutual sense of aliveness that a couple achieves during playful sex, for instance, reveals the dialectical tension between generating and surrendering to the moment and to each other. When theorizing about the infant's internal world, analysts refer to the infant's fantasies or omnipotent thinking, which are the first attempts to generate experience. Similarly, we conceive of the infant as being totally dependent on the parents. This dependence may be interpreted as surrendering to the parent's timely and good-enough ministrations.

A collapse of the dialectical tension results in a sense of emptiness or deadness associated with either pole. If, for example, a person is forced toward the pole of surrendering through impingement or deprivation, she loses, to some extent, the ability to create meaning, and surrender is transformed into submission (Maroda, 1999). In this moment of submission, in other words, the dialectical tension collapses as the "other" forces meaning onto the person, which Winnicott (1971, p. 3) called madness. A defensive retreat into the solipsistic world of omnipotent fantasies, for instance, may be survival, but it is also a distortion of the capacity to create meaning and value. Trauma represents the violent transformation of surrender into submission and, consequently, the loss of the capacity to generate experience (Ghent, 1990).

The collapse of the dialectical tension can be envisioned in another way. A person may move toward the pole of generating experience by refusing to surrender to an experience or event. Sadistic and compulsive behaviors represent persons' forced and rigid constructions of reality and concomitant refusal to give in to an experience or to the other. Too much sanity, one could say, represents the collapse of the dialectical tension between generating and surrendering to experience. "The madman," Chesterton wrote, "is not the man who has lost his reason. The madman is the man who has lost everything except his reason" (1959, p. 19). The madman relies on his reason to construct experience, to construct the other, to avoid surrendering to it. Unwittingly, the madman destroys the possibility of being alive. *Experiences of being alive during each phase of development depend on maintaining this dialectical tension between generating and surrendering to experience.*

Recognition and negation

The capacity to construct and surrender to another person or experience is closely related to a second feature of development – recognition and destruction (or negation). Jessica Benjamin (1988, 1990, 1995, 1998) has written extensively about the dialectical and paradoxical aspects of recognition and negation. A fundamental challenge in human life and development, Benjamin argued, is being able to recognize and accept the "other" as both different and like me. Negation, which means the other is not-me (difference), is "a vital moment in the movement of recognition" (1998, p. 83). It is vital in that the paradox of likeness in difference and difference in likeness is present, preserving the dynamics of a lively relationship. Indeed, negation is the condition for the possibility of recognition. Without negation, there is only sameness. Benjamin also suggested that the tension between recognition and negation is necessary for subjectivity and intersubjectivity to be realized. I would reframe this and state that this dialectical tension is constitutive for a subjective and intersubjective sense of being alive.

In terms of generating and surrendering to experience, recognition and negation play a necessary part. The construction of experience requires the capacity to recognize and negate. "I see you as like me" involves an interpretation, an active construction of experience, as well as active negation – you are not-me. Surrender is allowing the other to recognize and negate me, while constructing one's own experience. The paradox of surrendering to the other involves one's willingness to be moved by the other's active recognition and negation of me and, at the same time, constructing the other through one's own recognition and negation.

An illustration of this dynamic may be found in parent-infant interaction. Parents actively recognize and negate their children; that is, the parents construct meaning and value in relation to their child, without necessarily impinging on their child's own capacities for recognition and negation, and view their child as both like and different from themselves. At the same time, a good-enough parent accepts and surrenders to the child's active recognition and negation manifested in the child's assertions. The child's assertions, in other words, and the parent's accurate attunement represent the parent's willingness to be moved and transformed by the child's needs and assertions – a surrender to the child's active constructions of reality. The child is also moved and transformed by his parents' recognitions, manifested in the parents' ministrations as well as in other routine interactions. Development is frequently thought of in terms of the transformations taking place in the child, overlooking changes in parents. The mutual and dialectical engagement of recognition and negation in constructing and surrendering to experience, which is ideally present throughout human life, gives rise to a sense of aliveness in and between each half of the infant–parent dyad.

Trauma and a sense of deadness represent the collapse of the dialectical tension between generating and submitting to experience and, correspondingly, a distortion of recognition and negation. In the moment of trauma, the victimizer actively and omnipotently generates experience such that the victim is forced to submit to the reality of the victimizer and, in so doing, the victim's subjectivity is negated. The victimizer views the victim as not-me, as entirely different, either as a threat or something to be incorporated. The victimizer is attempting to force the victim to submit to and recognize the reality of the victimizer. "Violence," Benjamin wrote, "is the outer perimeter of the less dramatic tendency of the subject to force the other to either be or want what it wants, to assimilate the other to itself or make it a threat. It is the extension of reducing difference to sameness, the inability to recognize the other without dissolving his/her otherness" (1998, p. 86). Violence represents the collapse of the dialectical tension between generating and surrendering to the other and a resultant distortion of recognition and negation, two trends together leading to a momentary chimera of vitality that blurs awareness of a profound sense of emptiness. The cultural and religious rituals, myths, and doctrines that give rise to sexism, racism, terrorism, and ageism are macro illustrations of such a collapse.

The dialectics of care

When we consider these two attributes of human development and experiences of being alive, what feature of human relationships and experience helps maintain the creative and dynamic tension between generating and surrendering to experience? What enables persons to construct reality as well as to surrender to the other? What contributes to the paradoxical and healthy tension between recognition and negation? What prevents recognition and negation from becoming destructive? These questions bring me to the third salient feature of each phase of development, namely, the dialectical processes of Care. Martin Heidegger linked the idea of care to human existence, to Being. He believed that Dasein is the condition through which beings develop as phenomenal beings, and this condition or circumstance "is a meaning-context" to which he assigned the term "Care." "Care is not one possible meaning-context among others, but rather meaning-context itself . . . [B]eings cannot be except within the context of Care" (in Binswanger, 1963, pp. 122–123). Scottish philosopher John Macmurray (1961) used mother–infant interactions and, in particular, the mother's agentic care to illustrate the foundational features of Care in the child's movement toward self as agent and experience of being a person. A child's journey to personhood involves "seeking care and being cared for" (Young-Bruehl, 2000, p. 109). Care, then, is fundamentally social and is the circumstance and condition through which selfhood or personhood arises.

From the angle of experiences of being alive, Care is the field of the personal, which is a necessary condition for survival and vitality.

In the psychoanalytic realm, the idea of care was taken up by existentialist analysts (e.g., Binswanger, 1963) and indirectly by people such as Winnicott (1971, 1986, 1990) and Bollas (1991). Winnicott used the term "ruth" in referring to the moment in development when the infant realizes it can harm the beloved object and, as a result, develops a sense of care for the object. This realization is contingent upon the parent's care for the child. Bollas made a case for the unique interactions between parent and child to be an essential component in a human being's "personality idiom" (1991, p. 10). Care is constitutive for personality idiom and one's personality reflects the unique idiom of care (and carelessness) that takes place between parent and child.

Whether understood philosophically or psychoanalytically, Care is inextricably yoked to selfhood, to one's sense of *being* a person. Additionally, Care is yoked to generating and surrendering to experience, constructive recognition and negation, and concomitantly to the subjective and intersubjective achievement of being alive. Personhood and these dialectical attributes of development are connected to three interrelated pairs of processes of Care, which operate on a continuum – trust–distrust, loyalty–disloyalty (see Winnicott, 1986, pp. 137–141), and hope–hopelessness. Generally, a person develops a sense of trust when others have demonstrated loyalty to him, and this trust is the basis for the person's hope that surrendering does not result in annihilation of the self or one's capacity to generate experience (Winnicott, 1971, p. 102). Sufficient experiences of loyalty also support the belief that the other's recognition and negation of me will not lead to my destruction. Interpersonal loyalty, trust, and hope are foundational for a person to risk surrendering to experience, to the other, as well as to embrace the other's recognition and negation. Insufficient trust is linked to real or imagined experiences of betrayal and leads to a conscious or unconscious sense of hopelessness, making it difficult, if not impossible, to surrender to experience. Submission, a perversion of surrender, represents distrust and hopelessness that results from profound experiences of betrayal and fear of annihilation.

I wish also to make clear that the processes of care are socially constructed and contextual. Each family and culture conveys its own idioms of care. Trust, loyalty, and hope are universal aspects of being human; however, the meanings, objects, rituals, and motivations associated with these processes are diverse. This, in turn, suggests that individual, family, and community experiences of being alive will vary considerably. That is, the processes of Care will be expressed differently depending on the child's constitutional features, the parents' own past and present and conscious and unconscious constructions of these pairs, and communal constructions of trust, loyalty, and hope.

Disruption and repair

Naturally, the vicissitudes of human life include moments of distrust, betrayal, and hopelessness, which differ in intensity and length, and are associated with varying degrees of disruption in relationships and self-organization. In other words, while Care is essential to Being, indifference and hostility disrupt the personal field, and the absence of Care is implicated in non-being and depersonalization. Pick up the newspaper or read novels and myths and notice the manifold occasions of non-recognition, violent negation, and forced submission that disrupt and, at times, destroy relational harmony and persons' experiences of being alive. Disruption, however, is an inevitable and necessary characteristic of human existence, calling for real and imagined attempts at reparation. Indeed, disruption is necessary for the possibility of creative expressions of being alive. The fourth feature is the dialectic of disruption and repair. How do we handle and mend moments of distrust, betrayal, and hopelessness so they do not culminate in dehumanization, emptiness, isolation, and ennui? Can we embrace disruptions to make room for change and the possibility of feeling alive?

I understand this fourth feature of development to be linked to generating and surrendering to experience, as well as recognition and negation. Tronick (1989) noted, for example, that breakdowns in mother–infant interactions are followed by attempts by one or both parties to repair the relationship. Momentary or prolonged breakdowns may be the result of parental misattunement, misrecognition, impingement, and deprivation, rendering the infant distrustful. A parent, in other words, may generate experience such that the child's assertions are ignored or denied. If not corrected, the child will sacrifice his subjectivity for the sake of maintaining the attachment. Such a sacrifice may be understood as the child's attempt to repair the disruption. In this instance, the child's sacrifice is submission to the parent's expectations, which may lead to a false sense of trust, harmony or unity and a corresponding false self and pseudo sense of aliveness. For example, a depressed parent may misrecognize or not attune to the child's assertions, resulting in relational disruption or disconnection. The child is motivated to repair this disruption by trying to gain the parent's attention or by attempting to enliven the parent. The child sacrifices her subjectivity by submitting to the parent's "reality" to maintain (false) unity and attachment to the depressed parent. Submission, then, becomes the mode of repair and an avoidance of disruption. It also screens profound experiences of distrust and betrayal and the unconscious belief that trust and loyalty are equivalent to annihilation of one's subjectivity and sense of aliveness.

Happier occasions involve repeated breakdowns and timely repairs or "localized spoiling" (Winnicott, 1971, p. 97), which contribute to a person's sense of confidence that disruptions (Beebe and Lachmann, 1994), while inevitable, do not lead to submission, annihilation or deadness. Indeed, if a person obtains enough trust in his ability to repair disruptions, then he will be able to surrender to the event of disruption as he proceeds to repair it. Recall Diane Ackerman's (1999) delight and dread in observing the Hale-Bopp comet. Her realization that she would be dead long before the comet returned may be seen as a moment of disruption, threatening to upset her enjoyment. Yet, she was able to surrender to *both* the experience of joy and to the experience of dread – the disruption – without losing the aliveness of the moment.

Another example may be seen in a couple who experience a moment of disconnection that begins in a misunderstanding. Janet and Tom, both in their late thirties with two children, have sought help because of frequent, painful conflicts in their relationship. After several months, Janet and Tom arrived at the session with a renewed sense of confidence, intimacy, and vitality. Janet began by recalling an event from the previous week. She knew that her husband enjoyed flowers. One evening, she surprised him at the front door with a bouquet of flowers. Tom responded with something between a nod and grunt as he continued past Janet into the family room. In that moment, Janet felt hurt and angry, which was joined to a visceral sense of distrust and experience of feeling betrayed (past and present). Often, after these relational breakdowns, Janet would withdraw and later find something to yell at Tom about. This was Janet's unconscious attempt to repair the breakdown by getting him to attend to her distress. This approach, however, tragically and predictably exacerbated the disconnection between them. On this occasion, though, Janet withdrew to get a handle on her feelings, which she previously experienced as disruptive. She recognized and surrendered to (versus externalizing) her feelings and realized that Tom's response need not destroy her desire to give him a gift. Janet also entertained the possibility of some other explanation, such as Tom having had a difficult day at work. By containing and surrendering to her feelings and experiences, Janet was able to be present to Tom without trying to attack him. This enabled Tom to apologize and thank her, explaining that he was stressed about work. Janet's confidence and trust in the relationship enabled her to invite reparation through non-judgmental presence and, in turn, Tom was able to complete the repair by apologizing and expressing gratitude for the gift.

The routine importance of the dialectic of disruption and repair extends to the therapeutic relationship as well. Therapists know well the inevitable ruptures that take place in the cauldron of therapeutic work (Stolorow et al., 1994; Maroda, 2004). Safran and Muran (1996, 2000) have described this dynamic in terms of furthering the therapeutic alliance, developing hope, and as a royal road to the unconscious. The therapist's humility (Kohut, 1984), admitting mistakes, containing intense affect, and exploring the patient's behavior are all aspects of the ritual of repairing ruptures in the analytic relationship.

This feature of human development is also part of larger social, cultural, and religious systems. We understand, organize, and experience both disruption and repair differently, depending on the period of development as well as our family, cultural, and religious background. Families and cultures develop different rituals for mending real and illusory relational disturbances. One may expect considerable diversity in the ways people attempt to restore the balance between generating and surrendering to the other and correspondingly diverse expressions of subjective and intersubjective experiences of being alive. Mending moments of disconnection are as crucial as routine moments of connection, because they provide persons with confidence and a sense of loyalty in times of crisis or disruption. Sufficient trust allows one to surrender to the disruption without a loss of subjectivity and community.

Winnicott (1971) coined the term, potential space, to refer to an area of illusion, an area where spontaneity and play take place. I amend this to include the idea that potential space comprises generating and surrendering to experience, recognition and negation, disruption and repair, and the processes of Care. When these features are dynamically present within and between human beings, a space is fashioned wherein subjective and intersubjective experiences of being alive are co-created and organized. The collapse of potential space points to a loss of dialectical tension between these pairs, giving rise to organizations of experience linked to a sense of emptiness, deadness, and boredom.

Four modes of organizing experience

Whether conscious or unconscious, defensive or non-defensive, human beings continually perceive, remember, interpret, and organize what is occurring in the moment. A newborn infant is known to recognize and prefer the sounds of her mother's voice. A 16-year-old teenager eats breakfast with his parents in moody silence. Each represents instances of different, complex modes of organizing experience-in-relation. The following four chapters describe the characteristics of four modes of organizing experience that emerge sequentially in development and that continue to operate with succeeding modes. I rely primarily on, but alter considerably, Ogden's theory of developmental modes. Modifications imply a respect for and agreement with the theory as well as areas of divergence. The following survey of accord and difference provides a launching point for the next four chapters.

Ogden (1989), building on Melanie Klein's work, described the attributes of three modes of organizing experience – autistic-contiguous, paranoid-schizoid, and depressive positions or modes. Each of these positions "is characterized by its own form of symbolization, method of defense, quality of object relatedness, and degree of subjectivity" (Ogden, 1989, p. 10).

Ogden argued that "human experience is the product of the dialectical interplay of three modes of generating experience . . . Each mode creates, preserves, and negates the other" (p. 4). The collapse of "the dialectic in the direction of one or the other of the modes of generating experience" reveals the presence of psychopathology.

While this condensation does not do justice to Ogden's work, it does represent consistent assumptions that have several problems. First of all, the terms used to identify each mode refer to psychopathology. Depression, paranoia, schizoid, and autism are hardly "normal" or desirable when it comes to organizing experience. Of course, Ogden points out characteristics of each mode that are not pathological. My issue is not necessarily with his descriptions of how experience is organized in each mode. Rather, it is with assigning decidedly pathological terms to reputedly normal phases of development. A child may have some stranger anxiety, for example, but I would not wish to assign the term "paranoia" or "schizoid thinking" to the way she organizes experience. A child who relates to her parents in a paranoid-schizoid fashion is not healthy or normal and has come to organize experience this way because of traumatic interactions. Moreover, an adult who is deeply paranoid constructs reality in terms of his anxiety about and fear of others. This pattern of constructing experience, which is deemed pathological, does not necessarily mean that this adult's mode of organizing experience is identical to or even linked to a child's second stage or phase of development. The tendency to use adult pathology when depicting developmental stages or phases has been a problem in psychoanalysis (Peterfreund, 1983).[12]

I, therefore, steer away from using pathological concepts when identifying and describing the four modes of experience. Specifically, I depict four successive and interactive modes of organizing experience: corporeal-contiguous, taxonomic-object, symbolic-subjective, and narrative-communal modes. Each mode has particular characteristics associated with each of the four salient features depicted above as well as distinct organizations of being alive. Stated another way, subjective and, later, intersubjective experiences of being alive (and a sense of deadness) are organized in varying ways in each mode. Ideally, earlier modes are transformed by, shape, and are dynamically linked to later modes.

A second difficulty concerns Ogden's idea that human experience is the result of the interplay of these three modes (autistic-contiguous, paranoid-schizoid, and depressive). It is not clear what he meant by human experience or if he was simply associating human experience, in this instance, to adults. I would interpret this to mean that the *fullness* of adult human experience is manifested when there is dialectical tension between the three modes. Even with this clarification, confusion arises when Ogden suggested that psychopathology represents a collapse of dialectical tension between these modes whereby one mode seems to dominate. I believe it is more accurate to say that human experience, in general, and experiences of being alive, in particular, are the result of any or all modes. Health or pathology is not determined merely by the presence of one mode. In my view, the infant, for instance, organizes experience primarily in terms of one mode. If the four dialectical pairs depicted above are dynamically present, then the infant is able to organize and possess a sense of being alive. As the infant develops, other modes emerge and operate dynamically with earlier modes. So, for example, a child who now possesses the capacities associated with two modes of organizing experience is constructing experience relying on these two modes. Her reliance on one mode to construct experience may or may not be pathological. In a similar way, a person being swept up by the music of a Rachmaninov piano concerto may, for the moment, be organizing experience primarily out of the autistic-contiguous mode, to use Ogden's designation, and unconsciously feel very much alive. This suggests, then, that an adult may organize experience, non-defensively, primarily out of one mode and be considered healthy. Pathology, I propose, represents the *defensive and consistent use of one (or more) mode, an accompanying collapse of potential space, and a corresponding subjective and intersubjective sense of deadness, emptiness, or numbness.*

Another important aspect of Ogden's work (and others: see Bromberg, 1998; Pizer, 1998; Mitchell, 2000a) is the shift away from the authority of the analyst's truth and the patient's accommodation to external reality. This is a movement in psychology away from positivist approaches toward phenomenological methods. This shift from adapting to reality to experiences of being alive, I believe, has been fruitful.[13] In particular, a phenomenological and social constructionist turn in psychoanalysis significantly alters our conceptualization of the patient, analyst, and the analytic ritual. For example, focusing on how both the patient and analyst contribute (or not) together to subjective and intersubjective constructions of being alive makes the idea of analytic reality and truth more ambiguous and uncertain. Likewise, analytic authority and neutrality, which continue to be discussed and altered (Aron, 1996; Maroda, 1999), are more murky and fluid, happily I may add. When we shift attention to modes of organizing experience, we are concerned about the patient's patterns in organizing experiences of being alive and real and how the analyst's shifting modes shape the interaction. Put another way, what modes of organizing experience are operating between analyst and patient? How is the analytic couple creating or impeding subjective and intersubjective experiences of being alive and real? The final chapter of this book addresses some of these changes.

I wish to offer a final claim and comment about the paradoxical nature of human life and reality. Farley (1990) wrote that human beings are fundamentally tragic creatures because we distort reality in the very process of grasping it. Our prized stories, myths, legends, theories, and rituals are only approximations and it is an illusion to believe they represent *the* reality or *the* truth. Yet, these signifiers of reality are necessary in that, stories and rituals a community or culture holds represent not only "reality" but also their beliefs and hopes about what it means to experience being alive. The stories and rituals represent, in part, the telos of desire, of being alive with others. Human beings create these stories and rituals to possess structures and guidelines to nurture subjective and intersubjective experiences of being alive and real. Yet, tragedy invariably follows when individuals take the theories and rituals for life itself, as substitutes for the experience of being alive. Perhaps, we believe that we can capture being alive, removing its ephemeral and ungraspable nature. This illusion is as true of religion as it is of psychoanalysis.

Chapter 2

Embodied vitality

> The ego is first and foremost a bodily ego.
>
> (Freud, 1923, p. 26)

> The perceiving mind is an incarnated mind.
>
> (Merleau-Ponty, 1964, p. 3)

Poor Descartes, he receives so much blame for sundering the mind from the body and anchoring the security of human existence in knowing. We seem to have forgotten the Gnostics and later ascetic Christians who lauded and emphasized the spirit, viewing the body and "its" pleasures as impediments to union with God. A curious and illusory paradox exists when human beings differentiate body and mind. Organizing and representing experience depends on the cognitive ability to differentiate, and we come to believe that what we differentiate is, in fact so – that mind and body are in truth distinct entities. This illusion is *felt* to be real, giving rise to problems and questions regarding how the body and mind are related, which, in turn, can take on a *reality* of its own. For example, a patient may feel as if his body is lifeless, wooden, a drag on his existence. Another patient may believe that life resides in the mind and feels depressed and guilty when sexual feelings seem to arise without his control. These experiences feel real, but it is folly to believe that one's construction of experience is reality.[1] The paradox, though, is that the patient who feels disconnected from his body continues to organize experience in and through his body (cf. Corrigan and Gordon, 1995). The holy ascetic, who denies the pleasures of his body and feels closer to God, is able to do so because of the background unity of mind and body.

Freud's bodily ego and Merleau-Ponty's incarnated mind were attempts to awaken us from the illusion that we are dealing with *two entities*. Gradual recognition and acceptance of mind–body unity made way for questions, hypotheses, and experiments demonstrating the social nature of mind–body. During the second half of the twentieth century, philosophers (e.g., Macmurray, 1957, 1961; Johnson, 1987; Lakoff and Johnson, 1999), developmentalists (e.g., Stern, 1985; Fast, 1992; Greenspan, 1997), and neuroscientists (Damasio, 1994; Edelman and Tononi, 2000) have increasingly recognized and demonstrated mind–body unity, which is inextricably yoked to and contingent on the social field of personal interactions.

Given the idea of a mind–body–personal field, how are we to understand and describe the characteristics and dynamics of embodied experiences of being alive? This chapter is an answer to this question. Organizations of bodily aliveness appear first in development, although they are transformed by later modes of organizing experience. I call this initial mode the corporeal-contiguous (C-C) mode of organizing experience. The specific characteristics of this mode are identified prior to depicting the attributes of an embodied sense of being alive. It is important to note the distinction between the characteristics of this mode and embodied vitality. That is, when an infant organizes experience in this mode, this does not mean she has an embodied experience of being alive. Indeed, a baby may organize sensory experience defensively, leaving her with a diffuse sense of lifelessness in between periods of aliveness. The final portion of this chapter addresses how embodied aliveness is contingent on the fourfold dynamics of potential space – the field of personal interactions.

Characteristics of the corporeal-contiguous mode

Four related questions shape investigations into the infant's world. What does the infant "use" to organize experience?[2] What are the particular attributes of this organization? How is experience organized and represented? What does the infant perceive? Responses to these questions are manifold and perhaps best understood as ways of thinking about the inner world of the infant. The answers offered here fall under the heading of the corporeal-contiguous (C-C) mode of organizing experience. While the C-C mode appears first in development, it is neither surpassed nor left behind as the child achieves other capacities for organizing experience. As adults, the C-C mode continues to operate when making love, dining, playing, and fighting.

The senses, motility, and visceral emotions

An infant, broadly speaking, uses his body *and* the ministrations of the other to organize experience. Studies have shown that babies "are highly sensitive to the contingent relations between their physical responses and consequent stimulus event . . . [I]nfants possess an innate contingency-detection module for analyzing the degree of contingent relatedness between motor responses and consequent sensory event" (Fonagy et al., 2002, p. 208). Ogden understood this initial contingency-detection mode "as [a] sensory dominated, pre-symbolic area of experience in which the most primitive form of meaning is generated on the basis of the organization of sensory impressions, particularly at the skin surface" (1989, p. 4). The five senses (smell, touch, sight, sound, and taste), which are not separate and independent (Stern, 1985; Kumin, 1996), operate together as the infant organizes information in relation to a parent who responds to and mediates the interaction. An infant, then, has an innate capacity "to take information received in one sensory modality and somehow translate it into another sensory modality" (Stern, 1985, p. 51), and this capacity develops in conjunction with the parent's ministrations (Trevarthen, 1998). Uses of metaphors in adulthood are examples of this: The sound of her voice touched me. One excited patient declaimed, "Ah, the sweet smell of success." Another patient complained, "Everything feels gray."

Motility or physical movement is an important piece in the infant's active reception and organization of sensory input from the environment (Mittelmann, 1954). The infant is mind–body in motion in the interpersonal field, organizing data in and through senses. This means that soft, hard, rough, smooth, pungent, sweet, visual gestalt patterns, tone, rhythm are some of the sensory characteristics of the corporeal mode that are inextricably yoked to the infant's movements in relation to a parent's responses (contiguity and contingency). In other words, the corresponding physical tension and loss of tension associated with motility (physical resistance, pushing, pulling, sucking, yanking, grasping, relaxing, and kicking and lessening of resistance) are aspects of bodily organizations of experience in relation to objects. An infant's rhythmic rubbing of a soft blanket or snuggling up to and sucking on the breast are examples, representing motility in relation to organizing experience and the baby's rudimentary ability to regulate his emotional state through physical movement (Tustin, 1984; Anzieu, 1990; Tronick, 1989).

During the first weeks of life, visceral or precursor emotions contribute to and are part of sensory-motor organizations. Sroufe (1995) argued that "emotions proper do not exist in the newborn period" (p. 57). Instead, there are precursor emotions such as distress, physical arousal, pleasure, wariness, and frustration reactions. In a similar vein, Stern (1985) coined the term "vitality affects," which have "elusive qualities . . . such as 'surging,' 'fading away,' 'fleeting,' 'explosive,' 'crescendo,' 'decrescendo,' 'bursting,' 'drawn out'" (p. 55). Vitality affects are integral qualities of early organizations of experience, and the infant experiences these affects "from within, as well as, in the behavior of other persons" (p. 54). Activation and hedonic tone (Freud's pleasure–unpleasure principle), which are mediated by the infant's own constitutional configurations and actions and by parental responses to the infant's assertions (see Mahler, 1968, p. 43; Emde, 1980; Ornstein, 1997), are two dimensions of vitality affects that are also part of later categorical or discrete affects.

I prefer the term *visceral emotions* instead of precursor emotions or vitality affects, for three reasons. First, the term "visceral" suggests a close association between preverbal or pre-categorical somatic emotions. Emotion, during this period of development, is bodily and not a discrete iconic representation or idea. Damasio (1994) echoed this view, saying "the essence of a feeling may not be an elusive mental quality attached to an object, but rather the direct perception of a specific landscape: that of the body" (p. xiv). Second, one connotation of visceral is intuitive – something known deeply, in one's gut, but not formulated clearly. One knows, but the specific source eludes him. Many people, for example, are familiar with unbidden "body memories" that may be pleasant or terribly painful and frightening. An unconscious sensory perception or bodily posture or movement may evoke visceral-emotional memories. These emotions are felt in and through one's body and, like precursor emotions, visceral emotions are global or felt to be pervasive. Third, visceral emotions, unlike vitality affects, may be associated with a global and bodily sense of being alive *or* an enveloping sense of deadness. Carol, for instance, walked into the office looking bedraggled and depressed. She complained of feeling achy, while knowing that this was not a flu symptom. Later, Carol began to speak about the cold, cloudy winter weather and instantly saw images of a drafty farmhouse. She recalled lying quietly in bed, wintry weather seeping through the cracks in the walls and windows, while downstairs her controlling and dismissive mother and alcoholic father were yelling at each other. Before Carol linguistically formulated her present experience, she had a global, visceral experience – deadness – that was coupled with a diminished sense of motility, which she linked to painful childhood memories.

The senses, motility, and visceral emotions are three related aspects of the corporeal-contiguous mode of organizing experience. The infant "uses" these in organizing her experience at the same time she constructs experience mediated by the parent's responses to her assertions. The infant's bodily organizations of experience, then, cannot be separated from the infant's "use" of parental mediations. All of this presumes some rudimentary psychic structure and "representational" ability on the part of the infant.

Presentational organizations and differentiation

There is widespread agreement that infants clearly do not organize experience or memory verbally, symbolically, or autobiographically, but this is where consensus ends.[3] Mahler (1968) argued that the central feature of symbiosis was a "somatopsychic omnipotent fusion with the representation of the mother" (p. 9). Kumin (1996) believed that there is a pre-representational phase "that refers to an innate presentational capacity in human infants that preceded and makes possible the (later) development of semiotic and symbolic functions" (p. 25).[4] The infant, then, is not able to represent experience to himself nor is he able to differentiate one event from another. Fast (1992, 1998) calls these early presentational organizations "interaction schemes." Dynamic schemes represent "the particular way that the infant is interacting with its world" (Fast, 1992, p. 397) and these "different modes of interaction [that] are initially not integrated" (p. 398). In this mode, thought and action are one. "The baby can think only what it can do. More accurately, the baby can think only what it is doing at the moment" (p. 399). For example, "The still inchoate persons and objects involved in them (schemas) are defined in terms of the schema in which they occur . . . For the infant, the mother-of-nursing is essentially not connected to the mother-of-bye-bye" (Fast, 1998, p. 24). Early organization of experience is presentational – sensory-motor-visceral-emotional-interaction.

This perspective differs from the traditional analytic view of the infant as oblivious to the world outside its own body (narcissism or autism) and protected by a stimulus barrier. Freud (1911) used the analogy of a bird's egg in attempting to depict the infant's auto-erotic world where she takes her body as her own object. He said: "A neat example of a psychical system *shut off from the stimuli of the external world*, and able to satisfy even its nutritional requirements autistically . . . is afforded by a bird's egg with its supply enclosed in its shell; for it, the care provided by the mother is limited to the provision of warmth" (p. 220n; emphasis mine). Freud and other analysts conceived of the infant as psychologically fused with the mother, yet protected by a stimulus barrier. We can agree that the infant is not yet able to differentiate between him/herself and objects without having to posit a solipsistic, passive infant, incognizant of the world. In other words, Freud correctly recognized that the infant is not yet able to *represent* her experience to herself or others. Nor is the infant able to differentiate between senses, behavior, emotions, or interactions. However, the lack of "representational" ability does not mean that the baby is completely passive and unable to make use of her capacities to organize experience in relation to the ministrations of others.

This pre-representational capacity includes the ability to note differences in the environment. The infant, for example, shows preferences for her mother's voice, which indicates an elementary capacity for noticing auditory differences (DeCasper and Fifer, 1980; DeCasper and Spence, 1986). Eco (1997) calls this primary semiosis or indexicality, which "occurs when, amid the thick stuff of the sensations that bombard us, we suddenly (unconsciously) select something that we set against that general background" (p. 14). In short, the corporeal-contiguous mode of experience is pre-representational, which reveals the infant's ability to express preferences for and make use of sensory stimuli, motor movements, visceral emotions, and parental ministrations (e.g., caressing) in organizing her experience.[5]

Early perception of difference and pre-representational organizations of experience raise a question about the meaning of differentiation (and undifferentiation).[6] Negatively, the infant is not yet able to perceive discrete objects or represent objects in terms of me and not-me or I and not-I. In this sense, the infant is undifferentiated, which is then frequently seen as fusion or merger. As Fast, Kumin, Fonagy, and others argue, however, the infant has some rudimentary capacity to differentiate as she actively organizes experience in relation to the ministrations of her mother. The infant, then, is able to perceive differences in terms of preferences and expectancies (Beebe, Lachmann, and Jaffe, 1997), yet is unable to organize these via discrete representations; that is, the infant does not perceive and experience her mother as a separate object. Differentiation, at this point in development, then is understood as differences determined by global bodily hedonic experiences (Freud's pleasure principle) that are *contingent* with parental responses as well as global bodily aversions to stimuli and non-contingent parental actions (unpleasure).

It is difficult to imagine and describe this early world because our adult "imagination" is pervasively structured by distinct iconic representations, symbols, and language, and yet this "pre-object dimension of experience . . . participates actively in them as amodal, emotional, and psycho-physiological foundation from which all representational thought is constructed" (Kumin, 1996, p. 176). For example, I might find myself lost for a time while listening to a favorite symphony. The music moves me. It lifts me up. I feel it in my bones. During this period of listening, I am not actively differentiating one note from the other nor am I consciously aware of my surroundings. Yet, I am taking in auditory stimuli, organizing experience in and through a sensory-visceral-affective mode. It is only later, as I share my experience with someone else or attempt to write it down, that I have moved from a presentational mode to representational modes of organizing experience. Another illustration of this can be seen in Janet's initial experience upon hearing that her husband was having sex with her best friend. Janet was shocked and speechless, becoming physically ill for several hours after hearing the news. Janet's profound sense of betrayal, hurt, and rage was initially felt and organized somatically, which included other modes of organizing experience.

Attributes of corporeal-contiguous experiences of being alive

Greenspan (1997, p. 49) remarked that the earliest sense of self possesses a global aliveness, which gives rise to the question regarding the relation between the infant's "use" of sensory-motor-visceral-emotions (and her parent's ministrations) in organizing experience and attending attributes of bodily aliveness. I briefly identify five salient and interrelated conditions that are necessary for an embodied sense of vitality: bodily agency and spontaneity, rudimentary capacity to regulate emotions, sense of bodily cohesion and continuity, sense of bodily ownership, and visceral validation. Two important points need to be mentioned before describing each constituent. First, each of these five factors is evident in later, more differentiated modes of organizing experience and a concomitant sense of vitality, yet they take on different meanings and forms as a result of developing subjective and intersubjective capacities. Second, all five features of an embodied sense of being alive emerge within the matrix of potential space. Put another way, the fourfold dynamics of potential space, depicted later in this chapter, make it possible for a sense of bodily agency, spontaneity, cohesion, and continuity to arise. Conversely, the collapse of potential space results in a loss or diminution of each aspect and gives rise to various defenses, which represent failed attempts to recover one or more of these five features of aliveness. Implicit in this view is that vitality and psychopathology are inextricably yoked to the social-personal field and are never simply the sole property of an isolated individual.

Somatic agency

Freud (1923) believed that the ego is, first and foremost, a bodily ego, which means that "I" or nascent subjectivity is rooted in the body and that an embryonic sense of agency is originally somatic agency – the preverbal and unconscious capacity to move and exert power. In a similar vein, Winnicott (1965) said, "The True Self comes from the aliveness of the body tissues and the working of body functions, including the heart's actions and breathing" (p. 148). Since the mid-1990s, infant research and formulations would include the role of parental ministrations in achieving an embodied vital agency. For instance, when an infant's inchoate desires and expectancies are met by contingent or relatively contingent parental responses, the infant obtains a rudimentary, bodily sense of agency and capacity for spontaneity (Rustin, 1997; Beebe and Lachmann, 2002). Motility, then, represents the infant's internal desires and needs, that when recognized and met by the parent, lead to a sense of somatic agency (Sandler and Sandler, 1998). Balint (1993) carried this further when arguing that an infant's embodied instrumentality "can only arise out of a state of eager aliveness in two people; the infant with the potential for life and the mother alive inside herself and tuning to the emerging infant" (1993, p. 102). In brief, physical spontaneity and zest, which are part of a rudimentary sense of agency, are linked to somatic expressions of desire that are acknowledged and responded to by the parent who is "alive" herself.

Resistance and constraints are necessary aspects of the social achievement of embodied agency. The infant's movements are met by the routine constraints of other objects as well as the parent's actions. Pushing, grabbing, sucking, and pulling, for instance, can be understood only in relation to an object that resists along with an object that recognizes and responds to the infant's needs and desires. In this case, resistance is the nexus between the internal needs and the world that meets those needs, leaving the infant with an embodied, global, pre-representational sense of agency. In such instances, resistance is benign and not experienced or organized as an immovable obstacle or the source of intolerable anxiety. Embodied agency and spontaneity, then, include physical resistance that is, ideally, benign, global, and responsive.

As adults, this kind of global, bodily agency and spontaneity may be found when dancing with a partner, having sexual intercourse, taking part in physical competition or play, or entering into lively cultural or religious rituals. A bodily and global sense of agency is the necessary background presence of later, more consciously organized, expressions of agency and spontaneity, as well as a corresponding unconscious belief that resistance is benign and indispensable. Conversely, being physically constrained and confined such that one's desires and needs are ignored leads to a loss of physical agency and vitality, as well as profound and pervasive anxiety and fear. Indeed, physical constraint is psychological. Resistance, on these occasions, is experienced in conjunction with a loss of agency. For example, as mentioned above, Carol felt and looked physically depressed and passive. When Carol reached adulthood, her older sister told her that their mother hated Carol, which neither could explain or understand. Carol remembers her mother making her sit in one place or stand in a corner for what seemed like hours facing the wall, though she was at a loss as to why she was made to do so. Carol's posture was an embodiment of depression as well as a physical, iconic representation of cumulative experiences of not only being confined but also not having her internal desires and needs met by her mother. At one level, the world represented an absence of care and a seemingly insurmountable obstacle to an experience of bodily agency and freedom. In short, Carol's depression may be understood, in part, as a pre-representational, somatic manifestation of a type of global resistance that was disconnected from a world that honors one's passions, desires, and needs.

Regulating emotions

The achievement of physical agency includes a rudimentary capacity to "use" one's body to regulate emotions, which is the second component of experiences of being alive. This use of one's body to soothe or regulate arousal also depends on and is yoked to parental recognition and regulation of the infant's emotions (see Fonagy et al., 2002, p. 435). Put differently, an embodied sense of agency or somatic competence depends not "only to the degree of his or her cognitive and social development, but to the degree that capacities for emotional regulation enable engagement of the available environment" (Sroufe, 1995, p. 156). The course of emotional development, Sroufe argued, "may be described as movement from dyadic regulation to self-regulation" with dyadic regulation representing a prototype for self-regulation (Sroufe, 1995, p. 151; see also Sander, 1977, 1995; Tronick, 1989). The parent regulates the infant's arousal and hedonic tone by way of harmonious routines and the management of arousal in the face of novel situations, yet this is done in conjunction with the infant's own behavior and constitutional capabilities. While the parent plays a very large part in these "somatic concordances" (Lewis, Amini, and Lannon, 2000), the infant is not entirely passive or wholly dependent on the parent's regulation of arousal and physical tension (Silverman, 2003).

Dyadic regulation of affect, then, includes the infant's unconscious use of his body-in-relation-to-mother. Somatic competence or agency involves some ability for the infant to regulate (with the parent) her own arousal (Stern, 1995, p. 63). Specifying that the infant "uses" her body to regulate arousal doesn't mean she intends to do so nor does it imply that she possesses a discrete representation of her body-in-relation-to-mother that serves to soothe – for this is a later achievement of object constancy. An infant, for instance, regulates arousal by rubbing a piece of soft blanket, sucking on a pacifier, as well as participating with mother in breastfeeding. It is the interaction that is soothing, which corresponds to a pre-representational organization.

This early bodily agency to regulate one's arousal is often in the background of more adult, differentiated methods of soothing oneself. For example, I recall a patient remarking about the amount of stress and agitation she experienced during her previous few days at work. When she went home in the evening she would relax in a large, wooden rocking chair. The rhythmic action lowered her agitation and was deeply soothing. The rocking was associated with memories of being rocked and held by her mother and the comfort she had derived from their interaction. She even had pictures of her mother rocking her as an infant. While her adult behavior is not identical to being rocked when she was an infant, I suggest that there was an unconscious somatic competence that accompanied her ability to regulate her emotional state. Rocking and the experience of being soothed, then, reveal the presence of this earlier mode of organizing experience as it operates in conjunction with other modes.

Continuity and cohesion

A third necessary component of an experience of bodily aliveness is the baby's sense of a "non-self-reflective sense of 'going on being'" (Ogden, 1989, p. 54). A baby needs to possess a sense of bodily cohesion and continuity to feel alive. The idea of a bodily ego may be said to represent the relation of one's body to the mental function of maintaining cohesion and continuity. Esther Bick (1968), for example, wrote, "in its most primitive form, the parts of the personality are felt to have no binding force amongst themselves and must therefore be held together in a way that is experienced by them passively, by the skin functioning as a boundary" (quoted in Houzel, 1990, p. 53). Ego-skin (Anzieu, 1990), psychic envelopes (Houzel, 1990), and containment are metaphors that depict the relation between mental functions and bodily cohesion. Damasio (1994) argued that a "representation of the skin might be the natural means to signify the body boundary" (p. 231), which is a necessary part of cohesion.

This "skin" boundary depends on "good enough" parental care. "A mother with a baby," Winnicott (1989) said, "is constantly introducing and reintroducing the baby's body and psyche to each other" and, in the process, a baby attains a somatic and global sense of going on being (p. 271). A caregiver "who holds well gives her infant a feeling of unity within his skin" (Deri, 1978, p. 48). Happily, a parent who holds and protects his/her child enhances the infant's sense of bodily integrity (Fonagy and Target, 1997).

Not surprisingly, prolonged and unrepaired parental misattunement and nonrecognition disrupt the infant's experiences of mind–body boundedness or cohesion, resulting in primitive agonies (Winnicott, 1989, pp. 89–90) and "a feeling of being less alive in one's own body" (Looker, 1998, p. 241). Parental deprivation and impingement, then, disturb the infant's sense of bodily integrity, leaving the infant scrambling to obtain some sense of cohesion and continuity in the face of overwhelming disruption (Schecter, 1973). For an infant, penetration of the skin (or environmental deprivation) violates the infant's very mind and ability to organize experience. As adults, we can differentiate between skin and mind, external and internal, and we have the indispensable illusion that a violation of one's skin does not necessarily result in violation of one's mind and sense of self. And yet, a traumatic event may painfully demonstrate to us that this differentiation, if not an illusion, is tenuous at best. In short, our adult experience of cohesion is not separable from bodily-mind cohesion.

Consider, for example, Jean Amery's story of being bound and beaten by the Gestapo in World War II. Amery's poignant reflection illustrates the relation between the skin and mental cohesion in adult life. He was abducted by the Nazis and taken to a damp cell beneath a Gestapo complex before being sent to a concentration camp. Amery (1995) wrote of his experience of torture years later.

> The first blow brings home to the prisoner that he is helpless . . . Yet I am certain that with the very first blow that descends on him he loses something we will perhaps call "trust in the world." Trust in the world

> includes all sorts of things . . . the certainty that by reason of written or unwritten social contracts the other person will respect my physical, and with it also my metaphysical being. The boundaries of my body are also the boundaries of my self. My skin surface shields me against the external world. If I am to have trust, I must feel on it only what I *want* to feel . . . The expectation of help, the certainty of help, is indeed one of the fundamental experiences of human beings . . . The expectation of help is as much a constitutional psychic element as is the struggle for existence . . . But with the first blow of the policeman's fist, against which there can be no defense and which no helping hand will ward off, a part of our life ends and it can never again be revived . . . Whoever has succumbed to torture can no longer feel at home in the world.
>
> (Amery, 1995, pp. 126, 127, 136)

With the first blow, Amery realized that "boundaries of my body are also boundaries of my self." The policeman's fist violated his physical being and Amery's experience of mind–body integrity.

Bodily integrity is accompanied by the infant's sense of continuity, which is felt in terms of the body's duration. Bodily duration, which is not linked to linear time, depends, to a large degree, on the parents' ability to establish a relatively harmonious and consistent caring environment. Winnicott's depiction of the infant's sense of going on being and the environmental mother portrays the relation between care and the infant's sense of bodily continuity. In adult life, we see remnants of this in religious concerns and beliefs about bodily resurrection. Ancient Egyptian burial rituals and, later, Christian beliefs about bodily resurrection symbolically illustrate the desire and need for a sense of continuity and its relation to organizing experience. Even in the face of death and annihilation, these religious practices and beliefs represent the confidence in an idea of physical life persisting – eternity is going on being. Religious practices and symbols, like these, are not simply based in the wish to avoid the exigencies of life. Rather, they demonstrate the presence of and necessity for an embodied sense of integrity and continuity for individuals and communities to experience being alive in the present.

Owning one's body

The fourth feature of an infant's experience of being alive is the background sense of possessing one's body – bodily ownership. This basic experience is not associated with a discrete "me" or "I" representation. Rather, it is a global and pre-representational sense of possession. Embodied ownership is omnipotently created at the point of bodily desire and need and the caregiver's sensitive and timely holding. Good-enough attunement "facilitates the child's formation of a stable body-image, both of himself and of his nursing mother. This fosters the feeling of owning, of possessing both his own body and that of his mother" (Kestenberg and Weinstein, 1978, p. 87). If all goes well enough, the infant will begin to "believe" that agency and its derivatives are her own and, when the infant learns to possess her mind–body, there is hope for sharing it in the future (Gunsberg and Tylim, 1998, p. 120).

This is difficult for adults to envision because many of us do not often encounter circumstances that place this global, bodily sense of ownership into question. Debilitating old age, disease, torture and other forms of physical violence shatter this unconscious assumption. Jean Amery, for instance, realized his body, and hence his very being, was in the possession of the Gestapo. His profound sense of powerlessness and anxiety should not simply be understood as the result of a physical blow. The fist represented the violent disruption of his sense of bodily ownership. Implicit here is the connection between a bodily sense of ownership and one's unconscious belief that my cries for help will not only be recognized but met by a human response. In infancy, we obtain bodily ownership through good enough parental responses to our emotional states and needs.

Bodily validation

A fifth attribute of bodily aliveness is visceral validation. The baby's bodily, agentic assertions are ideally recognized and appropriately responded to by a parent who demonstrates interest, concern, and her own sense of aliveness (see Balint, 1993, p. 102; Meares, 2000). In this sharing, there is somatic competence, continuity, cohesion, ownership, and a global experience of validation – a confirmation of one's being and a somatic and pleasurable feeling of well-being (Sandler and Sandler, 1998). The baby unconsciously feels in its bones that she is valued. This confirmation is not external or internal in the sense that the baby can distinguish between the two. Nor is it a validation of "me" or "I." Rather, it is a visceral, global experience of endorsement that becomes a part of later more differentiated experiences of validation. *Self regard and self-esteem, for instance, are later expressions and organizations of this early experience of somatic, global validation.* A patient's deep sense of rest and relaxation in the presence of a therapist is, in part, linked cross-modally to a visceral sense of being validated. The enjoyment and pleasure obtained from mutual play is also an illustration of this. Negatively, dissociation (Davies and Frawley, 1994; Eisold, 1998), the absence of the lived body (Balamuth, 1998), and the mind as object (Corrigan and Gordon, 1995) are examples of the human capacity to treat the body as an object and concomitant experiences of one's body as worthless, numb, and lifeless.

Environmental impingement and deprivation (Winnicott, 1971) contribute to invalidation, which results in a loss of physical vitality. Robert's story of being ridiculed by his boss is an instance of this. Robert had missed his sales quota for the first time and his boss, jokingly, made reference to Robert's manhood in front of several other salesmen. Beneath Robert's anger was a deeper sense of being devalued, which he also felt physically (headaches, abdominal cramps). Robert remembered times when his father made fun of him because Robert was apparently not manly enough. "He was a vicious bastard who liked to crush things he didn't like . . . I always felt sick whenever I sensed he was going to start in on me. It was like that at work yesterday." This sadistic type of invalidation of his "manhood" was partly joined to a somatic invalidation. Robert's physical symptoms were evidence of this, also representing somatic loss of aliveness.

Presentational, bodily agency, spontaneity, emotional regulation, continuity, cohesion, ownership, and validation are attributes of an infant's embodied sense of being alive. These attributes, which depend on the infant's constitutional characteristics and the parent's ministrations, are organized in C-C mode. Just as achieving one attribute is linked to realizing the others, so too the loss or disruption of one affects the others. For example, parental impingement or non-attunement, if prolonged and not repaired, heightens the infant's emotional state, disrupting dyadic regulation and making it difficult for the infant to participate in soothing himself. The loss of contingency gives rise to helplessness and lack of felt control in relation to the infant's needs and desires, resulting in a loss of an embodied sense of agency. This is accompanied by a diminution of a bodily sense of continuity, cohesion, and ownership. Annihilation anxiety represents a massive loss of these attributes and the infant's defensive struggle to organize experience in the C-C mode.

The C-C mode of organizing experience, then, is not always associated with experiences of being alive. The infant who unconsciously perceives the environment as dangerously resistant will continue to organize experience using the C-C mode. In this case, however, the C-C mode is entirely defensive, split off from the ministrations of the environment, and focused on sheer survival. "Autistic" withdrawal or autistic rhythmic movements, for example, may be said to be the infant's use of the C-C mode to organize experience, but this is an entirely defensive use of the C-C geared toward maintaining some semblance of emotional regulation, agency, ownership, etc., which is split off from the perilous environment. In this scenario, the impinging and non-contingent environment is unconsciously perceived not as a benign resistance – necessary for one's experience of being alive – but as a malignant, global resistance that must be avoided to survive. Psychological and physical survival precedes and trumps the desire for an experience of being alive. An organized sense of deadness or numbness is better than complete annihilation.

Potential space and the emergence of embodied vitality

Achieving an embodied sense of vitality, organized in the C-C mode, is contingent upon potential space. The "potential" in potential space during any period of development is the emergence of those attributes that comprise subjective and intersubjective constructions and experiences of vitality. In the first chapter, I conceptualized potential space as comprising four interrelated, dynamic pairs – surrender–generation, recognition–destruction, Care (as trust–distrust, loyalty–disloyalty), and disruption–repair. These dialectical pairs represent the unity of the intrapsychic and the interaction, the individual and the interpersonal. Each pair is depicted from the perspective of how they potentiate pre-symbolic organizations of bodily experiences of being alive.

Surrendering to and generating experience

The infant is usually conceptualized in psychoanalysis as completely dependent on the parent for physical and psychological survival. A baby is indeed dependent, yet this dependency, beginning with Freud, typically meant passivity. Instead of passivity as a signifier of dependency, I reframe dependency in terms of surrender. In a relationship where the baby possesses a background sense of safety and well-being (Sandler and Sandler, 1998), she is able to surrender to the ministrations of the environmental parent (Winnicott, 1971), who is not yet perceived as a discrete object. The infant is surrendering to movement and environment. This is not, of course, "intentional" on the infant's part. Rather, it is a pre-intentional, global and visceral giving of oneself over to caring interactions. Using Lichtenberg, Lachmann, and Fosshage's (1992) motivational systems theory, one could say that, in this moment of surrender, the aversive motivational system is not activated or that the pleasure principle is at its height. Surrender, during this period of development, then comprises the bodily expectations and needs of the infant, a background presence of safety, and the timely and appropriate ministrations of the parent.

This pre-intentional does not mean the infant is passive. Surrender is accompanied by the active generation of experience in the C-C mode. Omnipotence and primary process thinking have traditionally been understood to be aspects of an infant's construction of early experience. Winnicott (1971, 1989) argued that the mother's near one hundred percent adaptation to the infant's needs provides the baby with a belief in and experience of omnipotence, attributes of primary process thinking. The breast appears at the point of need and, in that moment, the infant omnipotently creates the breast. Thus, omnipotence, Winnicott believed, was necessary for the infant's active construction of experience, which is contingent on the infant's giving into and being moved by the environment's ministrations – its holding environment. Omnipotence and primary process thinking, then, signify the active organization of experience in the midst of surrendering to the interaction. In this situation, surrendering and omnipotence are not defensive. Omnipotent thinking becomes defensive when there is a failure in the environment and the infant, instead of surrendering, is subjugated by the world. Put differently, the infant handles overwhelming anxiety by sacrificing her body to the environment and omnipotently retreating to the safety of her mind (Corrigan and Gordon, 1995).

Naturally, the parent is also a partner in maintaining this dialectic. In recognizing and responding to the infant's assertions, the parent is allowing himself to be moved by the infant. The parental act of recognition, accompanied by acts that meet the infant's embodied desires, may be understood as the parent's active construction of the experience as well as his willingness to be moved by the infant's needs and desires. The parent, then, surrenders to the infant's spontaneous expressions of desire and, in so doing, the parent creates a space for the infant to feel safe enough to yield to experience and obtain a belief in her own omnipotence. A parent who consciously or unconsciously views the infant's needs as burdensome, onerous or anxiety-evoking will respond mechanically, resentfully, or not at all. The parent's perception, in this instance, is one of being subjugated and not surrendering, which closes or narrows the psychological and interpersonal space the infant needs to surrender and denies the infant the belief in and experience of omnipotence necessary for generating experience.

Both parties support the mutual dialectic of surrender and generation, though the parent's surrender and generation of experience is of a different order. When an infant is able to surrender to caring interactions, a sense of bodily agency, continuity, emotional-dyadic regulation, cohesion, ownership, and validation is realized and organized in the C-C mode. For instance, at the moment of the mother's lively recognition of the infant's hunger and presentation of her breast to the baby, the baby magically creates the breast and surrenders entirely to the interaction. The sensory-motor pleasure of sucking the mother's breast, skin-to-skin touching, and hunger satiation accompany a bodily and global sense of liveliness. The omnipotent belief and experience, in other words, contains a presentational and unconscious "belief" in and experience of bodily agency, continuity, cohesion, and validation.

As adults, we carry the illusion that the dynamics and experiences of infancy have long been surpassed and thus we overlook the presence of this early mode of organizing experience and the accompanying presence of potential space in everyday life. Two illustrations reveal, in part, the presence of potential space, the dialectic of surrender and generation, and the C-C mode in adult life. Rachel, an intelligent, hard-working, single mother of three children, suffered from horrific flashbacks of sexual, emotional, and physical abuse, which she believed started when she was 3 years old. During the first two years of three to five times a week therapy, Rachel tended to neglect her health and hygiene. On more than one occasion, she angrily lamented that she felt damaged and dirty – the results of being tormented by her mother and older brothers. At some point in her third year of therapy, Rachel arrived in a more buoyant mood. Over the weekend, Rachel began to feel "bad," which foreshadowed an impending return of terrifying bodily memories and flashbacks. Previously, Rachel would wrap herself up in a blanket or she would simply lie on the floor as if she were a stone or piece of wood with no feeling. This time she drew a hot bath, lit candles, and listened to relaxing music. Without conscious intention, Rachel found herself putting lotion (her daughter's) on her body after the bath, which delighted her because she felt the sensual pleasure and comfort of rubbing lotion over her body. This represents a momentary restoration of the dialectic of surrendering to and generating experience. Usually Rachel felt powerless, subjugated and tormented by bodily memories. By becoming "stone" (the absence of sensory-motor-visceral emotions – "autistic withdrawal"), Rachel would sacrifice her body and retreat to some corner of her mind where she would not have to think or feel. For reasons that I discuss soon, Rachel was able to surrender her body to her own ministrations. She gave into, while actively constructing the experience – the pervasive pleasure and comfort of rubbing lotion over her body (C-C mode; motility and sensory pleasure) and a corresponding sense of agency and emotional regulation. In this moment there was a spark of vitality.

Mitch Albom's book, *Tuesdays with Morrie* (1997), provides another illustration. Albom narrated the journey toward death of a beloved friend and former professor, Morrie Schwartz. Morrie had amyotrophic lateral sclerosis (ALS or Lou Gehrig's disease), a disease that slowly and ineluctably destroys the nervous system. A person with ALS dies by stages, gradually losing control of bodily functions. In his first interview with Morrie, Ted Koppel asked what "Morrie dread[ed] the most about his slow insidious decay?" Morrie responded, saying, "Well, Ted, one day soon, someone's gonna have to wipe my ass" (Albom, 1997, p. 22). The understandable fear of losing one's independence and physical agency no doubt lay beneath this serious, though humorous, quip. It could also be said that his remark reflects some anxiety about being subjugated to his own body-disease. Later in the book, we discover that Morrie, despite pain and near complete physical dependency, enjoyed giving in to the pleasure of others' caressing, rubbing, and cleaning his body. Even while he fought to live, Morrie was able to give in to those moments of care. Being physically moved corresponded to a sense and act of allowing himself to be moved. Morrie's physical dependence-in-relation-to-people who cared for him and his concomitant pleasure were something he surrendered to as he faced his own death, without the loss of a sense of agency, cohesion, and validation.

Recognition and negation

A related feature of surrender and generation is the dialectic of recognition and negation of cognition and its importance in organizing experience (Sander, 1995). All forms of recognition include the capacity to negate, which together are twin aspects of identification (Benjamin, 1995, 1998). The psychoanalytic belief that the infant is merged with the mother, incapable of differentiating between itself and the mother, means that the infant is not able to recognize the parent as a distinct object, a separate self, or an equivalent center of subjectivity. Likewise, the infant is not yet capable of using negation to differentiate mother (not-me or not-I) from oneself. There is no "me and not-me" or "I and not-I." However, the infant is able to perceive and prefer sounds, smells, touch, etc. Infant researchers have clearly demonstrated that babies are able to *recognize* sounds, tones, smells, textures, and movements (DeCasper and Fifer, 1980; Meltzoff and Moore, 1998; Beebe and Lachmann, 2002). This is an elementary or primary form of recognition that we might call sensory-motor recognition or primary indexicality (Eco, 1997). Primary recognition is presentational, global, preverbal and somatic and includes a rudimentary capacity to differentiate, which is yoked to constitutional preferences and expectancies.

The presence of primary recognition begs the question regarding negation. Freud (1925) argued that there was no negation in the unconscious. Primary process thinking and early infancy do not include this secondary capacity to negate, to say no. In other words, the preverbal child does not possess a representation or the mental capacity to negate. If negation is conceptualized as a logical operation that emerges in concert with the achievement of symbolization, then Freud was indeed correct. I am suggesting that there is a precursor to "secondary" or logical negation. Primary recognition is accompanied by a somatic, presentational, prelogical negation that is manifested in avoidance, retreat, expressions of physical disgust and aggression (Spitz, 1965; Litowitz, 1998). The aversive system of motivation (Lichtenberg, Fosshage, and Lachmann, 1992), Freud's unpleasure principle, Winnicott's omnipotent destruction, I argue represent the earliest form of negation. For example, the infant omnipotently destroys the breast when finished nursing (Winnicott, 1971, p. 92). A baby turning away from the parent-world or closing her eyes can be aversive responses to the presence of something painful or simply a benign destruction (the world is not), both of which signify negation (Spitz, 1965, p. 193). Thus, primary negation, like primary recognition, is sensory-motor, global, and unconscious, having nothing to do with the logical operation of no. It is only with the achievement of symbolization that primary negation, the precursor to secondary negation, becomes a part of logical operations associated with secondary process and linked to discrete representations.

Surrender and generation, during infancy, comprise this early form of recognition and negation. To surrender to the ministrations of the interaction means that an infant recognizes the interaction to be safe, wherein safety is part of the belief in and experience of omnipotence in conjunction with meeting her physical needs. To generate experience, in the moment of surrendering to it, requires the capacity to negate. The creation of the world or the omnipotent construction of the breast, in other words, includes the capacity for destruction of both. This destruction may be benign or a part of the aversive system. The parent's ability to recognize and contain the infant's "creations" and aggression, which demands more differentiated and complex forms of recognition and negation, establishes potential space, whereby the infant can safely recognize and negate the world, all of which is necessary for the infant's sense of bodily agency, continuity, cohesion and attending embodied vitality. Parental impingement and deprivation represent misrecognition of the infant's needs and result in the infant's defensive use of primary negation to protect herself from subjugation and concomitant annihilation anxiety.

Let's return to Rachel's struggle to illustrate the points here. Usually, when memories threatened to return, Rachel felt out of control and subjugated to body-memories. She unconsciously recognized the impending danger, which was linked to past experiences of traumatic violence and deprivation. The world (of her youth) was too dangerous because the world had not provided recognition or acceptance of her physical desires, needs, and boundaries, disrupting her own budding sense of bodily agency, ownership, and validation. Parental negation was not benign, which evoked annihilation anxiety, making it impossible for Rachel, as a child, to feel safe enough to surrender to the interaction. By retreating into deadness (dissociation) or physical immobility, she omnipotently destroyed this earlier world and, at the same time, negated her body–mind. That is, when Rachel wrapped herself in a blanket and lay on the floor, as if dead, she omnipotently retreated from memories that stood for experiences of being subjugated and negated by powerful people upon whom she depended. This omnipotent retreat represented the defensive presence of C-C mode in that Rachel wrapped herself in a blanket to provide a sense of boundedness in the midst of annihilation. This also signified her visceral negation of a world that was too dangerous to live in (see Winnicott, 1971, p. 97).

A happier illustration of the presence of the C-C mode and the background presence of sensori-recognition and negation in adult life may be found in some religious rituals and related experiences. A believer walks through the doors of the church into the narthex, separating the world of the sacred from the profane. Incense, music, the rhythms of prayer and movement of a Catholic Mass invite the person to surrender to the experience, even as the person constructs his experience. If one is able to surrender, there is a visceral and global recognition of what a philosopher or theologian might term Being, and this recognition is quietly accompanied by an omnipotent negation that is represented in the term non-being. The church structure itself and the ritual represent a separation of worlds: the sacred and profane, being and non-being, life and death. Surely, there are numerous complex symbols manifested in the ritual itself and attending narratives. I would argue, however, that the ritual and symbols are accompanied by primary forms of recognition and negation as well as an embodied, global surrender to and generation of experience. Being and non-being, in other words, are not simply or necessarily mere cognitive abstractions that are separated from the C-C mode of organizing experience.

I believe we also see hints of surrender–generation, recognition–negation, and mind–body–world unity in William James' (1958) depictions of religious experiences:

> For when it is all said and done, we are in the end absolutely dependent on the universe; and into sacrifices and *surrender* of some sort, deliberately looked at and accepted, we are *drawn and pressed* as into our only permanent *positions of repose*. Now in these states of mind which fall short of religion, the surrender to is submitted to as an imposition of necessity . . . In religious life on the contrary, surrender and sacrifice are positively espoused.
>
> (James, 1958, p. 56; emphases mine)

The sense of being moved by some ineffable, benign, though recognizable, presence (Being) and accompanying bodily sense of rest represent, in my view, the background pattern of organizing experience in the corporeal-contiguous mode. The universe is, which accompanies the universe is not. In this instance, negation, like Winnicott's omnipotent destruction, is not defensive or necessarily logical and is only the "negative" aspect of the ability to surrender.

The dialectics of care

A third attribute of potential space, which is an essential piece for the realization of surrender–generation and recognition–negation, is the dialectic of Care (trust–distrust, loyalty–disloyalty). The caregiver's recognition and response to the infant's physical assertions, needs, and desires provide the matrix for bodily conviction and trust. Erikson's (1952) basic trust and Winnicott's (1971) environmental trust are metaphors for the infant's experience of a perceptually unified and embodied trust. The infant, in her multitudinous interactions, omnipotently organizes experiences that are not yet differentiated from each other. So, organizations of bodily conviction and trust are not discriminated from other contexts. For example, the caregiver-holding-the-infant-while-feeding provides a background of trust that is not yet differentiated from the caregiver-bathing-the-infant. Having said this, each of these and other contexts become the background of confidence and trust that are necessary for emerging bodily, unconscious experiences of being alive and real. This global, bodily sense of trust becomes the barely perceptible background of trust in all subsequent subjective states.

For adults, environmental or embodied trust is simply hidden from routine interactions and remains, to use Christopher Bollas' (1987) term, an unthought known. And yet when we experience a significant violation of trust, this organization of perceptually unified trust appears. "When I found out that John was lying, I was *crushed.* My *world* seemed to *collapse.*" "After I was assaulted, *the world* didn't seem to feel safe anymore. My *stomach* is always in a knot." Following the torture, Jean Amery did not simply say that he could no longer trust policemen. The policeman's fist shattered his global trust in "others," in the world. Being tortured also disrupted Amery's sense of bodily integrity and diminished his global and embodied sense of being alive and real. These and numerous other examples portray how trust is rooted in the body-in-relation and how it is woven into an unconscious, perceptually unified world.

Global, somatic trust is contingent upon the experience of loyalty or what Winnicott (1971, p. 108) called reliability, which serves as the ground of embodied hope. In the perceptually unified world of early infancy, loyalty, like trust, is not discrete or linked to a particular object. Instead loyalty, during this period, is an embodied and global loyalty that emerges from the caregiver's reliable recognition (and benign negation) and responses to the infant's desires and needs (Rizzuto, 2004). The infant develops a sense, knit into her psyche-soma, that the world is obliged to respond to her cries and needs, underscoring her sense of bodily cohesion and agency. This bodily conviction that the world is compelled to recognize and respond to desire and need becomes the foundation for other subsequent forms of loyalty. Again, as adults we tend to have little awareness of embodied loyalty until we experience recondite betrayal by others or by our own bodies. For example, Jean Amery's loss of trust in the world grew out of his existential sense of betrayal. He had, like most of us, held the conviction, which was not conscious, that someone would be obliged to recognize and respond to his cry of distress. "The expectation of help," Amery (1995, p. 127) wrote, "is as much a constitutional psychic element as is the struggle for existence." The absence of recognition and response gave rise to a global and physical sense of betrayal and hopelessness.

The background presence of a preconceptual and nonpropositional loyalty (and trust) is manifested in moments of disruption: that is, in the laments of people who struggle with a profound sense of betrayal. "I felt physically sick when I found out that Jane was having an affair. I don't know if I can ever trust anyone." "I spent years not getting close to men;

after all they either hit you or fuck you." "After I was raped, for months I looked at every person as if they were going to do something to hurt me. Still the world seems much more dangerous and frightening." These and similar statements portray the tear in the weave of a perceptually unified sense of loyalty, which disorganizes persons' experience of embodied cohesion, continuity, and agency, diminishing their ability to surrender to experience and their concomitant sense of being alive.

Global and embodied sense of trust and loyalty are yoked to a bodily hope, a hope that may be said to be related to Beebe, Lachmann, and Jaffe's (1997) notion of an infant's expectancies or unconscious anticipation of recognition and response to physically expressed needs. The bodily conviction of trust and loyalty makes possible the hope and confidence that my cries and desires will be met. This does not mean that the preverbal infant "hopes" as a discrete experience directed toward some future time. Environmental hope is born between the moment of felt need and desire and the caregiver's obliged meeting of the need. Hope in that moment is both global and embodied. An infant hopes in its very bones, sinews, muscles, and flesh. In adulthood, it is only in the darkest and deepest periods of hopelessness that we recognize the close link between hope and our bodies. Rachel's retreat to mind–body numbness or deadness may be understood as an iconic expression of global and overwhelming betrayal and hopelessness, which is linked to an inability to surrender to and generate experience. Put differently, the hopelessness Rachel felt in her bones was connected to a loss of mind–body agency, continuity, cohesion, and validation.

In brief, global and mind–body convictions of trust, loyalty, and hope in adulthood are rooted in early infant–caregiver interactions. In early infancy, the caregiver's recognitions, responses, and bodily availability and the infant's physical expressions of need and desire are all part of good-enough interactions. These caregiver–infant interactions, then, contribute to a global and incarnate sense of trust, loyalty, and hope and, at the same time, serve as the foundation for the infant's perceptually unified and bodily sense of cohesion and embodied agency. These preconceptual experiences make it possible for the infant to be at home in her body-world. Just as important, bodily and global conviction of trust, loyalty, and hope provide the infant (and adults) with the necessary background for embodied and unified experiences of being alive and real.

Disruption and repair

The vagaries of human life inform us that trust and loyalty are woven together with real and imagined moments of distrust, betrayal and hopelessness. It is not that distrust and disloyalty are, in and of themselves, traumatic or something to be avoided. Rather, what is important is that these disruptive moments are repaired (Safran and Muran, 1996, 2000). When repair occurs, each party gains confidence in being able to contain and handle disruption without a loss of self or relationship or aliveness (Tronick and Gianino, 1986). The dialectic of disruption and repair is a necessary component of potential space.

What does the dialectic disruption and repair look like with regard to the C-C mode of organizing experience and an embodied, global sense of aliveness? The parent's misrecognitions of the infant and non-contingent responses signify a disruption in the infant–parent dance. The infant's somatic experience registers a disturbance – a moment of bodily and global distrust – and she may escalate her response to obtain the "world's" attention and answer. "I'm wet not hungry." This is the infant's own unconscious attempt at repair. A good-enough parent realizes that her child's cries do not signify hunger and she seeks to repair the disconnection by searching for the difficulty. "Ah, you are all wet. Well, let's get you dry." The infant comes away from this interaction with a global and somatic sense of confidence and agency that relational, emotional disruptions can be repaired. Put differently, the contiguous world is safe even when there is tolerable unpleasure and anxiety. In my view, if we are fortunate as infants and children to have enough of these experiences, then as adults we are less likely to attempt to manipulate others or use violence to regulate our internal states and restore a bodily sense of cohesion. Massive adult distress and acting out, in other words, may be seen as distorted attempts to repair a global sense of distrust and betrayal. More positively, adults who, as children, had mutual, successful interactions of disruption and repair are more likely to experience a physical and emotional sense of centeredness in the midst of conflict and disruption.

I believe it would be safe to say that Rachel did not have many opportunities with her mother where relational disruptions were appropriately repaired. Rachel's actions of cutting herself or wrapping herself in a blanket as if in a cocoon may be understood as her attempts to handle overwhelming, tumultuous disorder using the C-C mode. Given Rachel's description of her mother, I believe it is likely that Rachel, long before she was sexually abused, was left on her own to handle relational miscues and disconnections. The absence of a relational dance of disruption and repair left her to rely on her own body, because the world-interaction was dangerous and unresponsive. Rachel's use of lotion was, in part, the result of many experiences of disruption and successful repair that she had had as an adult. Numerous interactions with me and two other important people who, over two years, displayed our trustworthiness and devotion by verbally and non-verbally recognizing, understanding, and responding to her distress, contributed to her sense of confidence that disruptions could be repaired (see Bacal, 1998b; Beebe and Lachmann, 1998). With Rachel, we created a safe enough place for her to express her suffering as well as her disappointment and disillusionment in me. In other words, Rachel had many opportunities to experience disruption and repair in therapy (Wolf, 1998) and other adult relationships, which led, in part, to her ability to regulate her distress without retreating into somatic numbness.

The presence and collapse of potential space: culture, disembodiment, and therapy

Corporeal-contiguous organizations of a global sense of bodily aliveness happily result when the web of potential space is preserved. A culture's ethos, stories, and rituals, at their best, function to maintain the viability of potential space and, in turn, the C-C mode of organizing experience, which is the barely perceptible background of subsequent, more complex subjective and intersubjective organizations of experience. In adult life, for instance, the sensory symphony of incense, bells, music, rhythmic prayers, wine, and bread of a Christian ritual may promote an unconscious sense of bodily aliveness in a believer. A football fan's deep pleasure in the pre-game ritual of grilling hotdogs, reminiscing about previous games, and the simple pleasure of the plethora of sounds and sights of the game itself offer moments of physical vitality. The pomp and circumstance of a graduation may tap into a person's bodily sense of joy and fulfillment.

Just as a culture's rituals and stories serve to protect potential space and bodily aliveness, they also may contribute to attenuation of potential space and, consequently, mar the capacity for somatic aliveness. Societal neglect of the needs of poor mothers, the absence of social recognition, support, and protection of women threatened by domestic violence, social minimizations of persons' grief (e.g., death of a pet, stillbirth), stigmatization of homosexuals and discrediting male expressions of tenderness are examples of the diminution of potential space. In more severe instances, people within a group may, for many reasons, traumatize others. If the trauma is brutal enough, early in life, and/or cumulative, persons become survivors, having lost the ability to possess and experience a bodily sense of aliveness. Before discussing trauma and its relation to the C-C mode of organizing experience and disembodiment, it is important not to lose sight of larger cultural factors in shaping potential space and bodily experiences of being alive. Two brief examples highlight the relation between culture, potential space, and embodied experiences of being alive.

Culture, potential space, and embodied vitality

At times, stories and treatises reveal a culture's real and imagined anxieties and fears, which, in turn, attenuate potential space and can lead to the partial loss of the attributes associated with bodily aliveness. Western Judeo-Christian preoccupation with negative views of sex and sexuality reveals significant anxiety and shame about sex and its integration into Christian life. Cautionary tales and moral prohibitions aim to influence people trying to live a Christian life. Yet, at the same time, these prohibitions often reduce or collapse potential space because of heightened shame, which contributes to sundering of the C-C mode from other modes of organizing experience. In other words, bodily pleasure becomes conceptually incompatible with being a "good" Christian, which makes it difficult to experience fully somatic spontaneity, pleasure, and validation in sexual play. Bodily pleasure must be controlled. One must not surrender to the pleasures of the flesh. The refusal to surrender to and make happy use of this aspect of bodily existence means that the generation of experience is attenuated because the "body" or physical pleasure becomes an object of distrust and betrayal. A partial or complete collapse of potential space, with respect to physical aliveness, leads to individual and group symptoms. In Freud's view, this is the return of the repressed.

Another more concrete illustration of a cultural artifact that reveals collective anxiety and its relation to potential space and the C-C mode of organizing experience is Star Trek's *Next Generation*, a popular science fiction series of the 1980s and early 1990s. In several episodes, the Borg, a mindless collective, threatens every civilization it encounters. It moves through space seizing other beings, who are then transformed into machine-body units and assimilated into an undifferentiated, mindless unity. Those who are captured function like zombies. Their faces, part machine, are ghostly and their movements are robotic and lifeless. The captain, Jean-Luc Picard, is captured and later rescued before he was fully transformed, leaving him with terrifying memory fragments of his experience and the near-total loss of his individuality. This is mystical oneness in the reverse. The Borg strikes fear in the hearts of crewmembers as they attempt to prevent this force from destroying all of humanity.

These episodes are cultural artifacts of our own story in an increasingly mechanistic and media-dominated world. That is, they represent in vivid ways our deep anxieties about the loss of a sense of aliveness. Will machines dominate us? Will we be absorbed into a collective mass that will obliterate our sense of vitality? Will we be subjugated to the dictates of a mindless commune? Picard's terror, as well as our own, is not simply about the loss of life, but of a living death – an existence without physical agency, spontaneity, somatic integrity, and sense of going on being. The Borg represents the joining of the technological and somatic in a lifeless unity that is as absolute as it is global. At one point in the show, one of the crew hesitates to destroy one of the Borg's functionaries because the crewmember recognizes him as a former comrade. Picard informs him that his friend is already dead. The crewmember cannot kill what is already dead. Picard knows that, after the transformation (more correctly deformation), there is no vitality left to salvage.

The show is not simply a trivial illustration of entertainment that is devoid of "real" cultural angst and loss of potential space. Concerned professionals (e.g., Lifton, 1993; Cushman, 1995; West and Hewlett, 1998) have weighed in on the dangers of technology, global market economy, and the increasing bureaucratization of everyday life. Greenspan (1997), for example, recognized that "modern institutions and much of the technology that supports them have come to threaten the conditions that nurture intelligence, compassion, morality, and creativity" (p. 167). The very tools and organizations that we construct to live better lives may obstruct the attributes (intelligence, compassion, morality, and creativity) that are part of a vital and embodied individuality and community.

Analysis, trauma, and the restoration of potential space

Religious and cultural stories and rituals, then, are connected to and shape potential space as it pertains to the C-C mode of organizing experience and concomitant experiences of being alive. One cultural ritual that developed in the late nineteenth century was psychoanalytic psychotherapy. The rise of this and other forms of therapy may be said, in general, to be a response to the decline of the hegemony of religion in organizing, interpreting, and responding to social relations and ills. More specifically, the advent of psychoanalysis brought heightened interest in understanding trauma and its developmental sources, as well as disturbances in imagination or fantasy. Even as psychoanalysis concerned itself with freeing sufferers from the bondage of symptoms, it is necessary to recognize a paradox of its origin: it emerged from within a patriarchal culture, which suggests the presence of elements of patriarchal narratives in both theory and therapy. Thus, cultural influences are brought into psychoanalytic theorizing and therapy, yet reinterpreted to bring to the fore what had been repressed, and restoring, in part, the possibility of potential space and somatic aliveness.

Consider, for instance, the Oedipal story Freud and others used. Before Freud drew on the Oedipal story to denote developmental struggles, it was a cultural drama manifesting the results of patriarchal systems of organizing families. To maintain his power and to possess his wife, Laius sought to have his son murdered. Laius' command to kill his son fails, unbeknownst to him, and the trauma of Laius' betrayal is manifested on Oedipus' body. Oedipus grows up unaware of this early drama and, thus, is unable to surrender to it and integrate it into his own story. Oedipus' experience of betrayal is organized in and through the body, which the analyst views as symptoms. The symptom represents the split between knowing and the body (Lear, 1998). Unwittingly, then, Oedipus acts out the earlier trauma by killing his father and possessing his mother. A psychoanalytic rendering of this story may be seen from the perspective of development and the analytic ritual. In development, there is a movement from organizing experience in and through one's body to narration that represents the integration of body and thought. The analytic ritual is not simply a movement from the unconscious to conscious, body to speech, but toward integrating the body into conscious formulations of experience. Consciousness and reason are not *the* goals of psychoanalytic therapy. The goals are the repair of trauma and the recovery of potential space so that vitality is experienced in and through embodied reason and consciousness.

Trauma and healing, or the restoration of potential space, are central features of psychoanalytic therapy. In general, trauma results from environmental impingement and deprivation and represents an abrupt tear in or diminution of potential space and, in this chapter, a dis-integration of mind and body through the defensive use of the C-C mode. The shrinkage of potential space is broadly defined as the loss of the dialectical tension between surrender-generation, recognition-negation, trust-distrust, loyalty-disloyalty, and disruption-repair. The C-C mode of organizing experience continues to operate, but it is accompanied by a global and non-propositional sense of subjugation and concomitant eclipse of agency and spontaneity, bodily negation and loss of visceral validation, pervasive somatic-environmental distrust and betrayal, and hopelessness of repair ever occurring. The absence of an embodied sense of aliveness brings to the foreground the necessity of physical-psychological survival, which compels the person's defensive use of the C-C mode. In psychoanalytic parlance, the person activates primitive defenses (e.g., projection, splitting, dissociation) to survive.[7] Pathological autism (Ogden, 1989), somatic defense (Green, 1972), primitive withdrawal (McWilliams, 1994), state of non-experience (Ogden, 1980, 1982a, 1982b), blank psychosis (Green, 1972), death in life (Laing, 1959), psychotic non-being (Grotstein, 1979), bodily dissociation (van der Kolk and McFarlane, 1996), desomatization (Krystal, 1997), and disembodiment (Ulman and Brothers, 1988) are examples of attempts to depict the defenses deployed to secure one's existence against intolerable anxiety associated with the collapse of potential space. In each case, the result is a profound and global loss of a bodily sense of being alive.

Given enough stress, anxiety, and violence, an adult may regress to a defensive posture with a defensive use of the C-C mode of organizing experience. Regression does not mean returning to an earlier period of development. Instead, *regression connotes the hyperactivation and dominance of the C-C mode in the face of overwhelming distress and loss.* Primo Levi's description of a Nazi concentration camp and how some people responded illustrates, in part, the annihilation of potential space and regression to primitive defenses.

> All the musselmans who finished in the gas chambers have the same story, or more exactly, have no story . . . On their entry into the camp, through basic incapacity, or by misfortune, or through some banal

> incident, they are overcome before they can adapt themselves; they are beaten by time, they do not begin to learn German, to disentangle the infernal knot of laws and prohibitions until their body is already in decay . . . Their life is short, but their number is endless: they, the Muselmänner, the drowned, form the backbone of the camp, an anonymous mass, continually renewed and always identical, of no-men who march and labor in silence, the divine spark dead within them, already too empty to really suffer. One hesitates to call them living: one hesitates to call their death death.
>
> (Levi, 1960, p. 90)

The arbitrary, pervasive violence of the camps tells us that vitality and potential space are more than simple metaphors. The absolute negation or absence of potential space becomes real when one is faced with such overwhelming deprivation and death. As Levi (1960) noted, some people responded by a kind of global, psychological withdrawal. Disembodiment, psychotic non-being, and death in life are apt terms for persons who tried to make one last attempt to survive in the face of overwhelming betrayal and hopelessness.

Children, because of psychological and physical dependency, are more susceptible to trauma than most adults and, in some instances, rely on so-called primitive defenses to survive in a world filled with danger. Rachel was severely traumatized throughout her childhood and, as an adult, struggled to bring bodily organized experiences and memories into emotionally regulated, mind–body integrated narratives. By wrapping herself in a blanket and lying on the floor as if dead, Rachel retreated into psychotic non-being by way of dissociation (Brenner, 2001). There were moments during the first two years of therapy when Rachel's non lively, rhythmic rubbing of the chair's fabric left me wondering where she had gone. On one occasion, she was furious that I had replaced a patterned rug with an all-white one. Rachel later told me that she would stare at the patterns, becoming lost in her own world or, more accurately, a world devoid of vitality and fantasy – only the rhythmic pattern of sensory experience. Rachel retreated from the world because it was too dangerous, though during these moments of defensive use of the C-C mode, there was no sense of inner or outer. Danger was global and overwhelming: there was no internal or external world. Rachel could not surrender to the environment nor even surrender to sensory aspects of her body. In other words, her recognition of the world as dangerous was yoked to global visceral negation and her survival depended on not being there. When I wondered where she was, it was not simply a question that involved her rational agency, subjectivity, or ego. Her body was present, but there was, in those moments, an absence of somatic agency, spontaneity, and mind–body cohesion, which is – disembodiment.

Over several years, these moments gradually lessened as we jointly enlarged the potential space. Her devotion to healing and the loyalty of me and several friends provided enough trust for her to risk surrendering to her own experience, to a couple of friends, to me, and to the ritual of therapy. With enough trust and confidence, Rachel's surrender was coupled with generating experience whereby she could somatically possess herself while facing painful memories. In the foregoing text, I mentioned Rachel's experience of putting lotion on after bathing – a seemingly trivial moment. Yet, I view this achievement as an indication of Rachel's integrating the C-C mode with other modes of organizing experience. On that weekend, when the storm clouds of horrific memories threatened to overwhelm her, Rachel did not retreat into psychotic, disembodied, and lifeless withdrawal. Instead, she retained a somatic sense of agency, validation, and continuity, which was accompanied by a sense of physical aliveness even in the face of distress.

Rachel may represent only a small percentage of people who suffer terribly and try to survive by using the C-C mode to isolate the body from the mind and the self from others, existing in a perennially devitalized state. There are many other "normal" or highly functional people who, because of anxiety and shame, supported by cultural narratives and rituals, are uncomfortable with physical pleasure and are not quite at home in their own bodies. I like to think that psychoanalysis, at its best, does two things. First, as a ritual, psychoanalytic psychotherapy invites the joint creation of potential space, which makes room for a somatic sense of aliveness that is integrated with other modes of organizing experience. Second, psychoanalysis provides theoretical frameworks that can be used to critique itself, in addition to debunking cultural stories and rituals that lead to the severing of one's body from one's mind and the severance of somatic liveliness from the social field of interpersonal relations.

Chapter 3

Living objects

> [T]he only possible metaphor one may conceive of for the life of the mind is the sensation of being alive.
>
> (Hannah Arendt, in Kristeva, 2001, p. 89)

> The first thing we instinctively strive to conceive is simply the experience of being alive.
>
> (Langer, 1942, p. 147)

John is passionate about collecting stamps. Sally takes delight in showing a friend the Hummels she has accumulated over the years. Professor Smith, with much excitement, has identified and named a new and rare species of butterfly. A baby squeals with glee upon being handed a toy zebra. On a less happy note, David ruminates over his coin collection, counting and re-tagging each coin in a seemingly endless and empty repetition. On the opposite side of the city, Julie anxiously scans newspapers and magazines, identifying and listing places, people, and things that represent some danger to her health. In a psychiatric hospital, Herb's incoherent word salad frustrates the staff's attempts to understand the significance of his utterances. Black slaves work in the field under the watchful eyes of white overseers. These moments of finding and sorting, of discovering and categorizing are occasions of joy or suffering, astonishment or fear, attraction or hatred. They reveal, in part, the presence of the taxonomic-object mode of organizing experience (T-O), which emerges from the foundations of the corporeal-contiguous mode.

During the first year of life, there is an incredible growth of neural networks, which develop in concert with social interactions (Siegel, 1999), making way for new capacities and more complex organizations of experiences of feeling and being alive. An infant's seemingly meaningless babble as she joyfully grasps a soft toy represents her ability to recognize, link, and organize sound, image, and object. It then becomes possible to represent, segment, and categorize experiences and objects. These preverbal, semiotic utterances precede parole, though they are the very basis of a child and adult's ability to communicate experience via complex and varied language games and symbols.

Before elaborating on the taxonomic-object (T-O) mode, it is necessary to begin with a brief definition and explanation regarding my reasons for introducing the terms taxonomic and primary semiosis. Derived from the Greek *taxis* and *nomia*, taxonomy means categorization or arrangement of items according to certain rules or laws. Taxonomy is usually associated with scientific classifications, which are more sophisticated, linguistic categorizations than I am using in this chapter. I use taxonomic to refer to the child's budding, preverbal abilities to identify objects and experiences and classify these according to rules, beliefs, and emotions that develop in the matrix of constitutional capacities and social interactions. Taxonomical organizations, whether in early childhood or more sophisticated scientific sortings, are contingent on semiotic processes. *Semeion*, yet another Greek word, means trace, iconic mark, distinctive feature, or index. Primary semiosis refers to the child's presymbolic ability to link image, sensory data, emotions, desire, and utterance even as she learns to categorize these associations according to the social syntax – the rules, cues, and roles of the interaction – and her own idiomatic syntax.[1] The capacity to sign is foundational for, yet precedes the capacities for symbolization, language, and narration. Primary semiosis, then, is a crucial component of the child's ability to classify and iconically represent objects and experiences that necessarily connote other attributes of the child's mental and social existence – identification, differentiation, valuation, inference, negation, and resistance. Primary semiotic process also means that to the child the classified object is what it represents. That is, there is no *as if* quality or multiplicity of meanings in the child's perspective.

I use taxonomy and semiosis for another important reason. Some decades ago, Fairbairn's (S. Mitchell, 2000a) schizoid condition and Klein's (J. Mitchell, 1986; Hinshelwood, 1994) paranoid-schizoid position were concepts – embedded in different theoretical orientations – that depicted and explained the intrapsychic and interpersonal dynamics of some patients. Fairbairn and Klein claimed that schizoid and paranoid processes could be detected during the earliest periods of an infant's mental development. And, more broadly, they argued that these processes represented fundamental aspects of the human condition (Grotstein, 2000). In the late 1980s, Ogden (1989) characterized the paranoid-schizoid (P-S) position as a mode of generating experience that appears in development after the autistic-contiguous mode. Omnipotent thinking, splitting, diachronic discontinuity, instability of object relations, and a sense of self as object dominate the P-S mode. Space does not permit a detailed depiction and criticism of their positions on theoretical and clinical grounds.[2] Instead, I use taxonomy and semiosis because I do not wish to pathologize experience or relationships.

Consider Diane Ackerman's (1999) account of glimpsing the Hale-Bopp comet burning in the darkness and feeling a sense of poignant awe. Or consider a deeply troubled young man who once said to me that his obsessive note-taking gave him a sense of security that screened his inner fear and emptiness. Whether we label one experience "healthy" and the other "neurotic," each portrays the capacities for categorization and signification. To make a case for this proposal, I begin by identifying the characteristics of the taxonomic-object mode of organizing experience and its relation to the corporeal-contiguous mode. Next, I turn to depicting the qualities of being alive in terms of this mode of organizing experience. That is, what are the particular attributes of being alive given the characteristics of this mode? A major claim in this book is that the fourfold dialectics of potential space are necessary for persons' experiences of being alive. In this chapter, potential space is portrayed in light of the capacities of the T-O mode of organizing experience and relating. A final consideration involves the collapse of potential space and a person's defensive use of the T-O mode.

Characteristics of the taxonomic-object mode

The primary, interrelated processes associated with the T-O mode are categorization and semiosis. The ability to classify objects and experiences is crucial for survival and, I would add, to a sense of being alive. Long before we experience the pleasure of naming objects, we derive satisfaction in sorting them, through linking image, sensory data, emotion, desire, and preverbal utterances. Given this, we still need to identify the particular features of this early mode of organizing experience and their relation to the C-C mode (and later modes). Four basic circumstances are integral to early capacities of categorization and semiosis.

Sorting me and not-me objects

Winnicott (1971) argued that the second phase of psychosocial development and the first type of sorting involves the child's ability to differentiate between me and not-me objects and experiences. This early recognition of the object as not-me accompanies a rudimentary sense of subjectivity, or, as Green (1978) noted, there is "no object without a subject, no subject without an object" (p. 170). Me-ness is "partly object and partly subject" (William James, in Meares, 2000, p. 9). This elemental, felt sense of subjectivity (or me-ness) is born when a child is able to recognize and categorize the object as not-me. It would be a mistake to suggest that this initial classification of objects and experiences includes the recognition of the object (or subject) as a person or an equivalent center of subjectivity (I-ness). This capacity emerges later in development.

Me-categorizations transform mind–body presentations of the C-C mode. Global-visceral organizations are changed by the ability to differentiate between me and not-me objects. A me-representation, then, includes the body, which, at the same time, presumes the ability to objectify, via discrete representations, one's body. For adults, this form of sorting is usually in the background of daily life, until some event abruptly brings it to consciousness. For instance, John, a construction worker, had an accident on the job that resulted in the loss of his hand. In therapy, John struggled with the loss of his body image and sense of self. John's previous coherent sense of self included his entire body (me-representation). At the same time, John knew that his severed hand did not define him (hand as not-me). The ability to categorize in this way helped him navigate the turmoil of losing his hand.

One may also treat one's body as an object to deal with traumatic events and memories. Mary's stepfather sexually assaulted her for years. As an adult, Mary often treated her body as an object of disgust, retreating from her body to the safety of her mind. One can also discover cultural beliefs and values that facilitate persons' categorizing their own or others' bodies (or parts). Preoccupation with women's breast size and men's "abs" and giving pet names to genitals are examples of the presence of categorization in American culture.

Not-me categorizations exist on a continuum. On the one side, benign or pleasing objects are recognized as not-me and the child is able to identify with the object. For example, the mother putting the child to bed may be sorted in terms of a benevolent or safe not-me object. The not-me object is acceptable or tolerable to the infant. On the other side of the continuum are not-me objects that a child disidentifies. The parent who yells at his child or consistently deprives his child may be categorized as a frightening not-me object such that the child fearfully disidentifies with the parent, classifying him as an intolerable not-me object. The fearful not-me object is absolutely different.

Me and not-me categorization is further complicated when one notes that there are not two basic categories (i.e., me and not-me), but three. The third type of "object" categorization is paradoxical, which Winnicott (1971) challenges us to tolerate, accept, and respect. For Winnicott, the transitional object is a categorization that is a *sign* of separation (from mother) and union, a me and not-me (subjective object) object, an object within and outside the baby's omnipotent control. This subjective object represents both internal and external reality as well as undifferentiated body–mind–environment and differentiated body-object (Deri, 1978). Notwithstanding important critiques of Winnicott's concept (Busch et al., 1973; Brody, 1980; Applegate, 1989), it is useful to conceptualize one aspect of semiotic and taxonomic processes in terms of the mixture of subjectivity and objectivity, fantasy and reality. This early (primary) transitional object is an important category because it signifies the baby's desires and needs, her construction and perception of an object – which represents the joining of these needs and desires – and her relation to an object whose function or role is to meet these needs.[3] The primary transitional object (PTO), then, represents the parent–child interaction of being cared for, hence the emotional and identificatory attachment to it.[4] In short, the PTO signifies a third type of categorization – me-and-not-me (like me and different).

Categorizing in terms of roles, rules, and functions

Me and not-me classifications are accompanied by a second related feature. A child initially recognizes and categorizes objects and experiences in terms of roles, rules, functions, and contexts as they relate to his needs, desires, and emotions. Tronick and Cohn (1989), for example, found that the parent's contingent and non-contingent responses are crucial to a child's "learning the rules of interaction" (p. 90). This suggests that me and not-me classifications and concomitant codes are more complex and varied. For example, the parent, who feeds her child, is a not-me object distinct from, yet related to, the category of the parent who puts me to bed (Stern, 1985). The me-object or primary transitional object may represent diverse functions, rules, roles, and contexts (e.g., self-emotional regulation, play, feeding, holding, containing, protecting, etc.). The child's representations of these distinct contexts and roles are not yet integrated or categorized into a unified representation of parent or a unified representation of self (I–you representation).[5]

The segmentation of objects and experiences by way of roles, rules, functions, and contexts can be seen in adult life. For example, in building a shed, the hammer one uses is clearly an object that is recognized and categorized in terms of its role-function. Or consider Alice, who is leaving to attend graduate school in a city six hours from home. One of the items Alice makes sure to pack is a favorite stuffed bear that her husband gave to her years before. While the bear represents a great many things to Alice, two features of the object and her experience are its role and function (comfort in the face of separation and the unknown). More bleak illustrations are found in cases of depersonalization, pathological narcissism, and paranoia. A therapist listening to a person who is deeply narcissistic may discover that the patient treats her as an object – an object whose only role is to meet some unspoken need. A profoundly paranoid person, who would fall within Klein and Ogden's category of paranoid-schizoid position, may be said to recognize and categorize the "other" as an object solely in terms of his/her role of persecutor and him/herself in the role of victim-object.

Emotional valuations and categorization

Klein believed that in early infancy, through the process of splitting, a child divides the breast into good and bad object, which she takes to be "an expression of the innate conflict between love and hate and the ensuing anxieties" (Mitchell, 1986, p. 216). Whenever anxiety arises, Klein said, "it is mainly of a paranoid nature" (p. 216). One does not have to accept the theory about paranoid-schizoid position to note that Klein recognized that infants are able to categorize objects and they do this in conjunction with judgment and emotion. Infants apparently are able to link emotion and valuation in relation to the object and their own bodies. A third feature of semiotic categorization, then, involves emotional valuations, which "are, if nothing else, semiotic mediators linking the body, the subject, and the social" (White, 1994, p. 220).

Emotional valuation in early life is not simply divided in terms of pleasure and paranoid anxiety. That is, the unfamiliar and strange are not always accompanied by or pervaded with anxiety-valuations of bad and dangerous. The primary transitional object and potential space suggest that a child may be able to organize experience in more complex ways than bifurcating existence, objects, and experience into the emotional valuations of good-bad, safe-dangerous. Surely, intense feelings of disgust, anxiety, and hate will be accompanied by evaluations of the object or part object and attending experience as bad. Yet, there are also more moderate feelings (e.g., interest-anxiety, early curiosity, or pleasurable astonishment) that attend judgments of the object as unfamiliar and safe-enough. It is more accurate to think of taxonomic and semiotic processes shaped by an affect-valuation that operates on a continuum of intensity.

Consider our own routine observations or participations in introducing a strange or different object to a young child. Certainly, the manner of introduction shapes the interaction. That is, the parent's own enthusiasm shapes the child's interest or curiosity as she evaluates the object as safe-unfamiliar. On other occasions, we might observe the child, on his own, reaching for and grabbing an unfamiliar object that he happens upon and initially categorizes as safe-strange. A low level of anxiety accompanies this preliminary judgment, which may change depending on other experiences that attend the interaction. A positive scenario would involve what Bollas (1992) called aleatory objects – unexpected objects. In this encounter, "we are played upon by the inspiring arrival of the unselected, which often yields a very special type of pleasure – that of surprise" (p. 37). The initial anxious-safe categorization changes to delight, surprise, or pleasurable astonishment, delight in novelty. If, however, the object hurts the child, pain and anxiety heighten and the object becomes categorized as bad-dangerous. When the child experiences pleasure or pleasurable astonishment in his exploration of the object, it is then sorted as good-safe. In brief, a strange, unselected (aleatory) object may not necessarily evoke troubling anxiety and fear. Instead, a strange object, a not-me object, may be an occasion of interest, curiosity, and pleasant bewilderment. This contrasts with the notion that there are only good and bad objects (P-S position).

Other types of categorizations shaped by emotional-valuations are primary transitional objects that the child idiosyncratically selects, discovers, and creates (Winnicott, 1971). This suggests that a subjective object (and I would argue benign not-me objects) can be both alien and familiar, strange and heimlich. A child can express excited attention and astonishment in relation to an object she omnipotently discovers and creates. On other occasions, a child can direct her aggression toward the object. In brief, the child's subjective representation of the object is a categorization that may be joined to and shaped by the pleasure of creation and destruction.

While there are, of course, important distinctions to be made between early childhood and adulthood, there are illustrations of this feature of the taxonomic mode in adulthood coupled with a sense of vitality (or deadness). A positive example may be seen in the excitement and astonishment Barbara shows upon sighting a strange outcropping of variegated rocks while hiking in the mountains. This aleatory object evokes interest and curiosity. In therapy, a patient's slightly anxious, though pleasurable, surprise upon hearing the analyst's interpretation may be seen, in part, as an unselected object that awakens and evokes aesthetic gratification instead of dread. Less happy occurrences are found when a patient finds the proffered interpretation to be upsetting and expresses an anxiety-tinged hatred toward the analyst, judging and viewing her as bad and dangerous.

One may also observe cultural beliefs and activities that manifest, to some degree, this feature of the taxonomic mode. In the recent past, US categorizations of Saddam Hussein as evil revealed heightened anxiety – screened by hostility and paranoia – that attended the judgment and categorization of the "object" as dangerous-evil. Saddam Hussein, for some Americans, did not *symbolize* evil. Indeed, the term "evil" loses its symbolic aspect when applied in this way. Freud (1924b, p. 179) and later Segal (1957) might have argued that this represents a collapse into a symbolic equation, but I would see this as an instance of taxonomic-semiotic processes dominated by anxiety-valuations. In this example, there is no *as if* quality nor are there multiple meanings and functions that accompany the capacity for symbolic classification. In the T-O mode, the sign is reality (facticity).

Animate-inanimate sortings

A fourth feature of the T-O mode is animate-inanimate categorizations. Abrams and Neubauer (1978) noted that infants are able to categorize the world into human and thing objects. In related research, Brazelton, Koslowski, and Main (1974) indicated that they could "detect whether he (the infant) was watching an object or interacting with his mother – so different was his attention, vocalizing, smiling, and motor behavior with the inanimate stimulus as opposed to the mother" (p. 53). Early in life, despite the child's ability to attribute fantastic aspects to the object, she is learning to recognize and categorize objects as living or lifeless. This period of development may surely involve a struggle to differentiate between inner and external reality, as Winnicott (1971) believed, but it also includes the child's learning to recognize objects as living or not. Having said this, the child values both animate and inanimate objects, depending on categorizations connected to roles, functions, contexts, and emotional valuations.

The category, animate, comprises a constellation of factors: *warmth, moisture, movement, softness, malleability, inhalation-exhalation, contingent parental responses to the child's affective expressions of internal needs and desires, parent–child utterances, and scents emanating from child and parents.* I would add that learning to categorize aliveness or animation is contingent, in part, on the eager state of aliveness manifested in the parent. The liveliness of the parent-object contributes to the child's ability to recognize the parent as distinct from inanimate objects. Thus, animate, as a category, is not related simply to the qualities of the object's (child or parent) aliveness, but includes the vitality or animation of the *interaction* between parent and child.

Naturally, a child may either confuse these two categories or project onto inanimate objects, via fantasy, the quality of aliveness. PTOs, which represent inner and external reality, also represent animate and inanimate categories. The primary transitional object is alive and not alive. The child imbues the primary transitional object with life, with her own vital idiom (Bollas, 1991, 1992). She omnipotently animates the object, meaning that the qualities of aliveness existing between parent and child, along with the child's unique constitutional characteristics (Bollas's idiom), are now assigned to the transitional object. To an adult, the child's prized blanket symbolizes separation and union and an inanimate object. To the child, however, the primary transitional object is alive – a semiotic, not symbolic, construction. There is no *as if* aspect here. The animated object *is* what it represents. This may explain, in part, the emotional response a child has when the object is changed or lost. It is not simply a blow to the child's sense of omnipotence, as Winnicott (1971) suggested. Rather, the loss threatens the child's ability to construct, perceive, and use an animated subjective object – to give life to the other.

We might observe a young child holding a soft toy as she falls asleep or dragging the toy as she crawls around the house. The toy, as a primary transitional object, is alive to the extent that the child creatively constructs the object. The rules, roles, and functions assigned to the object are created by the child, yet they represent (ideally) the rules, roles, and functions connected to the parent–infant interactions. One can find parallel examples in adult life too, though naturally there are significant differences. We often imbue the qualities of *human* aliveness to pets and to inanimate objects (planes, cars). Granted, healthy adults realize that they are using their imagination, but the early roots of this categorization and attending organization are part of the T-O mode. Indeed, this early categorization of animate objects is a first step toward a child's eventual recognition and sorting of the other as a person, as an equivalent center of subjectivity.

More problematic examples of animate-inanimate categorizations can be seen in racist or sexist behaviors. The object is recognized and categorized as an animate object, yet devoid of the qualities of personhood (e.g., dehumanization). To a white racist, the black person is an "other" that is unconsciously sorted in terms of anxious-dangerous evaluation as well as categorized consciously as a living object that is not recognized as an equivalent center of subjectivity. There can be no chance encounter with this "object" and only "pleasure" attends violent aggression to attain separation if not annihilation. Racist or sexist omnipotent constructions of the other point to the presence of the T-O mode such that the category of animate attends to and is shaped by anxious-dangerous-valuations. The taxonomic-semiotic processes are operating, dominated by anxiety, collapsing *as if* aspects of symbolization.

In summary, human beings are creative categorizers, sorting and labeling objects, persons, and experiences according to our conscious and unconscious desires and fears. Early pre-symbolic categorizations are classified and organized semiotically. More specifically, in the taxonomic-object mode of organizing experience, objects are categorized according to me and not-me, animate-inanimate, which, in turn, are sorted and shaped by the object's role(s), rule(s), function(s), context(s) and emotion-driven valuations.

Attributes of taxonomic-object organizations of being alive

In Chapter 2, I identified five interrelated attributes necessary for an embodied sense of being alive and real. Agency, emotional regulation, continuity and cohesion, ownership, and validation continue to be essential for experiences of being alive, yet they are significantly and qualitatively altered by the new mental and social capacities that emerge with the taxonomic-object mode of organizing experience. I briefly describe each of these attributes, leaving aside for the moment an elaboration of the dynamics of potential space as it relates to the achievement of the taxonomic-object mode of being alive.

Agentic me-ness

Accompanying nascent subjectivity is pre-intentionality, which means that the child's aims are semiotically organized in terms of me-ness. The child's behavior and utterances are discrete signs of her rudimentary intentions. Negatively speaking, one can note that the child's sense of agency with regard to the taxonomic-object mode is pre-reflective and pre-symbolic. There is no "I" schema that orders a child's behaviors and, as a result, she is not able to reflect consciously on her intentions or consciously *intend* to change her intentions. There are, however, semiotically organized me-representations that are joined to and give impetus to the child's more focused behaviors and intentions. In this phase, the child "uses" objects, though she does not consciously *intend* to do so. The child's use of a primary transitional object, for instance, represents not simply the interplay of omnipotent fantasy in relation to an external object, but also a more directed, agentic use of the object. One function of the primary transitional object is to help the child express and consolidate agentic me-ness, which includes various roles and rules that join one's interaction with and use of the object.

Naturally, the child, in expressing and developing a sense of agency, encounters resistance, which is a necessary feature of the development of me-agency. Psychoanalysts are accustomed to think of resistance negatively or, if positively, resistance is believed to represent a patient's understandable need to protect oneself. Instead of being depicted negatively or as protection, resistance is essential in supporting and limiting the child's nascent subjectivity and agency. Macmurray (1961) noted, "The Other is the correlate of the Self as Agent. It is that which resists, and in resisting supports, my intentions" (p. 79). Similarly, when Winnicott (1971) recognized that the transitional object is both within and outside the child's omnipotent control, he was pointing to the fact that the object (or Other as parent) qua object resists the child's absolute constructions, but still the resistance supports the child's emerging subjectivity and agency. The parent's good-enough responses to the child's assertions include resistance in that contingent responses are never perfectly coordinated with the child's needs and desires as well as the fact that the parent is recognized as an animate object and not a mere fantasy. Moreover, sensitive parents establish appropriate limits, rules, and expectations, all of which may be viewed in light of resistance that shapes and supports a child's burgeoning sense of agency and his semiotic learning of social codes and rules (Muller, 1996). Resistance becomes "negative" when there is parental deprivation and impingement such that the child loses hope and confidence that her intentions and desires are supported and can be acted upon. In these situations, the child becomes subject (me-ness) *to* the will of the object. Consequently, she experiences a loss of freedom and spontaneity and a corresponding distortion of agency. Agency, in this instance, is believed to be entirely derived from and contingent upon the Other.

Agency, in the T-O mode, is organized in terms of rules, functions, and roles. There is greater plasticity than previous somatic agency, because the child can extend and direct her intentions toward objects and she can recognize, possess, and manipulate the semiotic rules and roles associated with diverse contexts. In other words, not-me categorizations, as noted above, may be experienced and organized by various contexts that have specific social rules and functions, which support and limit the child's sense of agency. For instance, a not-me encounter with an aleatory object may enhance a child's sense of agency in that the object's function is yoked to the child's expressions of surprise and pleasure in this happenstance encounter. Likewise, the child's use of a PTO varies according to the context, function, roles, and the child's internal state.

Good-enough parenting enhances the child's organization of her budding sense of subjectivity and agency via the taxonomic-object mode. Obviously, children are not always and everywhere blessed by facilitating parents. Klein and Ogden's paranoid-schizoid position represents a taxonomic-object organization wherein the child's sense of agency is occluded. Subjectivity and agency are threatened because objects are perceived and categorized as dangerous and obstacles to realizing one's intentions. The object *is* a sign (not symbol) of danger and the transitional object is used to defend against internal or external peril. In the paranoid-schizoid mode, the child (or adult) semiotically organizes experience in terms of rules based on survival, protection, and avoidance of further subjugation to or annihilation by the object. Intention is restricted to survival and resistance is equated with subjugation. Sacrificing spontaneity and agency allows the child to maintain her existence in the face of danger. Fetishes and some obsessive-compulsive behaviors also represent a marked attenuation of agency and the dominance of the taxonomic mode where, for adults, words become objects to protect one from real or imagined danger and not to mediate intersubjectivity or to signify subjective experiences of being alive.

Phillip's story is an illustration of the T-O mode and agency. A tall lanky man, Phillip was very intelligent. He was a respected chemist and researcher for a pharmaceutical company. Married with two teenage children, Phillip was content with his life, until, that is, his wife left him, taking the children with her. He felt powerless and hopeless with regard to having his children back or the kind of life he had experienced as "happy." After the initial shock wore off, Phillip increasingly viewed his ex-wife as destroying his previous contentment and obliterating his chances of having a family in the future. The laboratory served as a refuge – a place where he could lose himself in his experiments. There was a great deal more to Phillip's story, but one view is that Phillip viewed his ex-wife as an obstacle that thwarted his intentions and agency. A place and activity where Phillip derived a sense of agency was at work, experimenting, classifying data, and researching chemical compounds. In therapy, Phillip also obtained some sense of agency, yet this was, in the beginning and at times, closely connected with him listing his grievances against his wife. It was in these self-states that the T-O mode dominated Phillip's organization of his experience, representing a sense of agency under threat by a bad object. At the lab, the objects and context did not represent insurmountable resistance. In therapy, when Phillip spoke about his wife, she represented an object that barred him from achieving his desires.

Agency and emotional regulation

A sense of agency is accompanied by more deliberate and discrete use of objects and, in particular, the use of PTOs for emotional regulation. White (1994) argued that "emotions are, if nothing else, semiotic mediators linking the body, the subject, and the social" (p. 220). Emotions are clearly important in shaping the child's organization of experience (Sroufe, 1995), yet the child now has the capacity to use discrete objects (and behavior) to regulate her emotional state. A reason why the PTO can be used by the child for arousal and soothing is that it signifies contingent, emotional regulation that originates in the parent–child interaction, which is the parent–child idiom of care. An adult, observing her child's use of a teddy bear for comfort, may say the object symbolizes good enough parent–child exchanges that led to calming the child. To the child, however, the bear signifies the experience of being soothed. In other words, it is not *as if* the bear represents these experiences. The bear is alive and real in its ability to calm the child. This does not mean the child confuses the two objects – bear and parent. *It is the soothing experience and attending semiotic code, rules, and roles (idiom of care) that link the parent and the teddy.* Whether the child uses the object for the arousal of desire and aggression or for calming anxieties and fears, the interactions with the PTO are yoked to semiotic rules, roles, functions, and contexts that the child learned in relation to the parent. The more varied the emotional regulation and the more control the child has in managing emotional states, the greater the sense of agency and being alive.

A child's sense of being alive depends not only on her agentic use of objects to regulate emotional states, but also on her response to aleatory objects – happenstance objects not within her omnipotent control. A sense of curiosity and surprise that are evoked when the child encounters a strange object already suggests an ability to be open to the influence of the object. The child does not use the object to induce surprise; the object itself evokes an emotional state. An aleatory object throws the child and the child is able to regulate his internal state to permit being thrown (see surrender below); as a result, she experiences pleasurable astonishment. One could say that the child is learning to tolerate ignorance and mystery – necessary components of adult joy, pleasurable astonishment, awe, and reverence.

Emotional regulation, then, includes the ability to be surprised, to experience awe and curiosity in the presence of an unfamiliar object. This capability is directly associated with the child's own sense of spontaneity. A playful and spontaneous child is able to handle and enjoy the spur-of-the-moment appearance of the unfamiliar. Use of the PTO and the aleatory object indicate the child's transition from somatic competence to object competence and this achievement represents her greater capability for semiotic agency and emotional regulation, which are necessary for experiences of being alive.

Objects and continuity and cohesion

The child's use of PTOs signifies as well the ability to extend a sense of bodily continuity and cohesion to objects (Kestenberg and Weinstein, 1978). Previous somatic, presentational organizations of continuity and cohesion are transformed. Prized objects now stand for a continuous and cohesive me. To the child, though, the object does not "represent" or symbolize continuity. Instead, she experiences the primary transitional object as me-continuity and cohesion. The object *is* what it signifies. A sense of continuity, however, is not exclusive to PTOs. Other objects, as well as behaviors, rules, roles, and social rituals, may also become linked to a continuous and cohesive me.

It is difficult to observe a child and try to determine what objects or behaviors provide a sense of continuity. Sometimes, the child's emotional response to the loss of an object or to being deprived of some customary behavior lends weight to this idea. With adults, it is also possible to observe this mode of organizing experience and, in particular, the relation between a continuous and cohesive me-ness and objects. Instances of adult trauma and deprivation reveal the background web of social and individual continuity and its relation to experiences of being alive. For example, Holocaust survivor Primo Levi poignantly narrated the close connection between objects and habits and their relation to me-ness and continuity:

> [C]onsider what value, what meaning is enclosed even in the smallest of our daily habits, in the hundred possessions which even the poorest beggar owns: a handkerchief, an old letter, the photo of a cherished person. These things are part of us, almost *like limbs of our body* . . . Imagine now a man who is deprived of everyone he loves, and at the same time of his house, his habits, his clothes, in short everything he possesses: he will be a hollow man . . . for he who loses all often easily loses himself.
>
> (Levi, 1960, p. 27, emphasis mine)

Levi's experience shows that human beings unconsciously extend their sense of me-ness to diverse, familiar objects and behaviors. These objects are like parts of one's body and, when deprived of these, a person loses a sense of himself, a sense of continuity and cohesion. I don't believe Levi was writing strictly in symbolic terms. These objects signified Levi's me-ness. His sense of hollowness and depression point to the link between routine objects that provided a background presence of continuity and cohesion – experiences of being alive. Being violently deprived of me-objects led to discontinuity and a sense of numbness, deadness, and emptiness.

Notwithstanding Levi's story, continuity, in the taxonomic-object mode of organizing experience, is not yet autobiographical (symbolic-subjective and reflective-intersubjective modes of organizing experience). The birth of the historical subject awaits the capacities for symbolization, narration, and self-reflection. Thus, a subjective sense of going on being is dominated by semiotic categorizations (me and not-me) of objects. Discontinuity is experienced as the loss or threatened loss of prized me-objects and behaviors and their concomitant roles, rules, and functions. A not-me object or behavior that is deemed dangerous to a sense of continuity and cohesion will activate the child's (or adult's) defenses and her motivation to secure a real or imagined safe object or activity. This is an important clinical point. Take, for example, Bob, whose diagnosis is borderline personality disorder. In his mid-thirties, Bob is marginally successful, though quite intelligent and gifted. Bob was the only child of two successful parents who alternated between indulging and neglecting him. Bob recalls his father as being kind and gentle, though Bob never quite knew when his father would "blow up." His therapist, recounting the previous session, remarked that Bob seemed to love him a minute ago, only to find that a few minutes later the therapist was deemed to be a dangerous and hostile person. His therapist believed that this change was precipitated by his interpretation about Bob's longing for and hatred of his father. After a brief outburst, Bob began to talk about his other therapist in glowing language, though the therapist recalled that in the past Bob angrily maligned the previous therapist. The therapist experienced and interpreted this interaction as discontinuous, though the patient, in my view, did not. What the therapist interpreted as discontinuous is the result of his ability to organize experience autobiographically – as a historical subject (Ogden, 1989). So the therapist might argue that patients, such as Bob, manage anxiety and pain "through the defensive use of omnipotent thinking, denial, and the creation of discontinuity of experience" (Ogden, 1989, pp. 18–19). In particular, Ogden wrote, "splitting defensively renders object-related experience of a given emotional valence discontinuous" (p. 19). This borderline patient, then, appeared to make his experience discontinuous, *splitting* off the bad experience-object. However, Bob, in this instance, was only aware of a threat and did not fathom his apparent contradictory behavior as manifesting discontinuity.

I argue, that in the taxonomic-object mode, experience is continuous but not in the same way that it is in later modes. That is, experience and objects are not integrated under an "I" schema and narrative. This means that an object (or behavior) signifies continuity and cohesion *in this context and with this emotional valuation*, which is not necessarily connected or integrated with other object-behavior-experiences (I-schema across time). Me-ness, then, does not denote an integrated, continuous, and cohesive me across *time and context*. Likewise, the object-parent is not continuous in the sense of narrative-time. All of this does not imply that the child necessarily experiences himself as fragmented. To return to Bob, we could say that, in this moment-context, he perceives and categorizes the therapist in the role of a dangerous not-me object. This particular taxonomic-object organization is not yet integrated with the taxonomic organization associated with the therapist functioning as a good me-(not-me) object. The patient *does not experience discontinuity* nor does he split off or evacuate bad representations to preserve continuity. Rather, we observe the hyperactivation of one strand of experience that is not integrated with the "good" therapist–patient experience. Anxiety is managed and continuity is maintained, not through rendering experience discontinuous, but through the defensive use of the taxonomic-object mode whereby an idea, behavior, or object is in the role of securing continuity in this context. For instance, the patient's discourse about his previous therapist serves, in part, to safeguard continuity in the face of threat.

In brief, borderline or paranoid-schizoid behaviors represent survival and *the defensive* use of the taxonomic mode in maintaining a sense of continuity and cohesion. A defensive and rigid use of the T-O mode to ward off anxiety attenuates agency and emotional regulation, leaving a person with a diminished sense of being alive and real. This differs from a non-defensive use of T-O mode in which continuity and cohesion are linked to agentic, non-defensive use of objects and where the emotions of pleasure, surprise, and spontaneity are part of the organization.

Object validation

Continuity, agency, and emotional regulation accompany an emerging sense of validation in relation to prized objects, such as the primary transitional object. A confirmation of me-ness and sense of being valued takes place in the emotionally contingent interactions between parent and child. As the child begins to use objects, the roles, rules, and functions of the parent–child interaction become linked to the child's use of objects. In this way, the child confirms and values an object and the object, she believes, reciprocates the favor. The experience of validation is now joined to a discrete object, though this experience is not one of recognized personhood. The child, in other words, in prizing and cuddling the object, gains and confirms a sense of being valued. Worth and validation are determined by the object's ability to fulfill a valued role and by its adherence to the rules of the interaction. If the child perceives the object as complying with expected rules and roles, the object functions to validate the child's me-agency.

Bob's struggle with his therapist illustrates this aspect of organizing experience in the T-O mode. One interpretation is that Bob values his therapist to the degree the therapist abides by those rules that accomplish the function and role of protector, which secures his sense of self. When the therapist made a strong interpretation about Bob's feelings toward his father, Bob felt threatened and viewed his therapist as violating unspoken rules. This was accompanied by anxiety associated, in part, with the loss of validation, of being valued, which not surprisingly was unconsciously yoked to Bob's numerous experiences of being invalidated by his father. By talking about the previous therapist, Bob was retreating to and making use of both an object and experiences of feeling safe and valued. It could be said that Bob was cueing his therapist about his anxieties and needs for a softer, more tentative, interpretation.

Primo Levi's experience also illustrates the relation between validation and objects (and behaviors). Levi's sense of hollowness represents a profound loss of being valued, which was inextricably yoked to a continuous and cohesive self. The violent and ruthless stripping of a person's possessions, ceremonies, and socially governed behaviors deprived Levi of his sense of worth and value. All of us obtain some sense of value as subject though prized possessions, behaviors, and rituals and, if all is well, this contributes to a sense of being alive. We can give these up if they are easily replaced or if our own agency is involved. In Levi's case, depersonalization (invalidation) was achieved by the systematic denial of his agency and by ruthlessly stripping him of even the smallest valued objects and ceremonies.

To summarize, being alive and real depends on a sense of agency, emotional regulation, continuity, cohesion, and validation. The child's use of primary transitional objects signals a transition from corporeal-contiguous mode to the taxonomic-object mode of organizing experience. Each capacity becomes joined to and shaped semiotically by rule- and role-based interactions in relation to recognized objects and behaviors. Greater flexibility in using and transferring contingent parent–child interactions to objects expands the child's sense of (me) agency, extends her ability to regulate and be open to emotional states, and increases her use of objects in securing continuity, cohesion, and validation.

Potential space, primary transitional objects, and the emergence of subject-object vitality

A sense of vitality, organized in the T-O mode, is contingent upon the fourfold, interrelated dialectic of potential space – surrender–generation, recognition–destruction, Care (as trust–distrust, loyalty–disloyalty), and disruption–repair. Each pair of poles is depicted from the perspective of the child's relation to and use of primary transitional objects and the child's concomitant use of the taxonomic-semiotic mode in her organizing experiences of being fully alive.

Winnicott (1971) noted that the child's healthy use of a transitional object represented creative omnipotence even as the child is learning to hand over omnipotence to an external object. From this, one could say that the child is generating experience via his preverbal, agentic use of the object. The PTO becomes subject to the child's desires, wishes, and needs. In this space, the child, in relation to the PTO, learns to generate and use the rules, roles, and functions – founded in and derived from the parent–child dyad – for emotional regulation, continuity, cohesion, and self (me) -validation. Yet, this is only part of the equation.

Surrender–generation and the PTO

Winnicott did not highlight the importance of the child's ability to surrender to the transitional object, which is a hallmark of creativity. Non-defensive use of the PTO includes moments when the child surrenders to the PTO, enabling the object to influence or transform his inner state. This pre-intentional me-surrender to a discrete (not-me) object is not separate from the child's constructing experience. The child constructs experience at the same time that he surrenders to the object. Winnicott's emphasis on play is a good example of generating and surrendering to experience and yielding to the ministrations of the object. Play requires an openness to be influenced, as well as the capacity to generate experience and make use of the object. Put another way, an aspect of abrogating omnipotence, which Winnicott believed was crucial for intersubjectivity, is precisely this ability to surrender to the object – to be a subject of the object's real and imagined care. This dialectic of generating and surrendering in relation to the PTO parallels the parent–child relationship. A child, who is able to surrender to the ministrations of the parent, so that he is influenced by the parent-object, is able to extend this to objects such as PTOs. This pre-intentional, dialectical openness and semiotic construction of experience gives rise to the child's felt sense of vitality and being real. Inner aliveness accompanies the aliveness of the object.

The defensive use of PTOs as well as Klein and Ogden's paranoid-schizoid position signify the refusal to surrender and the rigid generation of experience. Numerous objects are perceived to be dangerous and, therefore, the child protects herself against this danger by omnipotently constructing and using PTOs. Surrendering, from the child's perspective, is equivalent to being subjugated to the needs and wishes of the object, which is accompanied by anxiety linked to invalidation and the eclipse of me-agency. In these situations, experience is drained of vitality even as the child constructs experience in the taxonomic-object mode. The PTO, in this case, is a survival object, warding off intolerable anxiety and defensively maintaining a child's sense of agency, continuity, and cohesion at the cost of creativity, spontaneity, and curiosity.

Dave's struggle in love and work illustrates his tension between surrendering to and generating experience in the taxonomic-object mode. When Dave was 2 years old, his mother was diagnosed with a terminal illness. Shortly after this, his father left home, abandoning Dave and his older brother and sister to the care of his mother's sister and her alcoholic husband. Dave recalled many occasions when his aunt angrily threatened to leave them on the streets. There were times when his aunt would be kind, but only when Dave demonstrated ineptitude, weakness, or when he was ill. Not surprisingly, Dave quickly learned the rules and roles of this interaction and, as a middle-aged adult, he had numerous doctors and other people attend to his diverse ailments. One "game" Dave had become quite expert at was obtaining pain prescriptions from various physicians. Every evening, Dave would secretly take a pill, which would give him a sense of elation and the courage to be with his wife and child. For Dave, people were dangerous, yet he needed them – albeit at a safe emotional distance – to ward off terrifying feelings associated with abandonment.

To surrender to the care of his wife, to give in to being influenced and shaped by his daughter, to be open to being shaped by his therapist were too frightening for Dave because of his numerous early life experiences of being subjugated to the needs and wishes of his aunt (as well as the vicissitudes of numerous traumatic losses). One could say that Dave encountered too many occasions in childhood of having the environment and objects overwhelmingly transform his inner state. In these moments, Dave was subjugated to the whims of powerful others who treated him as an object of their desires and needs. In the process, Dave's sense and expression of agency in the social realm were killed off. To survive, Dave omnipotently made use of the pills (PTO), which I understand to be omnipotent, semiotic construction of experience, whereby he salvaged some sense of agency, continuity, and emotional regulation in the face of intolerable anxiety. The pills represented to me what did not happen (surrender to a loving, interested other) as well as what did happen (subjugation). This omnipotent construction of experience and use of objects occurred alongside his refusal to surrender to dangerous others. In securing prescriptions or using the pills, there was no sense of play or vitality. Put differently, the pills were survival objects that possessed certain functions and roles that secured some semblance of validation and solace in the midst of a frightening world. In addition, Dave's machinations in obtaining the pills represent rules he learned in his early relationships. Attention was purchased at the price of submission, yet he also resisted by duping a powerful figure (i.e., he was pretending). Physicians and therapist alike were treated as objects to be fooled, as he had been as a child. In short, the use of pills and objects of "care" represented Dave's terror in surrendering to the care and devotion of important people as well as his omnipotent generation of experience – defensive use of the T-O mode in organizing experience.

Recognition and negation

The second dialectic of potential space is recognition and negation, which is part of the process of secondary identification. As stated earlier in this chapter, the child is able to recognize discrete (animate and inanimate) me, not-me, and me-and-not-me objects. While the good-enough parent recognizes and treats the child as a separate subject, the pre-symbolic child is not yet capable of this form of recognition or identification. Instead, she recognizes the object and, semiotically and taxonomically, organizes experience in terms of roles, rules, and functions (Meares, 2000). The child recognizes the PTO, for instance, as a me-object that is subject to his needs and desires as well as an object to which she can safely surrender.

The negative pole of recognition is negation. Semiosis and categorization, which are capacities connected to secondary identification, depend on the child's ability to negate – to recognize the object (e.g., PTO or aleatory objects) as not-me. Negation, during this pre-symbolic phase, is neither a logical operation that Freud (1925) refers to nor a symbolic ability to represent "no." Spitz (1957), Ver Eecke (1984), and Litowitz (1998) noted that pre-symbolic rejection and refusal of another person represent types of negation that precede the semantic no. Because the child is not yet able to recognize the other as a subject (or person), his negation involves an object, not a person. Moreover, the ability to negate entails more than negative valuations associated with rejection or refusal. In other words, the child's use of the PTO involves a negation that does not involve rejection. As Winnicott (1971) noted, not every turning away from the object or PTO involves rejection or refusal. The PTO as a me-and-not-me object simply refers to the mental operation of semiotic negation, meaning the child knows the object is like-me-and-different-from-me. If the object is perceived to be disgusting or frightening, then the child negates it (spurned not-me object), perceiving it to be entirely different – the object is different and not like me. On other occasions, the child recognizes the object as not-me without rejecting or refusing it. The object is merely understood to be different-and-like me. So, secondary identification represents the mental operations that comprise perception of the object in terms of likeness (me-recognition) *and* difference (not-me negation), which is the precursor of symbolic identification that includes likeness in difference and difference in likeness (Benjamin, 1995).

Intense anxiety or feelings of disgust initiate defensive operations whereby recognition as likeness and negation as difference are semiotically divorced. For example, in the paranoid-schizoid position, the feared object is rejected (negation) as like me. To the child, the bad object is not recognized as like me-*and*-different. Rather, the object is recognized and semiotically categorized as dangerous and absolutely not-me (disidentification). While the capacity for negation is present with regard to the child's defensive use of the PTO, it tends to be hidden by a defensive "ratification of sameness" (Benjamin, 1995). The PTO is identical to me and operates to defend against any possibility that the dangerous object is like me. What we commonly call splitting (good and bad objects) is the taxonomic-object mode of organizing experience such that recognition is dominated by defensive negation (i.e., rejection of like me) of an object categorized as dangerous. Identification with the good object, in this case the defensive use of the PTO, means that semiotic negation of the dangerous object is accompanied by a hyperactivation of recognition of the PTO as me (ratification of sameness).

Let's return to Dave's struggle with intimacy. Dave certainly "knew" that his wife, daughter, and therapist were persons who cared about him. However, I see his behavior toward them and his physicians as a manifestation of his defensive use of the taxonomic-mode of organizing experience. In terms of secondary identification, Dave frequently recognized (and treated) his wife as a not-me object – an object that was entirely different from him (negation as rejection/refusal). Despite his anxiety about becoming subjugated to her needs and wishes, Dave also recognized her as an object who performed a needed role in his life – an illusion of intimacy and community. Put differently, Dave's aversive system operated in the semiotic mode such that he recognized the significant people in his life as objects and, because of his terror of abandonment, negated them as absolutely different from him. The pills sadly represented objects (not-me) that he could safely consume (me-object) to regulate his anxiety. In this case, the PTO functioned to ratify sameness and, at the same time, served to defend against recognizing others as like me-and-different.

Ideally, in the taxonomic-object mode of organizing experience, recognition and negation operate together when likeness (me-ness) is not separated from difference (not-me). If anxiety and fear are high, the child (or adult) may use this mode defensively, and safety is secured by keeping likeness and difference separated. When likeness and difference cannot be held in dialectical tension, emotional connection to significant objects becomes more difficult. Stated positively, intimacy and aliveness depend, in part, on the ability to hold in tension likeness and difference. In Dave's situation, it would have been intolerable to identify with his wife – to recognize her as like him. Dave once stated that he always expected some future disaster to happen to his wife and child, both of whom he desperately needed and feared. His semiotic categorization of them as not-me, was, as I understood it, a defense that served to keep him connected to them, yet on a long tether.

Care, disruption, and potential space

Care (dynamics of trust–distrust, loyalty–disloyalty), the third attribute of potential space, is a necessary part of both surrender and generation as well as recognition and negation. The child's recognition of discrete objects, in particular, the parent and PTO, occurs alongside his experiences of the object's devotion and trustworthiness. The parent's abiding interest in and appropriate responses to the child's utterances gives him a sense of hope and confidence that this devoted object will meet his desires. These experiences are organized in the taxonomic-object mode, which means that he is able to represent them (versus presentational organizations in the C-C mode). Thus the child's ability to organize trust and devotion semiotically is joined to his pre-intentional willingness to surrender to parental care as well as to the PTO or an aleatory object. The child's use of the PTO represents, in part, a semiosis of care that originated in the parent–child interaction. And this playful and creative use of the PTO manifests a sense of agency, spontaneity, continuity, cohesion, and validation, all of which are part of the child's experience of being alive and real.

Care naturally includes the child's and parent's ability to repair moments of real and imagined distrust and betrayal. A successful repair of the relationship is itself a contributor to the couple's deepening sense of trust and hope (Tronick and Gianino, 1986). Positively, a child in good-enough reparative interactions learns that the object can handle feelings as well as tolerate the child's desires and needs, which adds to his confidence in the devotion of the object. When this occurs, the child begins to realize that a sense of aliveness is not necessarily threatened by disruptions and, more importantly, the child unconsciously knows that disruption does not impede creativity. Rather, good enough disruption contributes to a flexible sense of continuity and agency.

A child, during this phase, also needs to learn that the experience of being alive does not mean the loss of the other person's vitality. In other words, the child, in these reparative moments, realizes that experiences of being alive fluctuate and that the object does not lose vitality, either as a result of his needs or momentary failures (e.g., non-contingent responses) in the interaction. A child who attempts to enliven a depressed parent, for instance, displays an effort to repair the object-interaction and restore a sense of vitality. When he fails, the child becomes aware of his experience of being alive and his attempts to enliven the object are costly to the object, which gives rise to a sense of despair and emptiness. What he can hope for is the survival of himself and the needed object.

The loss of both parents and the ongoing deprivation and impingement at the hands of his aunt and uncle left Dave with an overwhelming sense of betrayal, distrust, and hopelessness. Losing both parents would have been traumatic enough, though it could have been repaired if Dave and his siblings had been fortunate to have had surrogate parents who were emotionally consistent, devoted, and available in their care of the children. Tragically, Dave's experiences in relation to his aunt and uncle, which he defensively organized primarily out of the taxonomic-object mode, only confirmed that people in authority were unreliable in meeting his desires and emotional needs. What David could hope for from them was to gain their attention by feigning weakness, illness, and dependency. In those moments, he had confidence that people would fulfill their roles, though the cost involved sacrificing any hope that his desires and needs would be validated in the interaction or that the terrible pain of loss would be repaired. What was validated was a false self (or self-as-object), which involved his role as a slave to dangerous and powerful figures. Survival eclipsed aliveness.

The pills Dave obtained were PTOs and Dave was able to secure his sense of trust in them – a trust rooted in fantasy. The pills were (omnipotently) reliable and safe and they signified what he desperately needed, but was too anxious to surrender to in the social realm. Unlike PTOs that signify fantasy and good-enough care, Dave's use of the pills represented what did not happen with regard to care. Indeed, they pointed to a profound sense of hopelessness that past and present relationships could ever be repaired.

In summary, a sense of liveliness, organized in the T-O mode, relies upon the fourfold, interrelated dialectic of potential space – surrender–generation, recognition–destruction, Care (as trust–distrust, loyalty–disloyalty), and disruption–repair. The child's use of primary transitional objects represents, in part, the idiom or syntax of care that she transfers from the parent–child relationship to a me-and-not-me object under her omnipotent control. Vitality is extended to and becomes linked to discrete objects.

The presence and collapse of potential space: culture, trauma, and therapy

All cultures have ceremonies, rituals, and narratives that help participants categorize and semiotically organize objects and activities according to prescribed roles and rules (Muller, 1996, p. 47). At best, these rituals and interactions protect and preserve the dialectical tension of potential space, contributing to persons' sense of agency, continuity, cohesion, and validation. Put another way, a person's sense of aliveness corresponds to the vitality of the objects and rituals that she possesses and uses. At worst, rituals and accompanying categorizations are used to cement group cohesion by violently coercing hated and feared others to fulfill restrictive roles. Between the oppressed and oppressor, there is no potential space – only survival and death.

Whether life-enhancing or deadening, these cultural ceremonies and rituals, which are symbolic manifestations of the group's way of being in the world, reveal the background presence of the taxonomic-object mode. For instance, members of a group reverently face carved totemic figures in an elaborate ritual of thanksgiving. These objects, which the group animates, play roles within the community and these roles are accompanied by rules, all of which provide people with a sense of continuity, cohesion, agency, and validation. One particular object may be categorized by its ability to protect, while another may lie in the category of nurture. Both are rooted in the group's particular idiom of care. If all goes well enough, members recognize the totemic objects as like me and different (not-me object), and if the object is perceived to represent experiences of trust and devotion, group members will be willing, consciously and unconsciously, to surrender to it, even while generating experience.

Of course, many of us may be able to recall when rituals (psychoanalytic or otherwise) contribute to a sense of deadness or emptiness. Ritual objects and attending roles and rules devolve into rigid semiosis and mere lifeless routines. The defensive use of the taxonomic-object mode is evident when there is high anxiety and fear within a group, as well as in situations of trauma. The anxiety may be connected to a perceived (real or imagined) threat that the ritual and attending narratives are empty or meaningless or if the group feels as if it is under attack. For example, in some quarters of the Catholic Church, the seemingly obsessive concern with the rubrics of ritual and "right" doctrine represents, from this perspective, the presence of the taxonomic-object mode. In this situation, rules, roles, and objects are obsessively attended to, draining spontaneity and freedom. Personal aliveness and vitality are sacrificed for anxious and compulsive protection of rules, ritual behaviors, and objects. Freud's (1907) earliest article on religion, albeit flawed, points to such tragic and rigid use of religious rituals.

With regard to the taxonomic-object mode, this does not suggest that the rituals and attending objects are not symbols. Rather, in cases of high anxiety and fear, the symbolic mode of organizing experience is in abeyance and the taxonomic-object mode dominates. One notes a similar obsessive and compulsive preoccupation with orthodox rules and roles, at times, in psychoanalytic groups or schools. And I imagine most therapists have experienced moments during sessions that mirror this.

The collapse of potential space, whether from trauma or real and imagined threats to one's prized objects (e.g., rituals, narratives, beliefs), is a semiotic breakdown wherein surrendering to experience or to the other is too dangerous and there is a compulsive and anxiously defensive reliance on the PTO and its attending roles and rules. The person's self-protective use of the taxonomic-object mode signifies the generation of the "other" as absolutely not-me. Recognition of the other is dominated by negation and the tension between likeness and difference is heightened. The "other," as not-me, is omnipotently and rigidly perceived and constructed as playing a not-me role (e.g., victimizer). The idea that the other is like me *and* different (dynamic potential space) is intolerable because it threatens the person's semiotic *Weltanschauung*. This accompanies absolute distrust of the other as object, making the possibility of loyalty and devotion, as well as reparation of disruptions impossible.

Racism, for example, represents a complex, cultural collapse of potential space, the defensive use of the taxonomic-object mode of organizing experience, and devitalization of experience. The "black" person is omnipotently constructed and semiotically categorized as a not-me object *that* is given defined roles and rules. The black "other" is classified as an animate object, to the white racist, and not a person – not an equal center of subjectivity. A white racist is unwilling to surrender to the black "other" and is averse to perceiving the other as like me. The black other is tolerated and "trusted" only to the extent that she fulfills her omnipotently defined role(s) within the society. Thus, her "surrender" is, in actuality, subjugation. If there is any devotion directed to her, it is because the "other" plays the role and lives by white rules, which are timeless. The pseudo-repair of relational disruptions is determined by the black other's falling back into her prescribed and subjugated role, which parallels Dave's acquiescence to his aunt's unstated demand that he play the weak dependent other. Violence and shame, used by white power groups, are "reparative" in that they serve to enforce black others into adhering to white constructions of reality. The black other is used to confirm white reality and, in this way, provides white racists with emotional regulation and a sense of their own continuity and cohesion – not recognizing that they are defensively dependent on the black other for this emotional regulation as well as individual and social continuity and cohesion. The dynamics of racism, in short, embody the defensive use of the taxonomic-object mode of organizing experience, the collapse of potential space, and the concomitant loss of experiences of being alive.

The collapse of potential space and the defensive use of the taxonomic-object mode are also the result of traumas that people bring to therapy in the form of symptoms. Dave's compulsive attempts to secure medication from physicians and his preoccupation with using these pills represent the collapse of potential space both in his relationships at home and during therapy. Dave initially viewed me as someone who was powerful and who would almost certainly abandon and humiliate him, despite his need for new experiences of benevolent, devoted attention. This stemmed from childhood events whereby he felt subjugated to experiences of loss (abandonment) as well as subjugated to persons who defined and determined his world. Dave garnered a sense of object-trust by adhering to the rules and roles constructed by his aunt and uncle. Aggression and rage, which he may have used to rebel and construct his own experience, were understandably sacrificed to survive under the protection of his new "parents." In a sense, his aunt functioned to regulate his anxiety about abandonment at the cost of his subjectivity – his authenticity and agency – and his very sense of being alive and real. In the initial stages of therapy, I was the powerful other and he felt constrained to play the obsequious slave as I was ordained to play the master.

There were a number of moments with Dave when my anger was connected to my sense of being recognized and treated as, even subjugated to, an object-role. At times, I had fantasies of doing something provocative and "spontaneous," which I understand as a response to this collapse of potential space and my wish to play and to experience a sense of aliveness in otherwise monotonous sessions. My anger can also be seen as my (narcissistic) desire to be recognized and treated as a subject, a person instead of an animated object fulfilling an omnipotently prescribed role and function. Furthermore, it is plausible to suggest that my countertransference was, in part, linked to Dave's own anger and rage at being treated similarly by his aunt and uncle.

Dave trusted me as long as I fulfilled and remained faithful to the assigned role and abided by his rules, though this was unsatisfactory for both of us. For example, during one session, Dave triumphantly showed me how he had duped a physician into giving him pain medication. Believing he was playfully offering me a peek, I spontaneously reached for the prescription he held. Dave, at first, seemed shocked and confused, which was quickly followed by intense anger. I had stepped out of my omnipotently assigned role and broken a rule. He was terrified that I was betraying him by threatening to take his prescription (PTO) away, not unlike the numerous losses of precious objects in his past. Looking back, I now see that unguarded moment as one of the first steps to restoring potential space. Before this, it seemed as if Dave planned the session. Even his triumphant expression of victory over the doctor was premeditated, though Dave and I would later uncover his unconscious motivations. Yet, in this session, Dave expressed an emotion spontaneously, which was swiftly followed by fear of attack (by me) or abandonment. Dave was further surprised when I told him I was delighted to see that he was angry, which unconsciously communicated to him the possibility of both of us playing a different script – a script where spontaneous anger is not equivalent to loss, but instead can be contained and used to enhance a sense of vitality. I suggested to Dave that, when I observed his anger, I felt hopeful because there had been an opening for a different kind of trust as well as some freedom in our relationship. In the months that followed, we would return to and explore the diverse roots and meanings of this interaction.

Dave's paranoia toward powerful figures in his life was an expression of his defensive use of the taxonomic-object mode. During his childhood,

Dave was treated as an object of his aunt's needs and desires, while his own needs and desires were unrecognized. His aunt and uncle, for unknown reasons, were unable or unwilling to create and maintain potential space. Rather, their ongoing misrecognition of and misattunement to Dave and his siblings led to a collapse of potential space, leaving Dave to use defensively the taxonomic-object mode for omnipotently organizing experience and interactions. His defense enabled him to remain attached to powerful objects, but at the cost of his own agency and vitality.

Anxiety and the use of the T-O mode

The intense anxiety that leads to the collapse of potential space and the defensive use of the taxonomic-object mode differs from the corporeal-contiguous mode. On the one hand, in the T-O mode, anxiety is connected to the loss of a prized object and the rules, roles, and expectations that provide a person with a measure of continuity and cohesion. On the other hand, anxiety is transformed to fear by the person's ability to categorize the "other" as dangerous. Thus, anxiety is connected to semiotic organizations of experience that are part of the person's ability to recognize and categorize distinct objects. The anxiety of the C-C mode is pervasive and not tied to a specific object.

Paranoia (Meissner, 1978; Ogden, 1986), obsessive-compulsive disorders (McWilliams, 1994), schizoid behaviors (Gabbard, 1990), and borderline and narcissistic personality disorders (Kernberg, 1984) may be understood, in part, as representing the dominant and defensive presence of the taxonomic-object mode of organizing experience and the collapse of potential space. In the foreground of these disorders is the recognition and categorization of objects as dangerous *or* safe and the corresponding heightened attention to roles, rules, and expectations in interactions. The other is not perceived as an equivalent center of subjectivity, even though the other may be perceived and constructed as an animate object. Indeed, in these disorders, the other is absolutely not-me and surrender is impossible because one believes it leads to subjugation (real or imagined). The defensive use of the taxonomic-object mode is for the sake of survival and not life.

Before concluding, I wish to stress that the collapse of potential space and the dominant presence of the T-O mode are not always pathological. Winnicott (1971) once remarked, "It is of first importance for us to acknowledge openly that the absence of psychoneurotic illness may be health, but it is not life" (Winnicott, 1971, p. 100). There are many instances of the attenuation of potential space where psychopathology is absent, yet social interactions and personal experiences are drained of liveliness and spontaneity, and people survive by living lives of quiet desperation. Rampant consumerism, lifeless ceremonies, societal paranoia, racism, sexism, and cultural approbation of greed illustrate the diminution of the dynamic tension in potential space in larger social groups. By any standard of mental health, people within these groups may be diagnosed as healthy, but they may not feel alive and real. Rebellions and other forms of cultural resistance may be seen as attempts to restore potential space and create new or revitalize old objects, categories, roles, and rules that contribute to individual and group aliveness.

Chapter 4

Vital subjects

> To participate requires self-discipline and trust and courage, because this business of becoming conscious . . . is ultimately about asking yourself, as my friend Dale puts it, How alive am I willing to be?
>
> (Lamott, 1994, p. 236)

> Revitalizing grammar and rhetoric, and enriching the style of those who wish to speak with us because they can no longer remain silent and brushed aside: do such projects not mirror new life and new psyche that psychoanalysis wishes to unearth?
>
> (Kristeva, 1995, p. 10)

> Symbolization is the basis for all talents: that is, that it is the basis of those skills by which we relate ourselves to the world around us.
>
> (Milner, 1952, p. 194)

Parents often express excitement and delight upon hearing their child's first word. They intuitively know this achievement is a rite of passage – a birth into a world of symbols and language. Naturally, few adults possess conscious memories of their own passage, though Helen Keller poignantly depicts it in her book, *The Story of my Life*.

> She [Anne M. Sullivan] brought me my hat, and I knew I was going out into the warm sunshine. This thought, if a wordless sensation can be called a thought, made me hop and skip with pleasure. We walked down the path to the well-house, attracted by fragrance of the honeysuckle with which it was covered. Someone was drawing water and my teacher placed my hand under the spout. As the cool stream gushed over my hand she spelled into the other the word water, first slowly, then rapidly. I stood still, my whole attention fixed upon the motion of her fingers. Suddenly I felt a misty consciousness as of something forgotten – a thrill of returning thought; and somehow the

> mystery of language was revealed to me. I knew then that w-a-t-e-r meant the wonderful cool something that was flowing over my hand. That living word awakened my soul, gave it light, hope, joy, set it free! I left the well-house eager to learn. Everything had a name, and each name gave birth to a new thought. As we returned to the house, every object which I touched seemed to quiver with life.
>
> (Keller, 1954, p. 36)

Note the astonishing metamorphosis that took place. Keller "knew" that the hat signified (taxonomic-object mode) going outside and she felt pleasure and a sense of aliveness in anticipation of playing in the sunshine. A qualitative change took place when Ms. Sullivan tactilely spelled out the word for the sensory experience-object, which gave rise to thought and to Helen Keller's excited revelation that objects have names. The world and every object shivered with new life. Her soul was awakened and she was set free. The symbolic order carries with it the possibility of aliveness that is dramatically distinct from the order of signs.

The excitement, aliveness, and elation evoked in this excerpt from Helen Keller may be connected to dim memories of our parturition into the symbolic world. While the intensity of these experiences recedes as we move toward adulthood, the pleasure or jouissance (Lacan, 1977) of the symbolic order, or what Melanie Klein (1928) called the epistemophilic impulse (Freud's epistemophilic instinct), makes its appearance felt in numerous ways. Grasping a novel idea, developing a theory, arriving at a new understanding of oneself, encountering innovative melodies, creating songs, poems, and stories are examples of the joy and vitality attached to the use of symbols in adulthood.

Obviously, the passage into the symbolic realm is not all sweetness and light. "[L]anguage, art, morality, and science," Langer (1942) wrote, "have given us pain as well as power" (p. 294). An even less sanguine, or perhaps more realistic, view was held by Lacan. He argued that the achievement of language is accompanied by a split subject, who possesses the illusions of freedom, agency, and wholeness (Fink, 1995; Verhaeghe, 1999). Indeed, the "admission to culture and language," according to Lacan, "requires alienation from oneself" (Keylor, 2003, p. 228). Symbols, in this school of thought, "are the means by which we make tolerable our recognition of the limits of reality" (p. 238).

The freedom that Helen Keller experienced, when her world opened up to seemingly endless possibilities, also meant greater latitude in symbolizing and communicating aggression, hatred, and hostility, extended plasticity in making and using psychological defenses, and a heightened recognition of the inevitable limitations of human relationships (the other as subject) and life (e.g., death). Indeed, symbols and imagination, as Freud well knew, are linked to aggression (and pleasure), giving rise to lively, benign, and violent distortions of self and others. Philosophers and novelists have long known and portrayed the paradox of human freedom with regard to creativity and destruction. Aggression is a necessary thread of symbolization and of being alive, yet it may lead to harm, the diminishment of one's capacity to use symbols, and a loss of one's sense of aliveness. Thus, in the symbolic realm, we find – unlike our animal brothers and sisters – that *we can create* experiences of being alive and that this dawning realization is quickly followed by another reality and insight, namely, experiences of being alive can also be diminished or destroyed. What we create is impermanent. This truth gives rise to fundamental human questions, which are the essence of human creativity and destruction – *how alive am I and are we willing to be in a world of uncertainty, ambiguity, and death*?

Psychoanalysts, beginning with Freud, have been interested in symbols and language, and implicitly in the question above. Freud noted that a thing presentation comprised "a complex of associations made up of the greatest variety of visual, acoustic, tactile, kinaesthetic and other presentations" (1915, p. 213), which eventually become linked to and transformed by words. The relation between the verbal and non-verbal, the pre-symbolic and symbolic, continues to intrigue analysts, and the resulting literature is indeed voluminous. In this chapter I rely on this tradition, though my focus is on the relation between a sense of being alive and the symbolic-subjective (S-S) mode of organizing experience. In particular, I am interested in addressing the following questions: What characteristics of the symbolic order distinguish it from the C-C and T-O modes? How do these previous modes of organizing experience relate to the S-S mode? How are we to understand this extraordinary transition to the symbolic world? What are the characteristics of the experience of being alive as it is organized in the S-O mode? What relational dynamics facilitate this transition? What occurs in human relationships that invites and maintains persons' ability to organize experiences of being alive in the S-S mode?

Characteristics of the symbolic-subjective mode

Helen Keller's discovery of the symbolic world poignantly portrays the experiential aspects of being able to organize experience symbolically. I begin by briefly defining symbols, highlighting some of their characteristics. Once defined, I address two additional attributes of symbols – subjectivity and reality – that implicitly or explicitly attend psychoanalytic discourse. These two attributes are inextricably joined to and shaped by the social web of symbols, in addition to individual and social experiences of being alive. This excursus is not meant to be exhaustive, though it is intended to help differentiate this mode (S-S) from the C-C and T-O modes of organizing experience.

Symbols

Linguists, semioticians, and analysts (e.g., Lacan, 1968; Kristeva, 1980; Olds, 2000), interested in symbols and language, have relied on the works of Charles Sanders Peirce (1991, 1998) and Ferdinand de Saussure (1959). Ferdinand de Saussure, focusing more on speech and language and the detection of oppositions, wrote that the "word symbol has been used to designate the linguistic sign" (p. 68). The close relation between speech, language, and symbols, however, does not exhaust the nature of symbols, as Peirce well knew. For Peirce, a "symbol is a sign which refers to the Object that it denotes by virtue of a law, usually an association of general ideas, which operates to cause the symbol to be interpreted as referring to the Object" (1998, p. 292). Symbols comprise a signifying subject or interpreter, an object (its referent), and an interpretant, which "cannot be equated with the object or with the interpreter" (Muller, 1996, p. 33). Peirce had a triadic conception of signs, while Saussure had a dyadic notion (signifier-signified).

It is important to linger over Peirce's notion of interpretant, because it is central to his definition of symbol as a category of signs, as well as helping us understand the greater sense of freedom and creativity a person experiences when she is born into the world of symbols. The interpretant of a symbol is its significance (Peirce, 1998, p. 494). That is, it is the effect of the sign and, for Peirce, there are three interrelated effects. Peirce wrote that:

> The interpretant may be a *feeling*. Thus, an air for a guitar, if considered as meant to convey the genuine or feigned musical emotions of its composer, can only fulfill this function by exciting responsive feelings in the listener. But in the second place, the interpretant may be an *effort*. Thus, when a drill-officer gives a company of infantry the word command, "Ground arms!" . . . there must be, as in all action of signs, a feeling-interpretant,—sense of apprehending the meaning,—which in its turn stimulates the soldiers to slight effort required to perform the motion. In the third place, our categories lead us to credit ourselves, in expectation, with a kind of interpretant of a triadic character, while our acquaintance with signs enters upon the debit side of the account a kind of interpretant not included in either of the enumerated two, but which is, we know, the interpretant par excellence, I mean of course the *intellectual apprehension* of the meaning of a sign.
>
> (Peirce, 1998, p. 430; emphases mine)

The feeling effect or *emotional interpretant* of the symbol is always accompanied by its meaning, which is distinct from, yet related to intellectual apprehension or "*logical interpretant*." The effort a person puts forth as a result of the symbol's affect-meaning is the *energetic interpretant*, which is related to action that, in turn, can transform the symbol (Colapietro, 1989,

p. 35). The energetic interpretant is the effort that results from the emotional interpretant. Discursive and non-discursive or presentational symbols (Langer, 1942) give rise not only to thought, which is so frequently emphasized, but also to feeling and action. Put differently, symbols are forms of feelings, to use Langer's (1942) words, that evoke effort, meaning, and purpose (Peirce, 1998, p. 323).

This interplay of signifier, signified, and interpretants points to our ability "to *create* abstraction, without which we should lack a great engine of discovery" (p. 251; emphasis mine). Discovery and freedom are related to Peirce's recognition that a "symbol . . . produces an endless series of interpretants" (p. 323). In summary, Peirce's understanding of symbols and their interpretants shows the interrelation between affect, behavior (including motive), meaning, and abstract thought. Moreover, the interpretants of symbols help explain the profound sense of freedom, creativity, and sense of aliveness that *may* attend the achievement of symbolization and the representation of experience.[1] While an endless series of interpretants frees us from the facticity or is-ness of the C-C and T-O modes of organizing experience, the web of symbols we are thrown into also limits our ability to represent experience (Bucci, 2002, p. 58). There is no absolute freedom. Indeed, freedom and creativity, vis-à-vis symbolization, are inconceivable without limits and resistance.

Helen Keller's story provides an apt illustration of Peirce's definition of symbols and offers a way to distinguish between a symbolic mode and the C-C and T-O modes. The immediate joining of feeling, effort, and the *idea* of water evoked excitement, which accompanied her discovery of the seemingly endless possibilities of ideas – everything had a name and she could name anything. The symbol gave rise to thought, to a feeling of creativity, and to her motivation to discover and use more of these words. While the symbol was there to be discovered, there was also a dawning realization of the infinite combinations and meanings that she could experience. In being able to conceive of objects one is, like Keller, introduced into the realm of creating, finding, and possessing her own purpose, effort, meanings, and feelings in the symbolic web.

A difference between the *symbolic semiosis* and *taxonomic semiosis* is seen in Keller's vignette. Her hat was a signal. It announced to her that she was about to go outside to play. The meaning, feeling, and effort attended the sign-signal, but there was no intellectual apprehension of the hat as a symbol. Helen Keller acknowledged that this was not a thought. Rather, it was a wordless sensation, representing the interplay of the contiguous-corporeal and the taxonomic-object modes. Her visceral excitement was joined to her categorization of the hat as a signal for going outside, much as dog becomes excited when his owner reaches for a leash to go for a walk. There is no abstraction, no *idea* of walk. The hat (T-O mode) is equivalent to the walk and accompanying somatic sensations (C-C mode). For the hat to be a symbol, it must be an *idea* that has some independence from the walk itself.

Symbolization and subjectivity

It is clear that Keller experienced a sense of aliveness prior to her encounter with a world of words, yet symbolization qualitatively changed her experience of being alive. Her entry into the symbolic order meant the birth of a knowing and desiring, embodied *subject* (Lacan, 1977, p. 103).[2] Peirce put forth the idea that a person is "a species of sign; namely, a symbol . . . The subject in its inmost being is itself a form of semiosis" (Colapietro, 1989, p. 37). This is a bodily subject, meaning the body is the medium the human subject uses and "the use of all other media are mediated by this medium: For the human subject, semiotic consciousness is incarnate consciousness" (p. 39). The somatic, sensory, presentational organizations of C-C mode, then, serve as the foundation for an embodied consciousness, subjectivity, and symbolization (Bucci, 1997).

The semiotic processes of the T-O mode also play a role in this burgeoning embodied subjectivity and consciousness. Psychoanalyst John Muller (1996) echoed this, arguing that the very basis "for the experience of human subjectivity is an effect of semiosis" (p. 45). The elementary and pre-conscious sense of me-ness associated with the T-O mode is transformed by language into a subject – I-ness that is "a reflection of the differentiation of symbol, symbolized and interpreting subject" (Ogden, 1985, p. 131).[3] The capacity for symbolic representation and categorization of desire and experience accompanies an awareness of being a subject; "it allows one to experience oneself as a person thinking one's thoughts and feeling one's feelings" (Ogden, 1989, p. 12). In Helen Keller's story, not only did every *categorized* object quiver with life, she consciously felt alive. She knew desire and desired to know – the epistemophilic impulse – and both were distinct from its objects. Simply stated, "desire provides the motivation for entering the realm of signification" (Keylor, 2003, p. 233), subjectivity, and awareness.

While using different models and language, many analysts (Klein, 1930; Winnicott, 1971; Lacan, 1977; Stern, 1985; Ogden, 1989; Wright, 1991; Kennedy, 1997) note that subjectivity, a sense of I-ness, necessitates psychological separation. That, in turn, accompanies the capacity to recognize the other as a distinct other (object, then person). Indeed, the "other person is primal in relation to the construction of human subjectivity" (LaPlanche, 1999, p. 256). Separation from the other creates a symbolic space for the child to be an interpreting subject, using symbols to organize his experience (needs, feelings, desires, intentions).[4] For Lacan (1977), this separation is necessary for subjectivity as well as the humanization of desire. Additionally, separation makes possible an expanded sense of freedom that attends subjectivity and symbolization. This said, the birth of subjectivity also means that the child's identity, desire, and vitality are shaped by the symbol system into which he is thrown. Kennedy (1997), for example, wrote that the child is both subject to and the subject of the web of symbols. The symbols the child "discovers" are there to be found and this discovery molds the child's desires as he creatively uses and surrenders to them.

Symbols, society, and subjectivity

A number of analysts, beginning with Freud, view the shaping of subjectivity and desire through the web of social symbols with some ambivalence. Terms such as repression, alienation, and neurotic adaptation are laid at the feet of society's powerful symbols. Peirce's anthropology offers a different view of society's symbols and subjectivity. For Peirce, semiosis is the very foundation of subjectivity, Eros, thinking, and reality (Colapietro, 1989). I add that semiotic processes associated with symbolization make possible a deeper and broader subjective and intersubjective sense of aliveness. The introduction into the symbolic world means greater cooperation and not mere adaptation. Having said this, I argue that it is how symbols are used that determines the presence of alienation or communion, bondage or freedom, deadness or aliveness in human experience.

Notwithstanding the fact that the web of social symbols shape subjectivity, symbols become the child's own "only when the speaker populates it with his own intent, his own account, when he appropriates the world, adapting it to his own semantic and expressive idiom" (Bakhtin, 1981, p. 293). The child's unique, expressive idiom and sense of personhood are carved out even as she is initiated into and shaped by the cultural web of symbols.[5] The symbol system or web into which one is thrown, represents *my* desire, knowledge, and freedom, though I am subject to and a subject of these social, symbolically represented desires and knowledge. The symbolic web, essential for unique self-idiom, shapes, but does not necessarily determine my own desires and knowing.

To be sure, a culture's network of symbols is also subject to being shaped by one's desires. There is, then, a paradox in separation and the achievement of a symbolizing subjectivity – an involuntariness (Lacan, 1977) in the midst of freedom and creativity. Entry into a culture's linguistic and ritual webs represents the dialectic of generating and surrendering to the symbolic order, as well as the possibility of greater sense of freedom (and bondage), creativity (and destruction), and aliveness (and deadness).

Symbols and reality

Langer (1942) said that "out of signs and symbols we weave our tissue of reality" (p. 280), which echoes the Peircean view that "signs are part of the very fabric of reality" (Colapietro, 1989, p. 33). The vicissitudes of reality and truth are closely tied to symbols as well as to subjectivity, separation,[6] and freedom/creativity. A symbolically structured, subjective sense of aliveness is inextricably and necessarily joined to one's sense of and belief in truth and reality.[7] Persons feel alive when they have a secure sense of their own subjectivity *and* a belief and experience that their thoughts, desires, experiences, and feelings are real, valid, or true. Even a radical doubter like Descartes eventually secured some semblance of truth and reality to a foundational belief in identity and reason, though it is questionable whether his philosophical faith promoted a sense of vitality.

A symbol, Loewald (1987) wrote, "seems, in a special way, always to be a symbol for us" (p. 483) and *for-ness* is our belief in the symbol's reality. A symbol is for and by us because it is *given*, in the sense that we are born into a cultural symbolic system that is independent of us. As a result, we come to believe it is real and true. The symbol is also for us because it is *made*, in that symbols represent our creation of meaning. Put differently, we adopt the symbols of our culture by making them our own and we are adopted by the group's symbols in that they shape our subjectivity. Thus, the emotional, motivational, and intellectual interpretants of the social system of symbols become our reality, our truth. These malleable interpretants form our truth and reality, even as idiomatic desires shape our individual use and meaning of symbols. We could not function if core symbols were always in doubt and we certainly would not feel alive.

The relation between symbols and reality/truth is dependent, in part, on the pre-symbolic modes of organizing experience. The facticity or is-ness of somatic semiosis (C-C mode) and categorical semiosis (T-O mode) is the background, unquestioned presence of symbolic reality and truth. The child's somatic and categorical significations are her reality. In other words, the pre-symbolic child is not able to symbolize a no; she is unable to question or doubt the somatic or categorical signs on which she depends. There is no category for truth, right, wrong, or reality in these pre-symbolic modes. There is only necessity, facticity, and is-ness. Symbols retain this somatic and categorical facticity, but are not bound to it because of the capacity for symbolic negation and, hence, doubt (Freud, 1925; Parsons, 1999).

The power of symbolic "thinking" in human life is not solely linked to creativity and freedom; it is also the emotional, somatic, and categorical semiotic processes working in concert with the symbolic-subjective mode that imbue symbols with power and a felt sense of reality. The dynamic interplay between these three modes of organizing experience preserves the dynamic tension between facticity and creativity, between certainty and doubt, all the while providing a sense of somatic aliveness and playfulness to symbolic thinking. Of course, we also know that symbols can be used to promote rigidity, violence, self-deception, pseudo-innocence, and bondage (cf. Morris, 1964, p. 82). Rigidity and certainty, with regard to symbolic truth and reality, signal the presence of intense anxiety as well as symbolic equivalence (Freud, 1926, pp. 128–129) or what Segal (1957) viewed as a collapse into a symbolic equation, and what Bass (2002) called desymbolization – the symbol *is* the sign. This collapse, which is addressed in greater detail below, means that the facticity of the C-C and T-O modes is hyperactivated and symbolic negation is used defensively. Instead of an endless series of interpretants (emotional, intellectual, and energetic), there is a single interpretant. In adult life, this breakdown is observed whenever metaphor becomes dogma (e.g., God *is* Father; the flag is the United States), myth becomes unquestionably literal (e.g., Adam and Eve really existed), or the rubrics of a ritual become incontrovertible facts (e.g., real psychoanalysis is done on the couch). The hyperactivation of the C-C and T-O modes may serve to manage intolerable anxiety, but drain the transformative, playful, creative, curious, and spontaneous aspects of the symbolic-subjective mode.

Harry, a 33-year-old devout Catholic, illustrates the power of symbolic *reality* and the interplay of these three modes. During one session, Harry railed against a man who had suggested changing some of the rubrics of the Catholic Mass. Harry became incensed that someone would even suggest making small alterations to sacred words. Naturally, Harry's complex early history of parental deprivation, sibling rejection, and the current transference-countertransference dynamics were at play here. This said, Harry's heightened anxiety represents the collapse into a symbolic equation wherein the hyperactivation of the T-O mode forces the S-S mode in the background. Harry is using symbols (ritual and language), yet the dominance of the T-O mode manifests the ascendancy of facticity; that is, the words and rubrics of the Mass were, from his perspective, unalterable and unquestionable facts – one and only one interpretant need apply. The dialectical tension between the given and the made, between necessity and creativity was lost, occluding doubt, creativity, discovery, and playfulness.

In summary, symbols announce the presence of subjectivity and greater freedom, creativity, and discovery in relation to others and the larger world. With the advent of symbolization, we are no longer bound by the facticity of the C-C and T-O modes, because we can call upon the seemingly endless permutations of emotional, intellectual, and motivational interpretants of the symbolic web that we adopt (made) and are adopted by (given). The symbols, which we discover and create, are for us in that we trust that they are real and valid and that they accurately represent our knowing and desire. As Lacan noted, symbols represent the humanization of desire. Additionally, symbols signify the personalization of a human being and his/her sense of being alive. Defensive use of the symbols indicates a collapse into a symbolic equation, which constricts a sense of the real and diminishes subjectivity, freedom, creativity, and aliveness.

Attributes of symbolic-subjective organizations of being alive

It still astounds me to watch an earth-bound caterpillar create its chrysalis and to witness its transformation to a winged butterfly. To the caterpillar, all this seems quite common and routine – a matter of fact. By analogy, we often take for granted the transformation that takes place from the facticity of the C-C and T-O modes to the S-S mode. Stories like Helen Keller's provide a glimpse into the experience of transformation when one finds and makes use of symbols. The morning Helen Keller discovered symbols was the day she began to break out of her chrysalis and take flight. The attributes of being alive – agency, spontaneity, emotional regulation, continuity, and validation – undergo a radical change with the advent of symbolization, which precedes narrativity. Just as we might see the caterpillar and the butterfly as two different species, the changes that take place between earlier modes of being alive and the symbolic-subjective mode are so profound that an observer may wonder if they are not two different species. As Langer noted, "There is a profound difference between using symbols and merely using signs" (1942, p. 29).

Agency, desire, and I–you schemas

A child's agency, with regard to symbolization, means that her subjectivity is organized in terms of I–you schemas, which accompany budding capacities for self-reflection and recognition of the other as a subject (Fonagy and Target, 1997; Auerbach and Blatt, 2002). The child represents experience and *knows*, through the use of the symbols at hand,[8] that she possesses desires and intentions and is able to *act* on both. An I-schema, which represents desires and motivations in relation to the other as subject, orders her actions. This does not mean the child has free rein to represent or act. The "other" as subject and the cultural symbols themselves *resist* omnipotent expression and representation of desire. This resistance (see Chapter 3, pp. 65–66) is necessary not only for a subjective agency, but also for the child's ability to represent her desires and to act on these desires. Phillips (1993) once replied to a patient's query, saying, "We might be able to understand why he needed an obstacle to free his desire." In other words, "The desire does not reveal the obstacle; the obstacle reveals the desire" (p. 82). A child encounters environmental objects and other subjects as obstacles, which in resisting her desires reveal her desires by bringing them to consciousness and establishing the child's sense of subjective agency. Thus, resistance motivates the child to represent and act on her desires as an agent and these representations are organized into I–you schemas.

I am speaking here of the resistance that attends separation – the resistance of the other person or object of desire not perfectly matching the child's needs. There are environmental and parental resistances in the forms of deprivation or impingement. If the resistance is too high, if the obstacle is too frustrating and frightening, the child will sacrifice both desire and subjective agency for the sake of attachment and survival. Greta, for example, has been in and out of abusive relationships most of her life. A very quiet, nice, and complacent 54-year-old woman, Greta perceives men and women as formidable and frightening obstructions. In the face of physical and emotional abuse during childhood, Greta learned to survive by sacrificing (unconsciously) her desires and feelings (unclaimed passion, rage, and resentment) and, in the process, was unable to act on her wishes. She learned, however, to recognize and respond to the desires of the other, though it stultified her sense of agency and vitality.

The other subject is not simply an obstacle that educes one's agency via resistance. The parents' recognition and appropriate response to the child's assertions are key factors in nurturing the child's symbolically structured agency. By verbally and physically responding to the child, the parent represents the child's desire and the realization of the child's assertions provides an experience and validation of her independent subjective agency (Stern 1985; Fonagy et al., 2002). This independent subjective agency of the child "requires and is therefore limited by the independent subjectivity of the parents" (Auerbach and Blatt, 2002, p. 81). The obverse of this is seen in Greta's childhood experiences with her parents. Greta recalls her mother's violent and unpredictable rages, followed by withdrawal and silence. Her father would wake up Greta late at night, forcing her to have sex with him. This is an obvious and horrific example of parents who did not attune to their child's asserted desires. They were unwilling and, perhaps, incapable of recognizing and affirming Greta as an independent subject. Instead, Greta was to comply and represent the needs and demands of her parents. In this process, Greta was unable to experience, believe in, and act on her own needs and desires. This pattern, which was well established long before her first marriage, meant that Greta was in bondage to the desires and agency of others. Others' desires and agencies were more real and valid than her own hopes and passions and she perceived others, understandably, as insurmountable obstacles.

The emergence of the capacities for symbolization and self-reflection alter agency in another significant way. In the C-C and T-O modes, the child's agency is pre-intentional and unconscious. In the S-S mode, the child has some awareness of her intentions and, because she makes use of cultural symbols to represent her desires and intentions, there is the possibility of shared agency and intentionality. Mutual recognition and sharing of each other's intentions introduce an intersubjective and conscious sense of vitality. Of course, there is also a chance of greater conflict and disagreement due to the freedom and creativity in representing disparate intentions. While at the grocery the other day, I watched a mother and her 2-year-old child engage in mutual play. The mother turned shopping for food into a shared activity. Bustling down another aisle, a different mother and her toddler were engaged in a battle of wills, which was frustrating for both of them. The child kept reaching for items in the cart and on the shelves and each time the mother would angrily tell the child to stop. The analytic ritual is similar to both instances: the analyst and patient, for example, share, in part, their intentions to explore the unconscious together, to gain greater subjective and intersubjective freedom, and to grieve, heal, and place present wounds in the past. Negative therapeutic reaction, stalemates, enactments, and patient–therapist disruptions represent, in part, two people whose desires, expectations, and intentions clash. The advent of symbolization, then, brings with it the possibility of shared agency as well as conflict, which may or may not be a source of trauma that leads to the loss of both agency and vitality.

Other examples of the social-cultural aspects of the symbolic-subjective mode and their connection to agency and vitality can be seen in Erikson's (1952) description of the Sioux and Yurok Indians. The Sioux had been forced onto reservations and deprived of core symbols representing their (primarily male) identity as warriors, nomads, and hunters. These core symbols (for Erikson, ego-ideals) represented their desires and shared intentions; they were true and real. When these were violently stripped away, many Sioux men were left confused, angry, depressed, and isolated. Western European symbols simply did not represent their desires or aspirations and the Sioux men had difficulty being able to make use of foreign symbols and ego-ideals. Shorn of their core symbols, the Sioux's subjective and intersubjective sense of identity, agency, and vitality were disrupted and diminished. The Yurok, in Erikson's view, fared better because their cultural symbols, while different, were similar to the Europeans settlers. They were able to retain prized symbols that represented their values, intentions, and desires. Thus, European settlers did not significantly disrupt the Yurok's shared sense of agency and vitality.

Emotional regulation

A sense of aliveness that appends to a child's burgeoning subjective agency goes hand in hand with greater freedom and flexibility in experiencing, representing, regulating, and evoking emotional states and meanings. Symbols, in other words, are subjective and intersubjective objects that have emotional interpretants or meanings for individuals and social groups. As forms of feelings (Langer, 1942), symbols signify emotional coding, which both shapes and is shaped by the child's self-experience and agency. Nearly any cultural object may come to represent for the child some emotional state, yet these same cultural symbols also shape the child's experience. A 3-year-old child becomes excited when she spies Santa Claus in the mall. Santa Claus, as a cultural symbol, evokes an emotional state of delight and anticipation. Similarly, more idiosyncratic symbols of childhood are joined to the cultural and social web of symbols. For example, Allison carried around a stuffed animal that reminded her of a gentle and courageous ant in an animated movie she had seen. One could call this a secondary transitional object (STO) that was idiosyncratic to the extent that Allison used it to regulate and represent emotional states.[9] The emotional interpretants were, in part, unique to Allison, but the ant was as well a cultural artifact.

Allison's use of the toy – her ability to use objects to regulate and represent emotions – was also contingent on good enough parental attunement to her affective displays. This emotional attunement taught her to make use of objects to represent emotional experience (Fonagy et al., 2002, pp. 291–315). In short, representing and regulating emotional experience and the emerging capacities for self-reflection and agency are contingent upon the quality of parent–child interaction and attachment (Holmes, 1996; Siegel, 1999; Hesse and Main, 2000; Fonagy, 2001). From a less positive angle, the emotional deprivation Greta experienced at the hands of her parents, boyfriends, and husbands illustrates how the loss of a sense of aliveness accompanies diminishment of subjective agency *and* the ability to represent and regulate emotional experience. Greta knew early in life that she was to either regulate the emotional state of her depressed mother or absent herself from her physical and emotional abuse. Children like Greta are trained to attend to the emotional states and needs of others to salvage some level of attachment and emotional regulation as well as a semblance of subjectivity, however illusory. Not surprisingly, Greta, as an adult, struggled to identify and articulate her feelings, suggesting that significant people had not used language to mirror and soothe her emotional states. Additionally, she had difficulty making *use* of language to represent and regulate her own feelings. When Greta began therapy, her freedom and creativity with regard to emotional regulation were low and so, too, was her sense of vitality. The mutual work of therapy expanded her freedom in representing, expressing, and regulating a wide variety of affective experiences, which enhanced her range of subjective and social experiences of being alive.

Continuity: birth of the historical subject

A newfound aliveness that accompanies an expanded agentic use of symbols to represent and share emotions is also contingent upon continuity derived from the use of symbols. The achievement of symbolization transforms the facticity of a bodily sense of going on being (autistic-contiguous (A-C) mode) and the continuity of me-objects (T-O mode) to a more conscious and subjective continuity. Ogden (1989) argued that the depressive position, which signals the emergence of the capacity for symbolization, gives birth to an interpreting and historical subject.[10] This historical subject is embedded in a linguistic, semiotic logic of sociality (Kristeva, 1973, pp. 25–26). In other words, an earlier somatic sense of going on being becomes transformed, via symbolization, into a sense of continuity organized by the *idea* and *experience* of subjective time – by the idea of my and your past, present, and future. The "I am" of the present is joined to the "I was" of the past and the hope and confidence that I *will* be. This diachronic and synchronic "I am" is yoked to the emergence of a new semantic, episodic memory system (Siegel, 1999).

A historical subject makes use of symbolic objects (e.g., language and ritual behavior and objects) in securing a sense of I-continuity. Initially, the secondary transitional object (STO) is an I-object, helping the child negotiate the movement from the facticity and timelessness of me-objects to more separate, shared, and time-bound symbols. This transition depends, in part, on parents caring for their child not only as an independent subject, but also a continuous one. For example, Bobby's stuffed tiger represents his sense of self in time, indicative of his parents' seeing and treating him as a continuous subject. The idea and experience of time are thus contingent on Bobby's parents perceiving him as a distinct subject who is, was, and will be "Bobby." That includes good enough recognition of and response to his assertions. This pattern of mirroring becomes attached to the STO. Bobby imbues the stuffed tiger with personal continuity and subjectivity *and* the tiger-with-Bobby confirms and supports his time-bound identity. The loss of the STO is disruptive because of the loss of emotional regulation *and* because it disrupts the child's experience as a historical subject.

In adult life, the loss of symbols, which are linked to individual and social identity and ego-ideals, severely disrupts a person's (and community's) sense of continuity as well as his ability to act freely and regulate emotions – in short, a loss of vitality. This is seen in the experience of the Sioux and, in the previous chapter, Primo Levi's (1960) experience of the concentration camps. He and other Jews were violently stripped of their possessions and denied individual and communal expressions of a shared faith. Levi described people such as these as "hollow men." The Nazis created "hollow men" by robbing the Jews of their core symbols and rituals that had long provided a sense of individual and shared continuity and agency. Numerous Holocaust testimonies tell of persons' profound experiences of emptiness, deadness, and sense of timelessness. They had no past or future, only a limitless, lifeless present. The denial of their vital symbols – a prelude to murder – was the denunciation of their historical subjectivity and intersubjectivity, violently diminishing their sense of agency, continuity, and ability to regulate their emotional life.

Other less extreme examples are, nevertheless, painful. Greta appeared for our sessions wearing nondescript, ill-fitting clothes that she had purchased without zeal or interest. As a nurse's aid, she slavishly focused on the needs of the patients and the dictates of the nurses and doctors for direction. Clearly, Greta had a sense of identity and continuity, albeit impoverished. I often had the sense that she was non-verbally saying, "I am not important. I am not pretty or intelligent or interesting." On more than one occasion, she expressed surprise when I remarked that I had thought about her during the week. Greta did not think she existed for me outside of the session, because she believed she was insignificant. This is a form of historical subjectivity based on negation – the negation of desire, feeling, and agency – that accompanies the absence of vitality. Continuity, in her situation, was existence in an everlasting, insignificant present. Her survival was devoid of passion and significance. This began by virtue of parental deprivation and Greta obtained a form of continuity by meeting and conforming to the needs and desires of others. In representing others' desires, symbols were not *for* her but rather for others. Greta felt unable to experience and use symbols to represent her desires and feelings over time. Her unconscious idea of time was linked to an all-encompassing sense of emptiness.

Signifying validation

In remarking about Greta's sense of continuity and its relation to the experience of vitality, one notes the close connection between her feeling of insignificance and her experiences of being invalidated at the hands of her parents. A sense of significance and experiences of validation are just as necessary as agency, emotional regulation, and continuity in symbolically organized experiences of being alive. Earlier somatic and me validations are re-represented and transformed by way of symbolization. In the process of accurately representing a person's desire, symbols also provide a person with a sense of validation (Meares, 2000, pp. 68–70). In the S-S mode, symbols supply a subjective (I), personal sense of validation or worth, which becomes a part of individual and social reality. The validity of a symbol depends upon the congruence and derivative pleasure of one's inner desires as represented by external symbols. Symbols are *for us* to the extent that they provide a sense of our own individual and communal significance, which feels real and true.

Symbols become *for* a child when parents and others have appropriately recognized, represented, and met a child's assertions. This gives the child confidence in using the culture's symbolic objects (e.g., STO) to represent his desire, which in the act of representing his needs confirms both his desire and his subjectivity. The child, then, is not a mere passive recipient of parental or symbolic validation. Rather, his agentic use of the symbolic object to represent desire, motivation, and emotions is an important facet of his experience of validation. In addition, a child uses an STO to secure validation by conferring significance onto the imagined subject (doll) and the doll's imagined affirmation of the child.

The close relation between agency, emotional regulation, validation, and vitality is viewed negatively when a person believes and feels as if the world of symbols does not represent his desire and meaning. Kierkegaard's (1980) notion of despair as the will not to be oneself is an illustration of extreme invalidation. The will not to be oneself, according to Kierkegaard, is the ultimate form of despair (absence of vitality) because it represents impossibility. A person may will not to be himself, but he cannot not be himself. (Though his suicide may be the extreme attempt to "act" out the will not to be oneself.) Because of symbolization, consciousness, and the experience of subjectivity, only human beings can despair. In despair, the person believes that the world of objects, persons, and symbols does not and cannot represent his desires, needs, and feelings. The world, in this emotional state, only presents boundless insignificance, meaninglessness, purposelessness, and unreality. Indeed, the world of objects seems to mirror and evoke despair, invalidating subjectivity and draining one's will and desire.

A number of years ago, I worked with Charlene, a 45-year-old mother of two grown children. Unkempt, she sat across from me week after week deep in despair. Charlene did not want to be, but she did not consciously think of or plan her suicide. Most nights, she would lie down and simply wish that she would not wake up. Many times, the burden of life and the pervasiveness of meaninglessness clung to me long after she departed. There were occasions when I worked hard, trying to infuse a smidgen of desire and life in her, only to be met by an implacable emptiness that I was seeking to avoid and overcome. Naturally, this "infusion" was my countertransference and an avoidance of being with her in this dead space.

For Charlene, the world held no promise or desire. Neither therapy nor her therapist evoked or represented her desires, despite attempts to be empathic. She spoke and used symbols that were drained of desire and subjectivity. To Charlene, the world of symbols confirmed insignificance, draining her subjectivity of any glimmer of desire and verve. There were, in other words, no symbols that were for her.

An individual's struggle with making use of symbols to represent and validate desires and subjectivity also extends to groups – families, communities, and societies. Freud (1930), Fromm (1941), and Brown (1959) tended to see society as repressive of instincts and freedom, though necessary for protection and survival. While it is clear that collectively held symbols might invalidate individuals' desires, leading to repression or dissociation, symbols and group rituals are the necessary glue for subjective and intersubjective validation of desire and intimacy. A bar mitzvah, for instance, may be an occasion where the religious desires and subjectivity of a young Jewish boy are mirrored by the group and confirmed by a web of verbal and non-verbal symbols. A less happy occasion is apparent in the absence of societal and religious symbols and rituals that validate the desires and longings of gays and lesbians, leaving them to construct communities and symbols that represent and validate their subjective passions.

In brief, the birth into the symbolic world radically alters who we are and our relation to the world and others, though it is a faint memory for most of us. Our amnesia extends to the labor parents and others undertook in introducing us to or perhaps seducing us into the symbolic web, giving birth to subjectivity. This sweeping change in one's sense of agency, emotional regulation, continuity, and validation attends to a deeper and broader sense of freedom and vitality. And yet, the potential of greater agentic freedom in using symbols to represent one's desires and feelings is accompanied by the possibility of distortion, deception, and violence as well as a myriad of mechanisms used to escape freedom and drain vitality.

Potential space, secondary transitional objects, and the emergence of intersubjective vitality

Many of us go about our daily lives operating out of the illusion that our subjectivity and use of symbols are stable, permanent, or simply a state of being. Ortega y Gasset wrote, "being *man* [*sic*] signifies precisely being always on the point of not being man, being a living problem, an absolute and hazardous adventure . . . [In short] man lives in perpetual fear of being dehumanized" (in Colapietro, 1989, p. 42). The Holocaust, Cambodia, Rwanda, Bosnia, apartheid, segregation, terrorism, and numerous other atrocities show us how symbols are used to deny and deplete the other's vital sense of subjectivity, usually in preparation for his/her murder – real or imagined. We need not highlight such dramatic examples to awaken us to the precarious and dynamic aspects of symbolization and subjectivity. Any therapist can recount stories of patients who struggle with a sense of meaninglessness, deadness, or numbness resulting from past and present disruptions in personal relationships. A vitalizing subjectivity and use of symbols depend on what takes place between other human beings, which is always in flux.

Problems in the use of symbols reflect troubles in human interactions. Symbolic equivalence (Freud, 1926, pp. 128–129), a collapse into a symbolic equation (Segal 1957), and desymbolization (Bass, 2002) signify disturbances in subjectivity *and* relationships. Symbolic equivalence signifies a collapse of potential space and loss of vitality – subjective and intersubjective. Positively stated, the dynamic tension of the four interrelated pairs of potential space – surrender–generation, recognition–destruction, Care (as trust–distrust, loyalty–disloyalty), and disruption–repair – is necessary for the lively, shared use of symbols and accompanying sense of aliveness.

As discussed in the previous chapters, each mode of organizing experience shapes the particular attributes of potential space. The vitality that emerges from the potential space of the C-C mode, for example, is distinctly different from the T-O and the S-S modes. That said, the emergence and presence of a later mode do not imply the loss or eclipse of earlier modes. Instead, the advent and consolidation of the S-S mode depend on the cognitive processes of the earlier modes, even as the S-S mode re-represents experience by way of new semiotic capacities. So, for instance, the presentational organizations of a bodily sense of aliveness (C-C mode) form the basis of symbolization even as symbols re-present these earlier organizations. Some form of embodiment is needed for the symbol to function (Colapietro, 1989, p. 70). All of this is to say that the presence of potential space with regard to the S-S mode encompasses earlier semiotic modes, operating in the background. While the S-S mode builds on and interacts with earlier semiotic processes, the potential space of the S-S mode differs from earlier modes in three fundamental ways, namely, a budding intentionality (I-ness), awareness, and the possibility of sharing both.

Surrendering to and generating experience

Helen Keller's lively tale of being introduced to the world of symbols is a clear illustration of intentionality, awareness, and sharing as it relates to the dialectical pair of surrendering to and generating experience. Helen Keller yielded to the experience of having her hand placed under the water and her teacher spelling the word w-a-t-e-r on her hand. There was a nascent intentionality to her surrender and, when Helen Keller awoke to the power of symbolic thought, she consciously intended to learn the names of other objects. By allowing herself to be moved by her teacher's physical inscription of the word, Keller was able to use the symbol to begin to construct and share experience. To be sure, when Helen Keller "knew" that this soft flowing thing on her hand was w-a-t-e-r, she gained access to a qualitatively different type of consciousness and intentionality. The symbolic web that Helen Keller was introduced to stood for a shared world, a world of cooperation, and a world of mutual surrendering to and generating experience.

Winnicott (1971) believed that a child's entry into language presents another opportunity to hand over or surrender her omnipotence to a god principle or another object. He recognized that being introduced to the world of symbols meant a more conscious encounter with the limits of social life, frustrating the child's experiences of and belief in her omnipotence. Secondary transitional objects aid the child in learning to negotiate and preserve the dialectical tension between generating and surrendering to symbols and other subjects. By using and controlling the STO, a child can safely and imaginatively learn to surrender to the other while generating experience.

The STO, unlike the PTO, is itself a symbol, taken from the web of social symbols. That is, the STO – idiosyncratically selected and manipulated by the child – represents the child's desires, needs, and expectations as well as the values and expectations from the social field. In addition, the STO ideally signifies parental–child interactions wherein care has exemplified surrender and creativity. It is, in short, the confluence of the child's desires, the parent–child idiom of care, and cultural expectations and values. The child's use of the STO signifies his continued education in surrendering to and generating experience in relation to others.

An illustration is helpful here: 3-year-old Jan has a Barbie doll, named Sarah, which she carries everywhere. She adores this doll and the doll discloses and confirms Jan's desires whenever Jan imaginatively plays with the doll. The doll and the associated playful interactions represent, in part, what has taken place between Jan and her parents as well as the gendered desires and expectations of the larger social, symbolic field. Fortunately for Jan, her parents playfully interacted with her, allowing themselves to be moved by Jan's needs and desires. They also shaped Jan's subjective world when setting limits and engaging her in gender-specific ways. All of this gave Jan a background feeling of security that was necessary for her being able to risk surrendering to symbols and the subjectivity of others. Jan's interaction with her doll is a potential space where she safely learns to surrender to the created and imagined "subjectivity" of the other (Sarah): that is, she *intends* to be moved and shaped by the other (Sarah), who silently represents specific gender values and expectations. All the while, Jan is creating the interaction, shaping the other, and generating experience. Jan's use of the STO provides opportunities to shape and be shaped by the "other's" subjectivity and the symbolic web, which leads to cooperation, intersubjective play, and joint use of symbols in constructing shared experiences of being alive.

Similar examples can be found in psychoanalysis and adult life. When Winnicott said that a person cannot be creative except on the basis of tradition (Davis and Wallbridge, 1987, p. 27), he was saying that one must intentionally surrender to tradition. The tradition's symbolic web must shape one's subjectivity and yet a person (hopefully) shapes tradition in and through her creative use of it. Winnicott himself was shaped by the psychoanalytic symbols, myths, and stories even as he used them to generate his own theory (Greenberg and Mitchell, 1983). Unsavory instances of this can be seen in the history of psychoanalysis when analytic purity was guarded by denouncing heretics such as Sándor Ferenczi, John Bowlby, and others and when institutes operate as paranoiac seminaries (Kirsner, 2001), coercing candidates to accept blindly the doctrines and dogmas of a psychoanalytic tradition. In these circumstances, surrender is transformed into subjugation and generation is sacrificed for certainty.

A more routine illustration of the dynamics of surrender and generation is found in Robert's desire to play an instrument. During the first year of therapy, Robert would wistfully remark about his love of music and his unfulfilled desire to play the saxophone. As a child, his parents discouraged Robert from playing the sax because they said it was impractical, though it may have had more to do with the fact that they were poor. Emigrating from an impoverished country and repressive government, Robert's parents were understandably desperate for their son to have the "good" life. In therapy, Robert expressed his desire as well as his reluctance to learn how to play the saxophone. After some months, Robert bought a used sax and a beginner's guide. While he enjoyed practicing at home alone, Robert realized he wanted to learn from and play with others. One day, after a couple of years had passed, Robert elatedly told me that he and some friends had just played a gig at a local jazz bar. There are many ways to interpret all of this, but I believe Robert's therapy opened a space for him to begin to entertain the dream (versus wish) of playing the sax. His purchase of and playing the sax at home widened the space where he learned to surrender to and generate his own desires in relation to using the saxophone. The saxophone, lesson books, and the solitary play were part of a symbolic web that shaped Robert. In time, Robert was able to extend this space to include other saxophonists in a symbolic field of mutual surrender and generation of experience.

Recognition and negation

"Surrender," Ringstrom (2003) wrote, "allows that there is more than just me or just you, there is the 'us' of mutual recognition" (p. 199). Surrender in the S-S mode accompanies the recognition of the other as a *separate subject*, which necessarily entails negation (not-I). In fact, the child's own experience of being a subject is contingent on recognizing that the other's agency, judgments, and desires are *not* his own. The *resistance* of the other qua subject is necessary for the emergence of the child's subjectivity. The parent, who possesses his/her own distinct agency and desires, negates his/her child while also recognizing and validating the child's assertions. Subjectivity comes into being, in part, by virtue of the recognition and negation of other subjects.

Negation in the S-S mode differs from the previous modes in that it can now be represented linguistically, which, in psychoanalytic parlance, is secondary process thinking. Recognition and negation (e.g., naming the other), in terms of potential space, represents the paradoxical tension between likeness in difference and difference in likeness (Benjamin, 1995). The other as subject is like me and different (not-I). The collapse of potential space or collapse into a symbolic equation signifies two types of negation and recognition. One involves the recognition of the other who possesses no likeness – only difference (e.g., disidentification – absolutely not-I). The other type is an adhesive identification (Rocha Leite Haudenschild, 1997;

Grand, 2000), wherein the other is the same as I and difference is denied. Bob, a borderline patient, for example, angrily disparages his therapist. In that moment, the therapist is absolutely different from Bob. Several minutes later, Bob gushes with admiration, recognizing the therapist as like me (idealized self). Both instances portray the negation of the paradoxical tension between likeness in difference and difference in likeness.

A child uses the STO to learn how to negotiate the dialectic of likeness in difference and difference in likeness, which maintains a lively space of mutual subjective agency. When Jan plays with her doll, for instance, she recognizes the doll as Sarah (subject-like me) and Sarah is not-I (a subject different from me). Her negation of Sarah is devoid of denial or destruction, though not necessarily aggression. If, for example, Jan angrily throws her doll away, one could say that negation and aggression have moved to destruction.

Jan's playful recognition and negation of Sarah also means imagined reciprocity. The play involves *Sarah's* "recognition and negation" of Jan. In this play space, Jan's subjectivity (agency, desires, etc.) is validated in relation to the other. Jan is gaining confidence that recognition and negation can be tolerated and that mutual recognition and negation are necessary for intersubjective experiences of being alive and real. We can create and tolerate being alive together!

Dynamics of care

The dialectical tension between surrender–generation and recognition–negation of potential space is contingent upon the dynamics of trust–distrust and loyalty–disloyalty. Indeed, the symbolic web of a family or culture manifests and shapes the dynamics of Care, even as it depends upon it for creating a sense of shared aliveness. That is, the symbolic web represents diverse meanings and contexts of trust and distrust, loyalty and disloyalty. While overly generalized, young boys may grow up playing with toys and watching superhero movies and cartoons that inform them that care means protection of loved ones. Therefore, a trustworthy and loyal father is one who protects his wife and children. Freud's disappointment with his father would be an illustration of the violation of socially sanctioned expectations of how men were to care for their families (Rizzuto, 1998). Little girls, on the other hand, play with toys and games that inform them that care involves nurturing children, friends, and parents. Certainly, the US culture of the 1950s, through its web of symbols (toys, rituals, media) and in the verbal and non-verbal gendered care of parents, communicated to girls that being trustworthy and loyal meant taking responsibility for raising children, all the while maintaining emotional connections with spouse and extended family (Coontz, 1992). Girls and boys who violate social expectations are vulnerable to social shame (a form of recognition that demands likeness and negates difference) and are portrayed as untrustworthy or betraying their "sex" and the expectations of parents.

The child's use of the STO allows her to negotiate and manage the vicissitudes of cultural expectations of trust and loyalty. The trust and loyalty she has experienced in relation to Mom and Dad serve as an idiom of care that is transferred to another subject (STO) that she has selected. Jan's imaginative play with Sarah is a complex dance of trust and loyalty that is linked to the culture of her family. The *real* aspects of this play are present when the trust and loyalty between Jan and Sarah parallel the care between Jan and her parents. In those instances when distrust and disloyalty prevail in the parent–child relationship, a child's care of the STO may be unreal or defensively illusory. "Play," in this instance, is characterized by solipsistic fantasy and the doll becomes divorced from the reality of Care occurring between parent and child. Thus, the STO and its use signify what did not happen (Winnicott, 1971, pp. 23–25).

The STO and potential space offer an area of experience wherein the child learns to surrender to, generate, recognize, and internalize the symbolic web of trust and loyalty, which are necessary for the possibility of subjective and intersubjective vitality. Jan's trust in and loyalty to Sarah and Jan's imagined experience of Sarah's trust in and loyalty to her are real and foundational for shared creativity and aliveness.

Disruption and repair

Naturally, as human beings, we know too well the emotional and relational disruptions that result from real and imagined experiences of distrust and betrayal, even in the most loving and secure relationships. To handle these inevitable disruptions, cultures create and use symbols (stories, rituals) for repairing torn relationships and, when possible, restore subjective and intersubjective creativity, spontaneity, and vitality. The symbol itself, as Winnicott (1971) and Lacan (1977) noted, helps the child handle the disruption that entails her recognition of being separate from mother and may come to represent the possibility of reunion. In the depressive position, for instance, the child experiences the separation as alienation, though the achievement and jouissance of symbolization mitigates this experience. The symbol, in this case the STO, represents union in the midst of separation.[11] Taken further, this suggests that the repairs associated with the C-C and T-O modes become transformed by symbolic representation such that a child *intends* to use these symbolic idioms of parent–child repair in relation to the STO. In this potential space with the STO, the child safely initiates and imitates repair and she is, likewise, open to the reparative attempts of the STO, albeit imagined.

A child, for example, becomes angry at her doll for some imagined offense. After scolding the doll, she cuddles, soothes, and spoils her doll much like what she has experienced with her parents "localized spoiling" (Winnicott, 1971, p. 97). Adults also have and use symbols that represent disruption and repair. When Greta began therapy, she believed that God was always with her and loved her unconditionally. This common enough belief, however, was incongruent with her past and present interactions with others. The symbol, God, represented a wished-for repair and an avoidance of painful and life-draining disruptions – past and present. Because Greta had so many experiences of relational disruptions where there was no localized spoiling, it was safer to be in an imaginary relationship with a God who did not represent any threat. The first obvious sign of change occurred when Greta told me she hated me. Her expression of hate signaled to me that Greta had the confidence, trust, and hope that I would not leave her or retaliate and, more importantly, that we could repair this breach together.

Potential space in the S-S mode involves the child's use of the STO to negotiate the dynamics of surrender–generation, recognition–negation, Care, and disruption–repair. The imagined mutual play provides the child opportunities for intentional use of the STO and a concomitant symbolic representation of experience. Vital symbols are those symbols in which there is a subjective sense of aliveness between the person and the other subject and this vitality is maintained by the dynamic presence of potential space.

The collapse of symbolic potential space: culture, trauma, and therapy[12]

Within the psychoanalytic tradition, some analysts have focused on trauma that results from parental deprivation and impingement, while others have argued that the internalization of repressive social structures contributes to adult neuroses. Both views point to the collapse or severe attenuation of potential space, a defensive and rigid use of symbols, and an attending diminution of subjective and intersubjective experiences of being alive. With varying degrees of success, societies, families, and other groups establish rules, roles, and rituals to maintain and repair tears in potential space. In the West, psychotherapy has functioned as a cultural ritual that attends to the aftermath of trauma, ideally restoring the dialectical tension of potential space and providing a more flexible and creative use of symbols in representing and sharing experience. Keylor (2003), in examining Lacanian and Kleinian perspectives, said, "So fundamental is the use of symbols in communication with oneself and with others that the failure to develop this ability, or the loss of it, is in both theories a chief feature of significant mental disturbance and deep pathology" (p. 234). As in the previous chapters, I am interested in portraying the collapse of potential space in terms of the dynamics of the S-S mode and its relation to interpersonal interactions and the larger cultural field.

Trauma, whether a single event or ongoing deprivation, means that a person is subjugated to the desires and expectations of the other (or event). To be subjugated is to be articulated by the other, to be inscribed by the other's needs and cravings, having imposed on oneself the symbolic meanings and values of the other. In trauma, the victim is unable to find her desires represented in the social-symbolic realm and is coerced to sacrifice her agency and longings for the judgments and expectations of the more powerful other and his/her symbolic world. The hysteric, for example, lives out her life using the symbols of the social world, but these symbols represent the other's desires and not her own (Bollas, 2000). It is no accident that this diagnosis is most often attributed to women in Western history. The "wandering womb" signifies a female hysteric's search to discover and generate her sexuality in a patriarchal society – a society that seeks to articulate and determine female sexuality while silencing the spontaneous and erotic speech of women. Of course, there are male hysterics, as Freud recognized, and they, too, find it difficult to discover and use their own idiom in the social symbols. Whether the result of parental impingement or a repressive patriarchal society, hysterics struggle to use symbols to represent their own desires, because they have been subjugated to the needs, demands, and desires of the other. The result is a loss of vitality.

The difference between surrender and subjugation is that in subjugation there is a denial of the other's agency and passions; this differs from negation that involves recognition of the other's desires as different from, yet like, my own. We are used to thinking about secondary negation as various types of no. However, the act of calling out a friend's name is a form of negation (not-I) that preserves and validates her subjectivity. Derogatory names like nigger, gook, frog, raghead, spic, bitch, and fag are symbols of negation that represent the collapse of potential space – the refusal to be moved by the subjectivity of the other and the real or imagined subjugation of the other's identity. Symbolic recognition, in these instances, comprises the other as absolutely different.

Symbolic negation may also be found when using the verb "is." What "is" always implies what is not. In terms of the diminution of potential space, the verb "is" is yoked to the facticity and omnipotence of the previous modes. In the collapse of potential space, it is as if the S-S mode has been captured by the earlier modes, though retaining the veneer of symbolization. For instance, "He's a nigger," signifies the presence of omnipotent negation by way of symbolic speech. The speaker's use of language is omnipotently denotative. The other is *not recognized* as an equivalent center of subjectivity. Subjectivity is negated and the other is dominated by the constructions of the powerful other. The symbols and cultural rituals surrounding racism, sexism, and ageism are illustrations of omnipotent negation and the shrinkage or absence of potential space. The use of symbols to negate the subjectivity of the other is not necessarily pathological or traumatic, though it is certainly an anxiety-driven and hostilely rigid use of symbols that results in a continuum of violence and exclusion.

A tragic example is seen in John's story of his relationship with his mother. When John was a young towheaded boy, his mother took delight in his curly hair. She played dolls with him and dressed him as a girl. John, like most children, desired his mother's attention, which was necessary to his physical and psychological survival. Initially, he "played" along. Whenever he resisted, his mother would withdraw emotionally or become violent. His mother's speech and behavior were traumatic, because John was forced to submit to his mother's symbolic representations of him – representations that did not mirror his own idiom, making it exceedingly difficult for John to find and use language to represent his own desires, agency, and needs. Maternal speech, in this instance, negated John's subjectivity even as she inscribed her longings onto him. This severe attenuation of potential space drained John's experience of being alive.

Being subjugated to and inscribed by a powerful other does not lend itself to feelings of confidence, trust or a sense of loyalty. Experiences of trust and loyalty give us the courage to risk surrendering to and being moved by others and the symbolic web. Moreover, these experiences make it possible for us to handle the negation of the other, while remaining a subject. Subjugation and negation of subjectivity, however, represent the loss of trust and fidelity as well as an underlying sense of hopelessness regarding the restoration of trust. A person may respond by holding onto an illusory "trust" in the powerful other, which maintains the relationship at the cost of sacrificing one's own desires, hopes, and needs. In other words, in oppressive contexts I obtain loyalty and am deemed trustworthy as long as I remain a subjugated other. Acts of rebellion and resistance manifest a glimmer of hope for freedom and life, though sadly both may repeat the legacy of domination, distrust, disloyalty, and negation of the other's subjectivity.

As a child, John learned that trust and loyalty in relation to his mother demanded his subjugation to her commands to play the role of a little girl. Whenever he displayed resistance, asserting his own desires, his mother would either attack or ignore him. Asserting himself was tarnished with experiences of betrayal and distrust. Trust and loyalty were not affixed to recognition of his subjective desires and needs. This severe contraction of potential space led to a distortion of trust and loyalty, and profound anxiety and confusion with regard to surrendering to an other. Not surprisingly, John carried these traits forward into adulthood. Women would initially be attracted to John's charm and attention. He intuited their wants and needs and, quite naturally, women were lulled into a feeling that they were loved. The honeymoon would be quickly shattered by John's rage at their selfishness, leaving a long line of confused women in the wake of John's abandonment. As an adult, John's rage and hatred toward his mother can be understood as his way of trying to free himself from bondage, and, in the process, find and establish his subjectivity in the social symbolic field. This is an arduous and complex process, because at an unconscious level, the symbolic field is his mother's tongue. If one's first introduction to the symbolic web involves subjugation and the denial of one's personal idiom, it becomes extraordinarily difficult to trust one's use of language. The symbolic web, in other words, unconsciously represents, for John, painful experiences of distrust related to the negation of his subjectivity.

When John was a child, it was horribly confusing being conceived of as a girl while having the idiom of a boy. His work in therapy was finding his sexuality in the cultural field of masculine symbols, but this was made more difficult because surrender meant subjugation and negation. I understood John's "resistance" in therapy as his attempt to bring his subjectivity into play, though notably distorted because of anxiety and painful prior experiences of betrayal. The arduous and lengthy work of restoring potential space involved cooperative efforts at containing his rage without attacking or withdrawing, and by building trust so that John could surrender to and trust his use of language to represent his sexuality.

The collapse or attenuation of potential space is not merely an interpersonal event that occurs in families. All too frequently, we unwittingly and naively separate the trauma a child experiences in her family from the larger cultural milieu. A woman who is beaten up by her husband most likely grew up and resides in a patriarchal culture that possesses symbols, stories, and myths that celebrate female submissiveness and relegate female sexuality to the status of possession and servant-hood. She, as other, is trusted only to the extent that she submits to this norm. If she resists, violence and ostracism can be expected. A middle-aged man, who drags himself to the assembly line five days a week, is weighed down by a sense of meaninglessness and purposelessness. He lives in a capitalistic society that worships profit, but not the needs, desires, and aspirations of the individual worker. While patriarchal and capitalistic symbol systems do not, in and of themselves, represent the attenuation of potential space, they are easily used to subjugate and inscribe the less powerful (Foucault, 1972).

I am not sanguine about the possibility of any social, political, economic, or religious system being free of traumatic forms of subjugation, denial, distrust, and betrayal that annihilate or drain away individual and communal experiences of being alive. Indeed, human beings have a remarkable ability to distort and use available beliefs, values, and meanings to insure their own survival by way of subjugating others. Perhaps we unconsciously believe that others' survival and experiences of being alive threaten our own. In any case, the liveliness of our individual and interpersonal use of symbols requires attending to attributes that maintain the dynamism of potential space, whether that is in the analytic space, the family home, or the larger society. The challenge is not only to identify sources and accomplices that lead to anxiety-driven use of symbols and a draining away of subjective and intersubjective experiences of being alive, but also to create and use symbols (rituals) that provide a restoration of symbolizing potential space.

Psychoanalytic therapy, at its best, is a cultural ritual wherein the patient's particular idiom is recognized and met by the analyst's curiosity and devotion. In this meeting, the patient finds and represents her desires in the symbolic field. One could say that therapy is a drama, wherein two people continually cooperate in creating trust and repairing real and imagined moments of distrust and betrayal. In this play, the analyst recognizes and is moved by the patient's subjectivity, offering recognition and negation free of annihilation and bondage. In time, the patient experiences enough trust and hope to surrender (free association). In surrendering, the patient begins to use language to find and represent her own desires and sense of agency as well as discovering, experiencing, and sharing a greater sense of aliveness. If all goes well, the patient discovers and recovers vital symbols.

Ideally, psychoanalysis moves a person toward giving voice to silent longings, either because the dominant social system denied these yearnings and/or because parents and others refused to recognize and affirm them. The methods and rules of psychoanalysis are the tools employed to maintain and restore potential space and the vitality of symbolization. Unlike many other cultural rituals, psychoanalysis does not attempt to replace the patient's symbol system with an analytic one, though certainly this has been a problem in the history of psychoanalysis. Rather, analysis loosens a patient's hold on the specific symbolic web of one's youth and culture, which she used to create symptoms for survival, and creates a space to either find new vitalizing symbols to represent meaning and desires or to discover new meanings and desires in old symbols. This said, I end with a caution: "The one thing psychoanalysis cannot cure, when it works, is a belief in psychoanalysis. And that is a problem" (Philips, 1993, p. 121). The symbols used to free can, in turn, be a cage.

Chapter 5

Enlivening stories

> All sorrows can be borne if you put them into a story or tell a story about them.
>
> (Isak Dinesen, in Arendt, 1958, p. 175)

> Action reveals itself fully only to the storyteller.
>
> (Arendt, 1958, p. 192)

> What life have you if you have not life together? There is no life that is not in community.
>
> (T. S. Eliot, 1999, p. 154)

Circling a crackling fire, children listen with rapt attention to an adult telling a story of the legend of the bog monster. Two lovers share stories about each other, feeling a burgeoning sense of aliveness and intimacy. Cradled in a mother's arms, an infant, without understanding, attends to the tones and rhythms of his mother's voice as she tells her friend the story of her pregnancy, birth, and her baby's charming personality quirks. A patient begins the session with a characteristic, affectless tale of loss and pain, leaving the therapist wondering how his story functions to defend against desire and hope. With the background din of a nursing home, a woman reminisces on her long life to a chaplain.

Human beings are forever telling and listening to stories. Indeed, we might say that human beings are *homo fabula*, creating and being created by stories (MacIntyre, 1983). We are born into the stories of our parents and culture. Before we can speak, before we utter our first words, before we stumble in telling our first story, others are narrating us into existence and into life. The developmental movement from symbol to weaving symbols into intricate narratives represents the successful integration of a complex array of semiotic processes and the achievement and possibility of community and communion. In other words, semantic, lexical, syntactic rules and meanings of the narrative system make possible the forms of subjectivity and intersubjectivity wherein community is found.

Stories have always been a part of psychoanalytic practice and theorizing. Freud was an accomplished storyteller and his theory was informed, in part, by Greek myths along with various cultural, scientific, and religious stories that shaped his work (Gay, 1988; Sulloway, 1992). Notwithstanding Freud's (Breuer and Freud, 1895) early remark that his medical histories read like novellas, he and many of his followers thought of themselves as scientists, ostensibly distancing themselves from narrative forms of knowing (see Polkinghorne, 1988), and ignoring the idea that a "scientist is before anything else a person who 'tells stories'" (Lyotard, 1999, p. 66). It was not until the late 1970s and 1980s that hermeneutics and narrative rose to the foreground of psychoanalytic thinking (e.g., Spence, 1982, 1987, 1989; Schafer, 1983; Messer, Sass, and Woolfolk, 1988; Morris, 1993). Since then, the literature on narrative in psychoanalysis and cognate fields has expanded exponentially. The purpose in this chapter is not to review, summarize or critique psychoanalytic perspectives regarding narrative in human development. Rather, it is to address the relation between semiotic processes associated with the narrative-communal (N-C) mode of organizing experience and individual and communal experiences of being alive.

Narrative, community, and time

A few background comments about narrative, community, and experiences of being alive are necessary before attending to the specifics of the N-C mode. I am reminded of Winnicott's famous remark, "There is no such thing as a baby," when I aver that there is no such thing as an autobiography. Certainly "I" can construct and convey my tale, but my story is a story of others. Before I could tell my story, parents and siblings told stories that shaped how I would eventually recount my story. A child, Lyotard (1999) realized, "is already positioned as the referent in the story recounted by those around him, in relation to which he will inevitably chart his course" (p. 15).

The absence of solipsism in autobiography is also bound to the fact that telling a story implies listeners who respond and in turn shape narrative discourse. For Bruner (1990), "'the-story-of-a-life' as told to a particular person is in some deep sense a joint product of the teller and the told" (p. 124). Thus, when I am able to tell my story, it is not simply "my" story. It is a story of interlocutors – family, friends, enemies, and culture. Indeed, Kenneth and Mary Gergen argued that "the culture is speaking through the actor, using the actor to reproduce itself" (in Polkinghorne, 1988, p. 119). I would add that other cultural actors shape the storyteller by listening and responding.

The fact that "I" am formed by stories and tell my story in the midst of interlocutors suggests something fundamental about narrative, identity, and being human. Heidegger (1971) believed that language is the house of being. I would put it differently. Narrative (and the act of narration) is the house of being-in-community. A reformed Cartesian might say, I narrate, therefore *I am and we are*. Acts of narrating have always undermined Cartesian epistemological and anthropological claims. Having said this, alienation, violence, oppression, and destruction of communion and community have been supported by totalitarian narrations and narratives (Barratt, 1993). Though, in their distorted forms, there is nearly always a faint echo of hope and longing for being-in-community. In situations where narratives are used to exclude or divide, for example, there is a wish for (and fear of) community that lies in the shadow. When we recall the frightening and vicious stories the Nazis told *ad nauseam*, it is noted that they had a vision of community, albeit formed through and dependent on the hated "other."

Implicit here is the intimate connection between narration and community. It is not narrative itself that binds people together (or sets them apart); rather it is the ongoing acts of narrating, of affective telling, retelling, creating, and listening to stories that make communion and community possible. "Narrativity," Ricoeur wrote, "from the outset, establishes repetition on the plane of being-with-others" (in Polkinghorne, 1988, p. 134). The absence of narrative, narration, and listening points to the demise of culture and the eclipse of community, as well as the loss of experiences of being in communion.

It is important to note that I differentiate between intersubjectivity and community, though they are cognates. In psychoanalysis, intersubjectivity may mean a field of mutual influence (Stolorow et al., 1994), a capacity that emerges when an infant is able to share subjective states (Stern, 1985), or a field of mutual recognition and regulation (Benjamin, 1988). Despite important differences in definition, each refers to verbal and non-verbal interactions between self and other. While intersubjectivity is the basis for telling and sharing stories, the concept, in psychoanalytic discourse, tends toward a general and abstract depiction of the intricate dynamics of social behavior and communication. Interest in and use of this concept is shaped by the desire to move away from a one-person to a two-person psychology. The idea of community necessarily moves the conversation to three or more persons. The experience of communion may take place between two people, but community, which is the basis for communion, connotes many different people who share a common life together. It is in this common life that we become persons-in-relation (Macmurray, 1949).

The movement from a one- to a two-person psychology accompanied growing attention to the myriad of intersubjective exchanges between parent and child. While the intersubjective interaction between a parent and an infant (or young child) may be profoundly intimate and a part of the web of interactions that form community, it is only a piece of the various intersubjective forms and activities that create community. The concept of community refers to complex social rituals and communications, as well as diverse ideas about and meaningful experiences of friendship, fellowship, camaraderie, companionship, and communion (Kirkpatrick, 1986). The concept of intersubjectivity can be appended to all of this, but, in psychoanalytic discourse, intersubjectivity tends to refer to the dyadic exchange between parent and child or analyst and analysand.

Another reason for distinguishing between intersubjectivity and community has to do with the relation between time and personhood. The dynamics of intersubjectivity tend to be portrayed synchronically and, when there is disruption, one searches the past to explain the present. Narrative and the idea of community, in my view, connotes the *personalization* of shared time past, present, and future, which, in turn, depends on diverse forms of promises that establish and maintain communal continuity (Macmurray, 1949; Arendt, 1958). We tell stories that say these are (were, will be) my people who keep and break promises, as well as repair disappointments and betrayals. Time is profoundly personal and communal. In brief, the capacity for intersubjectivity, which I identify with S-S mode, is foundational for, but not identical to, the achievement and possibility of community – the *personalization* of history and the hope for future generations.

Narrative knowing: communal survival and vitality

Narrative time, storytelling, and community are yoked to individual and collective knowledge and experiences of survival and being alive.[1] For Lyotard (1999), "narration is the quintessential form of customary knowledge" (p. 19). Without a doubt, human beings "think, perceive, imagine, and make moral choices according to narrative structures" (Sarbin, 1986, p. 8). To "adopt and be adopted by a particular story, we are in fact assuming a set of practices which will shape the ways we relate to our world" (Burrell, 1977, p. 36). And this relation to the world and others is largely informed by narrative knowing and its customary knowledge – the rules, roles, moral codes, and conventional practices that inform us and provide directions regarding survival and life.[2]

The stories that we tell about our ancestors and ourselves comprise customary knowledge that informs listeners about how to survive *in this* environment and *in this* community. These narratives may be moral tales, heroic legends, sagas, fables, or cautionary vignettes that provide listeners the practical wisdom (phronesis) needed to avoid the pitfalls and dangers if she or he and the community are to continue. Knowledge for survival, while essential, is one aspect of human existence that is usually motivated by fear. Whereas fear may hold a people together, it is never the basis of experiences of communion.

Narratives and narration also possess knowledge that shapes the possibility of shared experiences of being alive – communion. Communion connotes narrative discourse that makes possible a lively and relatively free people with a shared identity, a shared history, rituals, and stories. Communion signifies what Buber (1958) called I–thou relations or what Dilthey (1989) labeled *Gemeingefuhl* – feeling of community – which he joins to *Lebensgefuhl* – feeling of life, which has its own forms of logic. And T. S. Eliot juxtaposes the painful struggle for survival and the deep yearning for life with others. "What life have you if you have not life together? There is no life that is not in community" (1999, p. 154). Both community and the diverse modes of being alive in community are in-formed and maintained by narrative knowing.

Given this, I view the tools and ritual of psychoanalysis, at their best, as enabling patients to deconstruct the absolute necessity of the epistemology of their survival narratives, which are often shaped by deprivation and impingement, for the sake of re-telling stories that are open to and expressions of communitarian epistemology and its attending experiences of being alive. *Psychoanalytic goals of insight, bringing the unconscious to consciousness, deconstructing totalitarian narratives, moving from symptom to story, from showing to telling, helping patients achieve a coherently meaningful story, are empty if not informed by and leading to forms of narrative knowledge related to individual and communal experiences of being alive.*

Characteristics of the narrative-communal mode

Since we grow up in an ocean of stories, we intuit narratives. Nevertheless, before plunging into the relation between narration and experiences of being alive, it is helpful to define more clearly what narrative and its relation to other modes of organizing experience mean. For example, what do we mean by narrative? What comprises narrative? What are the functions of narrative? When and how does the skill for narration emerge in development? How do the C-C, T-O, and S-S modes operate with the N-C mode?

Narrative semiosis and plots

In general, narrative consists of a complex web of cognitive, semiotic processes "that organizes human experience into temporally meaningful episodes" (Polkinghorne, 1988, p. 1). Put another way, human beings, through use of narrative semioses, impose a form(s) on the flow of experience, organizing episodes, actions, and accounts of actions into a coherent form of knowing (Sarbin, 1986). In this way, narrative and narration enable human beings to give "meaning to their experience of temporality and personal action" (Polkinghorne, 1988, p. 11). This narrative meaning, which is personal and social, "functions to give form to understanding a purpose to life and to join everyday actions and events into episodic units" (p. 11), providing both personal and social continuity (Crites, 1986, p. 159). The semiotic processes implicated in narration include retrodictively revising, selecting, and ordering "past details in such a way as to create a self-narrative (and group narrative) that is coherent and satisfying and that will serve as a justification for one's present condition and situation" (Polkinghorne, 1988, p. 106). Giving form and meaning to experience in the present and past includes intending, consciously and unconsciously, a future action. In everyday parlance, we expect stories to have a plot (Ricoeur, 1984) and this plot, ideally, is the achievement of the intersection of semiotic processes of all four modes.

The plots of complicated, as well as uncomplicated, personal and group narratives comprise a web of stated and unstated beliefs, themes, meanings, expectations, emotions, desires, rules (or moral codes), scripted roles, and values that are constituted by and emerge from a group of interlocutors. Stories, in other words, are more than forms of meaningful episodes. Narration and narrative represent, organize, and regulate individual and group desires, values, intentions, and emotions, which takes place with real and imagined partners. For instance, Marc, a 25-year-old single man, begins the session with a story about his frustration with being late due to heavy traffic and difficulty in finding a parking place. On the manifest level, one hears his desire to be on time, because he values our time together and he holds to a family and cultural code of punctuality. Obstacles, like heavy traffic, frustrate his desire, expectation, and moral self. And yet, there is another layer here. To whom is Marc speaking (Heimann, 1956)? What script is he beginning to play? His father was a stern and punitive man who did not tolerate mistakes. Perhaps Marc is beating me to the punch, fearing that I will lash out for his tardiness, overlooking (by way of narration) my desire for his safety and my pleasure that he is here. For Marc, there is a rule, one of many, and consequences for breaking it in this ritual about being on time. I hope, in time, not only that he tells the story of his father, but also that we construct and narrate other meanings and emotions about timeliness and tardiness.

Narrative competence: relationships and co-constructions

Implicit here is the reality that stories are co-constructed and the attainment of narrative competence depends, to a large degree, on relational achievements.[3] When coming across a person whose story seems incoherent and disorganized, we become confused and may attribute something wrong with the person. There is some disorder of the self. Likewise, overly rigid narrative enunciations reflect a relational disruption and a closing off of creative doubt and ambiguity. Stories and narrative competence are fundamentally relational achievements that encompass a certain amount of ambiguity and uncertainty. Chaotic or excessively rigid narratives nearly always point to disordered relationships – past and present. Recent research (Main, 2000; Hesse and Main, 2000) demonstrates that a severe problem in the parent–child relationship leads to difficulties in a child or adult's ability to tell a coherent, comprehensive story.[4] As a child moves from a preverbal to a verbal, from a verbal to a narrative world, the parent's ability to organize and narrate experience shapes the child's ability to do the same. A child will have difficulty narrating experience if she lives with others whose recitations are disorganized, lack reflective attributes, or who inhibit the child's story through acts of minimization, denial, and rejection.

A good-enough parent helps a child tell his story by recognizing and responding to the child's assertions. This includes introducing the child not only into the language of the culture, but also the storied plots and scripts of the culture and family, which the child, in turn, assimilates and uses to order, represent, and articulate her desires and meanings. A child comes to *know* her desires not simply because the other recognizes them, but also because she is able to tell stories that represent her desires. Parents who are dismissive of their child's assertions and who do not actively facilitate their child's ability to use the cultural symbols at hand to construct and enunciate her story will make it difficult for the child to narrate her experience in a meaningful, coherent, and comprehensive way. All of this suggests that semiotic processes that make narration and narrative possible are inextricably yoked to interpersonal communication that takes place between the child and others (Bucci, 2001).

Narrative, mentalization, and reality

The co-constructive reality of narrative also includes the interrelated capacities for self-reflection and recognition of the mind of the other – what Fonagy and Target (1997) called mentalization or reflective function. They maintained that, by age 5, children are able "to conceive of others' beliefs, feelings, attitudes, desires, hopes, knowledge, imagination, pretense, plans, and so on" (Fonagy, 2001, p. 165). A child's

> acquisition of reflective function . . . depends on the opportunities that he had in early life to observe and explore the mind of his primary caregiver. The parent of the secure child engages in behaviors such as pretend play, which almost obliges the child to contemplate the existence of mental states.
>
> (Fonagy, 2001, pp. 166–167)

The emergence of the reflective function and self–other consciousness coincides with the child's competence in understanding stories and constructing experience narratively. As Simone de Beauvoir nicely summed up, "Self-consciousness is not knowledge, but the story one tells about oneself" (in Clavell, 2000, p. 518).

The reflective function, self-other consciousness, and narration are intertwined and each is shaped by the lifelong play and struggle of reality and fantasy, veracity and falsity. We know that the myths, fairy tales, and legends, as such, are not true, though they may point to some valuable and hence true meaning about human life or necessary customary knowledge. When we move into the realm of science and, in particular, the human sciences (e.g., history, psychoanalysis), the lines between reality-truth and imagination are blurred. Donald Spence (1982) attempted to articulate his view of the continuum between narrative and historical truth, which evoked a flurry of articles critiquing his position (Eagle, 1984; Freeman, 1985; Sass and Woolfolk, 1988). Whether Spence is right or wrong is not the point I wish to address. With the exception of intentional fabricators, all human beings, in telling their stories, possess some belief that the story they tell about themselves and others is true/real and, yet, there is also, most often unacknowledged, an underlying uncertainty that attends every story. The story I tell cannot fully capture reality. There is always a remainder that niggles at our belief in fact and truth. This remainder, which undercuts our certainty despite our denials, is a necessary disruption for a creative and open narrative. Otherwise, narrative (and community) becomes ossified and totalitarian.

The dynamic struggle between what is true/real and false/unreal (e.g., fantasy, pretend, imaginary), while lifelong, has roots in earlier modes. From a developmental perspective, a young child

> generally operates in "psychic equivalence" mode, where ideas are not felt to be representations, but rather direct replicas of reality, and consequently true; however, at other times the child uses a "pretend" mode, in which ideas are felt to be representational but their correspondence with reality is not examined.
>
> (Fonagy and Target, 1996, p. 219)

I suggest that the facticity or psychic equivalence of the C-C and T-O modes continues to operate dynamically with S-S and N-C modes. That is, the facticity of somatic semiosis (C-C mode) and categorical semiosis (T-O mode) is the background, unquestioned presence of individual and collective experiences of narrative reality and truth. One could say that there is underlying omnipotent thinking in all autobiographies and especially in every group's self-narrative, wherein certain meanings, beliefs, scripts, roles, and values are unquestioned, unexamined, and unconsciously presumed to be *the* truth and felt to be real. Indeed, the very narratives that comprise a group's customary knowledge contain criteria and codes for adjudicating what the group deems real and unreal, true and false, which points to an underlying tautological, if not tyrannical, aspect of group narrative claims regarding truth. The stories Freud and his followers told about Breuer (Breger, 2000) and the stories religious groups tell about their founders are examples of this. Challenge the veracity of these stories and one can expect to be the recipient of hostility that is connected to the facticity and omnipotence of earlier modes of organizing experience.

One further point about reality-truth and narrative concerns their social and communal functions. Philosophers from Plato to Macmurray have recognized and struggled to show the relation between truth, reality, community, and life. Truth and claims about what is real do not simply reside within an isolated individual's narrative declarations or in the rigid codifications of a single group. Rather, truth and declarations of reality emerge in discourse of agents seeking to organize experience for the sake of survival and life. As children, we begin to grasp the truths of our clan in the stories we are told and in the storied answers we are given to our queries. These stories and our own tales retain a sense of reality, not only because they represent forms of customary knowledge needed for survival and life together, but also because we need to have a sense – individual and communal – that what we narrate is real – or at least more real than unreal.

In sum, narratives, which encompass a complex confluence of semiotic processes, organize self–other experience into temporally meaningful episodes. These narrative organizations comprise conscious and unconscious scripts, rules, roles, meanings, beliefs, values, desires, feelings, and intentions that are contextual, time bound, and social. The achievement of narration includes the self-reflective function and self–other consciousness – which depend on a child's constitutional capacities and her parents' skills in constructing stories and facilitating her stories. Consciousness and self-reflection, found within group narratives and narrations, include the diverse individual and shared epistemologies that manifest ways of being in the world as well as communal experiences of survival and being alive. While human beings can imaginatively and self-reflectively construct all types of stories, there is a varying mix between fact and fiction, reality and fantasy, in all stories, which is necessary for creativity. Narrative semiotic processes include experiences of and claims about what is real and not real, and these experiences and claims are dependent on and linked to the semiotic facticity of the C-C and T-O modes.

Attributes of narrative-communal organizations of being alive

While it is an overgeneralization, it seems to me that many of the contributors to psychoanalytic literature depict the "other" as an existential or anthropological reality and as a psychological and developmental necessity. For Freud (1917a), the "other" is the source of identifications that casts a shadow on the ego, which may be used to deny loss, dependency, and the lack of omnipotence. Phillips (1993) views the "other" as an obstacle, a source of necessary frustration for psychological growth. The "other" looms large for Lacan (Verhaeghe, 1999) and LaPlanche (1999), though depicted differently. For them, the "other" is implicated in an alienated subject or alienated consciousness. To be sure, there are instances of alienation, denial, lack, and obstacles in human life. Yet, I wonder if the "other" qua mystery, shadow, object, obstacle can distract us from the "other" as essential to the possibility of human personhood, unified consciousness or subjectivity, and communion. In discussing the attributes of the N-C mode, I am arguing that the good enough "other," ideally speaking, is necessary for achieving a unified and unifying narrative and attending experiences of being alive with fellow human beings. Moreover, the "other" is not only an equivalent center of subjectivity; the "other" represents the possibility of person-in-community-with-other-persons (Macmurray, 1961). Buber's Thou, for instance, is not an impersonal other, but a personal, narrated thou in community. This significantly alters the meaning and forms of being alive, in general, and the ways that agency, emotional-regulation, continuity, and validation are understood and organized, in particular.

Narrative and agency

In the previous chapters, I portrayed agency as something that resides in the individual and is largely dependent on the ministrations of the other. Even with the emergence of I–you schemas in the symbolic-subjective mode, agency, while, at times, shared with the other, is experienced primarily in terms of I-ness. We could say that agency moves from somatic, to monadic (me-ness), to dyadic, to triadic (quadratic, etc.) forms.[5] Agency in the narrative-communal mode is, at the very least, triadic ("we" as in more than two) and is represented and organized as such. For example, when Helen Keller wrote about her awakening to the symbolic world, she recalled moments of pleasure and excitement of shared intentionality with her teacher. Once she knew that water represented w-a-t-e-r, there was a shared intention to learn. It was much later that Helen Keller was able to narrate her experience, which implies a group of people who can share in her experience and in her intention to learn about and experience the wider world. Put differently, in the background of her story are the stories of her family, of her teacher, and of all the other agentic interlocutors who depend on language to construct and narrate stories. Helen Keller's passionate intention to learn was connected to a larger story of others who shared in this passion.

When Helen Keller discovered the world of symbols, she was able to represent experience and *know*, through the use of the symbols at hand, that she had desires and intentions and was able to *act* on both. In the N-C mode, she knew and shared the narrated desires and intentions of other persons, as well as her own desires and agency. Keller's and our own introduction to the symbolic world and the world of stories necessarily includes others. For instance, the parent as "other" who reads stories to his child may indeed contribute to an alienated subject or consciousness, which means that agency is experienced and organized as split. However, parents may also read stories to their pre-narrative child that cement relationships and introduce the child to "other" desires that may be used and shared (triadically, quadratically). The "other," through a myriad of stories, introduces and seduces (in a positive sense) the child into the family and cultural narratives that manifest collective intentions and desires.

When a child feels loved, accepted, and valued, she is able to internalize, as well as match, her desires and agency to the community, while retaining an individual and shared sense of spontaneity, flexibility, and creativity. The "other's" agency and desire (as story and narrator), then, may be experienced as a communion (not union) of personal agents and not fundamentally alienating, repressive, or oppressive. Put differently, personalization and intersubjectivity, which begin in the S-S mode, are deepened and broadened in the N-C mode, making possible a *community of agents that rely on narratives*. Without stories, there is no community of agents.

Recently, I spent a week with friends and their four children. Given the expectable vicissitudes of everyday life, the parents, who are well educated and secure in who they are, interacted in countless ways with their rambunctious, creative, and playful children. The father, an accomplished storyteller and novelist, would frequently tell his children stories and they, in turn, would clamor for more. The older children (10 and 11) also told their own stories or emended Dad's stories by way of questions and observations. Naturally, the tales he told varied, but all of them were rooted in their particular culture. Despite the very different personalities of the children, it was clear to me that these children were internalizing the stories of their family and culture such that their own individual agencies were expressed (narrated), fit within, and shared with the community of agents. The conflict that any person would have in this family or group does not necessarily spell an alienated agency. Indeed, in this family, conflict and its resolution become part of the family narrative such that agency, even in the midst of conflict, retains the possibility of community – a community of agents and shared agency.

Less happy occasions may be found in the overly rigid or incoherent stories patients tell their therapists. Agency is present in the narration, although it is desiccated, lacking individual and shared flexibility and spontaneity. Whenever Lana, a middle-aged woman who suffered from trichotillomania, experienced any "negative" affect (e.g., anxiety, anger), she would return to familiar storied themes. In those moments, it was as if there was no possible way for her to tell a different story, which was an overly restrictive manifestation of her agency. But there is more. The way Lana told the story did not allow for retelling the story from other perspectives or simply telling another story. That is, during those times, Lana also worked to keep us from creating and telling another story that would have expanded her agency. Her idea of shared agency was my conforming to this, and only this, story. The boredom and frustration I felt, while having several sources and other interpretations, had to do with the loss of mutual participation in creating and discovering meaning together – a momentary loss of shared agency.

Narratives and emotional regulation

Lana used her story to protect herself from being overwhelmed by anxiety and hopelessness. Stories and the way we tell them are inextricably linked to emotional regulation. As children, we are enthralled with stories of the macabre, because they heighten our anxiety. Of course, we listen with others to both heighten the pleasure of playful anxiety as well as to reassure ourselves that there is safety in being together. The ritual of bedtime stories may help a child relax, soothing him in the face of being separated from his parents through sleep. After a natural disaster, we want people to tell their stories over and over again, because it facilitates meaning and helps them contain and work through loss and terror.

Cultural narratives may function to transform an intolerable or troubling affect into one that is bearable, all the while shaping group motivation and behavior. For example, after 9/11, the Bush administration and the US media told stories about the "axis of evil," not only fueling anxiety, but also transforming anxiety into hostility toward real and imagined threats. In this example, we see how political narratives function to regulate and transform affect(s) and, at the same time, we see the relation between narrative and collective agency – a community of fear and hostility aimed toward controlling or attacking actual and imagined foes. On these occasions, one observes the heightened preoccupation with survival and an attenuation of spontaneity, flexibility, openness, and creativity – loss of shared experiences of being alive.

Closer to home, the psychoanalytic ritual can be viewed as a process of narrative construction (Schafer, 1983) that transforms, gives voice to, and regulates the affective life of both analyst and patient. One aspect of this shared story is the patient's ability (or inability) to narrate and regulate a wide variety of emotion with others. This narrative process is not simply dyadic. The intersection between therapist and patient comprises the cultural stories they share, which regulate and give meaning to their emotional lives. More specifically, the analytic couple share, in varying degrees, analytic stories – tales about Oedipus, Freud, consciousness, gender, etc. And these familiar stories often provide shared meaning that regulates affect and shapes mutual intentions.[6]

Individual and social narration, which channels, transforms, and regulates emotions and motivations throughout life and at all levels and venues of social life, represents the activation and dynamic interaction of semiotic processes associated with S-S, T-O, and C-C modes. A parent reads to her child a story of different types (T-O mode) of animals who band together and comfort each other in the face of a dangerous foe. The parent's voice, tone, rhythm, which is embodied narration, and the contiguity of bodies or intercorporeality (C-C mode) are all part of the action (N-C mode), evoking shared interest, soothing the child, and forming a sense of physical and psychic communion. This complex interaction – and associated semiotic processes – is one of the many possible forms of emotional regulations and communion.

Narration, then, is itself a form of affect regulation, and the stories patients tell often reveal the variety of idiosyncratic, yet familial, ways they have learned to regulate affect. Indeed, in listening to others, one can hear the echoes of childhood stories and parent–child affective regulation. Idioms of affective interaction that are laid down before a child can tell her story are, in part, present in adult renditions of their autobiographies. For example, Lana told me, with some anger and resentment, that people couldn't understand what it is like to have trichotillomania. I heard stories of how people, like her ex-husband and friends, had failed to grasp the suffering and humiliation that attended her illness. These tales of her more recent past were linked to numerous stories of her father's indifference toward her. Her mother, who was certainly a more benevolent figure, was preoccupied by her husband's parsimony and violence, making it difficult for her to join with and meet the emotional needs of Lana, as well as the other children. So, when Lana narrates, in the present, her anger and frustration toward people (including me, of course) who do not understand, this echoes earlier stories of losses and numerous failures to regulate her distress as a child.

Individual and mutual constructions of stories, which evoke and regulate diverse emotional responses, are necessary aspects of individual and communal survival and experiences of being alive. Narrow and rigid formulations reflect the presence of intense negative affect and the hyperactivation of narrative semiotic processes, which are motivated by survival (physical and/or psychological). The result is constricted, shared agency, impoverished emotional regulation, and attenuated forms of being alive in community. More flexible, spontaneous, and open narrations represent low anxiety, the capacity to contain, express, and share troubling affects, and the possibility of narrating experiences of being alive with others. Three years into therapy, Lana told me that she had taken her three grandchildren to the park. It was a cloudy, sultry day. When they arrived at the park, it began to rain. Lana jumped out of the car and invited the children to play in the rain. Lana laughed as she recalled dancing with the children in the rain and their hilarity. "People who drove by probably wondered about this crazy woman dancing in the rain." When Sally, her granddaughter, came home, she excitedly told her dad what they had done and how crazy grandma was. As Lana recalled this story, there was a sense of aliveness, which paralleled the aliveness that was created and shared at the park and carried home in the form of a story that had become part of the family lore. This did not spell the end of Lana's tendency to repeat the same themes to regulate intense anxiety, but it represented one of a number of new stories that expressed diverse emotions and communal experiences of being alive.

Narrative and continuity

The various plots of stories represent, evoke, and regulate all manner of affect, which would not be possible without autobiographical and shared memories that provide persons with a shared sense of continuity. Plot and memory go hand in hand, creating a sense of individual and shared continuity across time and space. Indeed, human beings are quite adept at telling and keeping alive stories of ancestors long dead, of events centuries old, and of places never seen. The sense of shared continuity derived from these tales may or may not contribute to experiences of being alive in the present, but a sense of continuity is necessary for communal experiences of survival and being alive. A positive example of this is found in Neville's childhood recollection of his mother telling him humorous stories of her father, whom Neville had never known. Neville's grandfather came alive in the stories his mother shared. His memory of these events and her stories bound him to his mother and his grandfather, giving him a lively sense of continuity and experience of communion with a loved one long dead.

Of course, the sense of shared continuity derived from paranoiac or xenophobic tales may depend on the hated "other" for a sense of communal continuity. A negative instance can be seen in the visceral hatred Bosnian Serbs held toward Croatians, which was carried and nurtured by stories of many events that occurred a decade or centuries ago. Societal continuity and community – which were linked to a shared identity and a common motivation of a community of agents to commit or overlook acts of brutality and murder – were maintained by narration and narratives that created and preserved affective memories of exclusion (see Volf, 1996). There are an infinite number of examples of survival narratives and the sense of continuity and community that is obtained by constructing a hated or feared other. Indeed, some of these examples may be found throughout the history of psychoanalysis.

Clinical settings are rife with stories wherein a person's sense of continuity is yoked to a deadening plot and memory of the "other's" abuse and neglect. A person's compulsion to repeat may be his way to carry on with a plot that has familiar, though unsatisfactory, actors, scenes, and endings. His story is the one that was inscribed on him and, while deeply unsatisfactory, it gives him some semblance of going on being, as well as connection to and continuity with others. Sometimes this story, this rigid way of being with others, trumps the horror of discontinuity and nothingness.

One gentleman, for example, had grown up in a household where his mother was manic-depressive and his father was an alcoholic. In his late thirties, Mark was terrified of "losing it," which meant becoming crazy like his mother or violent like his father. To protect himself and others, Mark retreated to the safety of his laboratory, which suggests the prevalence of the T-O mode in the N-C mode of organizing experience. Mark had an obsessive and rigid manner in telling stories about himself, but the fact that he sought therapy suggested a yearning to include and be included in the stories and lives of others. This longing, however, was too anxiety-evoking for two reasons. First, Mark unconsciously believed that what little sense of continuity and identity he had would be annihilated if he stepped on the thin ice of opening himself to expressing and sharing his desires and longings with others. Who would be there to recognize, respond, and share in his expectations and passions? Second, to be open to the other's narrative (desires, expectations, etc.) was linked to being overwhelmed by their needs and feelings, losing a sense of continuity with his needs and desires.

Narrative, desire, and validation

When experience is organized by the N-C mode, a shared sense of continuity is accompanied by validation and, at times, invalidation of desires, identity, motivations, affect, and values. The stories we tell and the rituals we participate in shape and support who we are as a people and what desires may or may not be enacted and shared. Every culture and group creates narratives of exclusion and prohibition that are inextricably linked to prized values and desires. These moral and cautionary tales, positively stated, point to real and imagined dangers regarding both survival and what it means to be alive. For example, the diagnosis of hysterical neurosis during the nineteenth and early twentieth centuries cannot be divorced from Western, patriarchal narratives that invalidated women's aspirations and sexual passions, all the while rigidly validating what women should desire. Paradoxically, these patriarchal narratives, in part, also supported shared visions of what it meant to survive and experience being alive in community. Indeed, Freud used a patriarchal story (e.g., Oedipus Rex) to depict human psychological development and the child's struggle for freedom (versus castration). The narratives and ritual that Freud and his followers constructed, which cannot be divorced from the patriarchal narratives extant in the culture, enabled some women to begin to tell stories of forbidden desires and thoughts, which, in instances of good-enough psychoanalytic work, were validated and woven into the patients' stories.

Psychoanalysis has played an important role in altering cultural narratives, helping patients speak more freely about invalidated desires and experiences, providing opportunities to narrate and validate latent passions and dreams, and enabling people to experience a greater sense of freedom and aliveness with others. Having said this, in the history of psychoanalysis, we can find examples of psychoanalytic narratives that invalidated patients' (and other analysts') experiences and desires. Freud's well-known antagonism toward religion (Rizzuto, 1998), expressed in letters and publications, was carried forward by many of his disciples and, in some venues, lingers to this day. Analysts who consciously or unconsciously agree with Freud's narrative about the illusory foundations of religious experience will often subtly or overtly invalidate a patient's desire to talk about his or her religious or spiritual beliefs and experiences (LaMothe, Arnold, and Crane, 1998). If religious faith or spirituality is important to a patient, then invalidation will almost certainly kill off the possibility of these desires and experiences becoming part of the analytic couple's shared narrative (Sorenson, 2004). There will be no lively validation of, communion around, or story of the patient's religious values and desires. The analyst's countertransference finds its support in psychoanalytic narratives (theories) that can serve to kill off the patient's desires from being narrated and shared.

A clinical illustration serves to highlight the connections between narrative-communal mode, validation, and experiences of being alive and the interactions between therapist and patient. Years ago, I had the good fortune to meet and work with Jan. Married with two young children, Jan talked about her desire to go to graduate school and become a lawyer. Jan's family of origin and her husband, Dave, believed that mothers should remain at home, raising the children until they left for college. These beliefs were supported by Jan's and her husband's family stories as well as by their religious narrative traditions (as they interpreted them). Not surprisingly, this created conflict within Jan and between her and Dave. Jan felt hurt and disappointed by her husband's resistance and minimization of her desire to obtain more education and seek a profession of her choice. The fact that Jan sought therapy and was able to articulate her desire suggests the presence of cultural narratives that supported women's aspirations in the public spheres. Therapy included validation of her feelings, experiences, and desires, some of which had been crowded out by the stories she had learned and internalized growing up.

We worked well together and Jan, after a couple of years, felt confident and secure enough to begin living out her dreams and writing new chapters of her life. Therapy was successful, yet toward the end of our work, Jan revisited an unfinished story. I had never encouraged her to re-narrate her religious life. This one important aspect of her life-story was excluded from shared discussion and exploration. While I tend to value religious stories, I judged her religious tradition to be excessively rigid and patriarchal. My lack of curiosity and interest, which were linked to my own storied perspectives, reflected my unconscious hostility toward and secret invalidation of her stories of faith, resulting in this part of her life not being shared or reconstructed in the therapy relationship.

To review, the complex integration of the semiotic processes of earlier modes with the N-C mode results in a significant transformation of persons' capacities for and experiences of agency, emotional regulation, continuity, and validation. With the appearance of the N-C mode, there are greater opportunities for shared agency, emotional expression and regulation, and continuity. There can be shared intentions, emotions, continuity, and valuation in the present, which is also shaped by the stories of our ancestors. Indeed, stories can lead to shared agency and a mutual sense of continuity with people we do not know and have never seen. The social and communal achievement of N-C mode means that we recognize we are part of a larger story and plot than simply our immediate families. Of course, this achievement and the capacity for community and communion do not mean one can expect to discover shared experiences of being alive. Stories where the plots are characterized by survival, violence, hostility, and fear tend to be rigid, exclusive, and boringly repetitive and predictable. The forms of community manifested in these stories exemplify organizations of experience that are dominated by psychic equivalence, connected to collective anxiety, and motivated by survival against real and imagined threats. Yet, there are also shared stories that are characterized by openness, flexibility, freedom, curiosity, playfulness, discovery, and creativity. These narratives are linked to a coincidence of shared representations of desire, knowing, and acting together. A derivative sense of communion is founded upon shared experiences of being alive – organizations of being alive that are communal.

Potential space, tertiary transitional objects, and the emergence of communal vitality

Human beings are creatures of massive contradictions. We, as individuals and communities, are capable of courageous feats of sacrifice and tenderness, as well as astonishing acts of brutality and malice. Paradoxically, we tell stories that create cooperation and, at the same time, painful divisions. The stories we tell and use in forming community may, at the same time, negate, subjugate, minimize, deny, and even destroy others and their stories. These communal tales of exclusion represent apparent and hidden human motivations, desires, and affects. Whether the stories are inclusive and life-giving or exclusive and deadly, the communities and experiences of community we form through these narratives are dynamic and precarious. We are always, consciously and unconsciously, forming, re-forming, telling, retelling, repairing, creating, and destroying experiences of being in community. Narrative and community, in short, are both potential and actual.

Winnicott's ideas of potential space and transitional phenomena can, with playful emendations, be used to understand the transformative leap from a child's first use of symbols to narrative competence – the ability to organize symbols into complex, temporally meaningful episodes, which is connected to her sense of shared agency, continuity, emotional regulation, and self–other validation. In other words, potential space, with regard to the process of narration, represents the dynamic aspect of creating stories wherein the possibility of communal experiences of being alive is made real. The presence of intense anxiety, fear, hatred, and hostility signals a collapse or attenuation of potential space, which does not mean that community is obliterated or that there is a loss of narrative competence. Rather, attenuation signifies rigidifying narratives, the narrowing of community, and the loss or diminishment of shared experiences of being alive with others. There are, for example, dead and dying communities, families, and groups wherein the stories told have lost flexibility, spontaneity, and openness. In this book, I have argued that potential space is an aspect of each mode (with its own characteristics) as it appears in development, and comprised of four interrelated pairs – surrender–generation, recognition–destruction, Care (as trust–distrust, loyalty–disloyalty), and disruption–repair. The creative, dynamic tension of these pairs makes possible a lively, communal use of stories in organizing shared experience and an accompanying sense of vital communion with others.

Surrendering and generating narrative experiences

Tertiary transitional objects (TTO) and potential space facilitate this transition from symbols to narrative competence.[7] In the area of play, where parsing out reality from pretense is of little concern, a child chooses and creates a toy taken from the cultural field. A difference between this object and earlier objects (e.g., STO) is that the child pretends and imaginatively and omnipotently constructs a story that includes herself and the personal object. That is, the object is omnipotently animated and personalized by the child's narration, which emerges out of the cultural stories the child has at hand. This created "person" is necessary in that the child is learning to create and tell her own story – using the stories of her family and culture – with an other. In addition, a child uses the TTO in learning to surrender to the story of the other. She imagines the other as a full participant in the drama, which requires her willingness to surrender to the other's story as they "mutually" construct a shared narrative and experiences of lively communion. This joint, imagined play of surrender and construction enables the child to develop narrative competence in sharing agency, continuity, affect regulation, and self–other validation.

An amusing illustration of this is seen in the popular comic strip *Calvin and Hobbes*, though I imagine we can all recall examples related to our own childhood or our own children. Calvin is a 6-year-old boy who carries around his friend, Hobbes, a stuffed toy tiger. Whenever another person enters the picture, Hobbes is simply a stuffed animal. On all other occasions, Hobbes is very much alive as they explore strange worlds, plan strategies for attacking Suzie Derkin, and comfort each other in the face of real and imagined dangers. Even though this is pretend, Calvin is involved in omnipotently generating diverse stories that represent his desires, motivations, emotions, and needs. While there is an omnipotent aspect to his creation and a seemingly solipsistic sense of play, we understand his world because he uses symbols and stories of our culture.

Included in Calvin's omnipotent personalizing and animating of Hobbes is his willingness to surrender to the imagined needs and expectations of Hobbes – as any good friend would do. This is all a tad paradoxical because Calvin is surrendering to the very personalized object he omnipotently creates. While true, this is a way of playfully practicing what will need to occur and is occurring in the social realm – mutual generation and surrender in creating and using stories together to establish and maintain shared agency, continuity, affect regulation, and self–other confirmation.

We need not relegate this experience to childhood. Robert Zemeckis' movie, *Cast Away* (2000), features Tom Hanks stranded on an island for seven years. During that time, he creates a friend, Wilson, out of a volleyball. This "friend" is very much alive to Hanks and, when Wilson is lost in a storm, Hanks despairs as if he has lost a cherished friend – a friend that represents "mutual" surrender and generation. His creation of and friendship with Wilson represents a profound human longing for community and shared stories.

Winnicott (1971) believed that potential space and transitional objects were used throughout life to handle the struggle between one's internal and external world. Calvin or a real child struggles with this, to be sure, but one could also say that the struggle is between generating and using one's own narrative, which represents one's desires and needs, and constructing and using shared stories that represent the group's desires, expectations, and needs. Will surrendering to the story of my family/culture require me to lose what is precious to me, leading to a desiccated agency, a false self, and a pseudo sense of vitality? Will "I" be constructed by the larger cultural story so that my desires remain unarticulated?[8] Can we construct a story together such that mutual surrender will represent a communion of desires, instead of alienated subjectivities? Potential space and the TTO provide the child (and adult) with opportunities to surrender safely, all the while generating narrative experience with the other. There are, of course, times when generation is sacrificed for the safety of being subjugated by and to the other's story, leaving a devitalized sense of self and a distorted sense of communion.

In the history of psychoanalysis, Ferenczi's (1988) mutual analysis with RN was, in my view, an attempt to attend to this dynamic of surrender and generation. Ferenczi, in other words, was prepared to risk surrendering to the patient's interpretations in the process of co-constructing a therapeutic narrative. The willingness to be moved by the patient, to surrender to the patient's perspectives, and to co-construct a shared narrative, has been and continues to be a focus of attention for many analysts (Bollas, 1987; Mitchell, 1988; Jacobs, 1991; Aron, 1996; Pizer, 1998; Maroda, 1999; Black, 2003; Chused, 2003). For example, Bollas (2002) wrote,

> The method of free association subverts the psychoanalyst's natural authoritarian tendencies as well as the patient's wish to be dominated by the other's knowledge. This is all the more reason, then, to reflect on the extraordinary wisdom of the method which demands that the analyst dispense with his or her conscious memories and intentions, instead to surrender to a form of listening that actively dispossesses the analyst of the ability to impart his or her own ideology.
>
> (Bollas, 2002, pp. 36–37)

Dispensing with authoritarian tendencies means the analyst retains the dialectical tension of surrendering to the patient's and his/her experience while also constructing formulations.

Recognition and negation

The mix of surrender and construction in narration accompanies the dynamic dialectic of recognition and negation. "Surrender," Ringstrom (2003) wrote, "allows that there is more than just me or just you, there is the 'us' of mutual recognition" (p. 199). In the previous chapter, I argued that surrender in the S-S mode accompanies the recognition of the other as a *separate subject*, which necessarily entails negation (not-I and secondary process thinking) and the dialectic of likeness in difference and difference in likeness. In the N-C mode, the capacity to surrender and construct stories together depends on the ability to recognize the distinctiveness of the other *person's* story, which implicitly involves negation. One realizes that our stories are alike – that we share a common story even while we each have unique stories. Thus, recognition that previously involved the other as separate subject is transformed to recognition of the other as a separate *person* with a distinct story – a story and person that are different, yet like my story and me.[9]

There are two other important attributes of recognition and negation of the N-C mode. First, recognition and negation include the capacity to know that I am (and we are) not *the* story I am telling, which leaves open the possibility for creating new meanings. I am and I am not this story. We are and we are not this story. Complete identification of the self or the community with a story reflects the attenuation of potential space and the foreground of facticity associated with the C-C and T-O modes. The person and community, in other words, in this context, deny negation and are, therefore, not open to creating new stories, or including others with stories that are perceived to challenge or threaten the individual's or group's prized story. One often experiences this in analysis when the patient (or therapist) rigidly grasps his own story, refusing to recognize the validity or possibility of other stories and experiences. A false self, for instance, is understood as a person's negating other renditions of his experience, sequestering aspects of himself from narrative discourse and community.

Schafer (1983) and Mitchell (1993) rightly believed that the ability to hold together and to be open to multiple histories or storied selves is a relational achievement. Bromberg (1998) called this the ability to stand in spaces (dialectic of unity and multiplicity; change and continuity), which I argue depends, in part, on the dialectic of recognition and negation. Standing in spaces, in other words, is understood as the dialectic of likeness in difference and difference in likeness, which means that the individual and group have a sense of openness, curiosity, flexibility, and discovery in relation to the "other's" narrative, as well as in relation to constructing new narratives regarding one's own (and the group's) experience. To be moved by the other's narrative, all the while retaining a sense of continuity, requires the ability to handle the tension between recognition and negation.

Having said this, Bromberg was speaking about individuals. I am including two or more people. Can the analytic couple, for example, begin to move into this potential space where there is no single story, but rather openness to multiple stories and many possible forms of narrative and communion? Can an analytic community (or institute) recognize the likeness and difference of a strange person and his theories? Can the analytic couple or analytic community co-create and maintain potential space, rather than retreating to the omnipotent security of master narratives and totalitarian discourse? Can families and communities recognize and be changed by the stories of strangers?

The second and related aspect of negation and recognition involves the triadic and quadratic nature of the N-C mode. The story, which we create together, is my story, your story, and our story. It is both mine and not mine. The story itself is a separate object, if you will. It possesses its own existence that may outlive you and me. I don't absolutely own the story I tell of my family, of my work, and of experience as a therapist, husband, professor, etc. This is one reason why there is no such thing as an autobiography. Put another way, the communion that we create together and that is supported by our stories is something that is both internal and external. Winnicott's point about lifelong epistemological struggle between what is inside and outside takes on a different and more personal and communal meaning. The stories I-we create belong to me-us, but are separate from us. So, when a child transitions from the S-S mode to the N-C mode, she is using the potential space – between herself and her personalized object (TTO) – to figure out what part of this story is hers and what belongs to others. Calvin, we might imagine, recognizes Hobbes (and the stories) as his own creation, which involves negation. At the same time, Calvin believes Hobbes is an equal participant in the construction of a shared story – a story that does not entirely belong to one person and a story that is linked to others (e.g., parents, teachers, etc.).

Consider Jan's story. As her children grew, Jan wanted to become a lawyer, which conflicted with the dominant story the couple had held regarding the role of mothers. Her husband's initial resistance means that the story he held onto did not have room for recognizing Jan's newly emerging story. Jan said that Dave felt that she had betrayed him, and this betrayal is inextricably linked to the story that they had constructed earlier in their marriage. In this story, recognition–negation was linked to a story told about wives and mothers caring for children at home, which did not include stories about wives and mothers in the public sphere. Jan, though, had not entirely rejected the religious stories she previously held, which had supported a more traditional role of mothers. However, there was enough negation (not-I), in tension with recognition, for her to begin entertaining another story – a story that, early on, her husband rejected (not-I and not-us). Therapy provided a space for her to begin to play with and construct other narratives.

Dynamics of care

The ability to preserve the creative tension between surrender–construction and recognition–negation, such that there are communal experiences of being alive, depends on the dynamics of Care (trust–distrust, loyalty–disloyalty). Mutual surrender to the other's narrative constructions requires shared trust, which is supported and maintained by beliefs in and experiences of fidelity. Loyalty in the N-C mode comprises a commitment to recognize and affirm the other person with his unique storied agency, desires, motivations, and needs. Distrust and betrayal, which are informed by stories, accompany the myriad ways human beings minimize, deny, and reject the other's (and our own) passions.

In childhood, the TTO and potential space between the child and his toy have everything to do with his initial narrative construction and learning about fidelity and trust with others. A child omnipotently creates both Sally (her doll) and the stories that include imagined beliefs about and experiences of trust and loyalty, which attend shared, albeit imagined, recognition of each other's desires and hopes. *Yet this is not all imagination.* Cultural narratives that contain conscious and unconscious rules and expectations about trust and loyalty serve as the background for the play that takes place between the child and his imaginary friend. Potential space involves the joint narrative construction of trust and fidelity necessary for communal experiences of being alive.

Of course, mutual narrative constructions of trust and fidelity continue to be both potential and actual throughout life. There are countless examples in adult life of the mutual struggle of creating and maintaining shared experiences of trust and loyalty. Indeed, the very stories we tell and listen to are implicitly linked to and depend on how trust and loyalty are understood and lived out. For instance, the background questions regarding the trust and loyalty of the analyst are part of the patient's initial story. The patient's story is often replete with experiences and expectations regarding trust and loyalty (and their opposites). A task for both therapist and patient is to negotiate and create a shared story where desires and needs are recognized and narrated against the backdrop of beliefs in and experiences of trust and loyalty, making possible new stories and new experiences of being alive with others.

Jan's difficulty with her family is an example of the relation between the dynamics of Care and potential space. In Jan's immediate family, there was a shared story about the roles of women and men as justified by shared religious stories. This initial, shared loyalty to these religious narratives provided Jan with a sense of being able to trust her husband and her family of origin. When she married Dave, Jan believed that the stories they shared represented her desires and needs and, as a result, experienced some sense of communion with her husband and her own family. That is, Jan surrendered to the stories of her childhood and young adulthood because of a felt sense of trust and fidelity. When Jan began to dream about going back to school, she was on the verge of telling another story that was not in synch with the expectations of the religious stories she held. She began to question and doubt the relevance of previously held (and surrendered to) religious beliefs about women, contributing to a growing sense of distrust.

Eventually, this internal conflict led to relational conflicts in her marriage. Dave believed Jan was betraying the covenant that they had both agreed to when they were married and tried to pressure Jan to remain faithful to old stories. Jan felt hurt that Dave was not moved by (i.e., did not recognize and support) her newfound hopes and desires (story) and she, increasingly, felt subjugated by the religious stories about women and marriage. This marital friction contributed to a mutual sense of distrust that was fueled by shared experiences of betrayal and a corresponding attenuation of potential space. Dave was operating out of the original story they shared when they were married. Over the years, Jan had generated and was generating a new story that she wanted her husband to acknowledge, support, and respect.

When Jan began therapy, she often expressed guilt, feeling as if she had betrayed her husband, her parents, and God. These thoughts and feelings were in conflict with her growing interest in constructing and surrendering to those cultural stories (and people) that located trust and fidelity in women's ability to give voice to dreams and desires in public spheres. Acting on her desires meant that Jan was confident in cultural narratives that recognized and affirmed women's desires to play a role in the public sphere.

Disruption and repair

The changes that took place in Jan's life included real and imagined experiences of distrust and betrayal, which points to relational disruption and the necessity of repair. Potential space is an area where disruption need not lead to disconnection or loss because there is the possibility or hope of repair, which is embedded in narration and narrative. Indeed, disruption is necessary for the possibility of new meaning and new stories. In the transition from the S-S mode to the N-C mode, the child is learning how to use stories to repair inevitable moments of disruption, as well as disconnections linked to distrust and betrayal. The play that takes place between the child and her prized toy reflects this dance between disruption and repair. The child omnipotently narrates the interaction and thus has control over both the disruption and the repair. She is working out and internalizing her own culturally and family-informed rituals of repair and disruption. One can see this when a child berates her doll for some imagined offense, and this behavior parallels her countless experiences within her family. If all goes well, the child will learn that disruption is not something to be feared. Indeed, disruption is a necessary part of the vitality of narrating one's experience with others because it represents the possibility of change in the midst of continuity. Without disruption, there exists only rigid narratives and experiences drained of vitality.

Relational disruptions, ideally, involve the presence or emergence of new desires, expectations, ideas that evoke anxiety related to change as well as trust and fidelity. A tolerable amount of disruption, accompanied by rituals of repair, contributes to and strengthens trust and fidelity, solidifying communion and experiences of being alive together. Overly rigid narratives reflect unconscious anxiety about disruption and the hopelessness of repair.

Repair, in these instances, is attained by way of submission and violence, which one finds in sadomasochistic relationships.

In Jan's marriage, her acting on and speaking of her desires led to conflict. These disruptions, while painful and, at times, intense, were handled by Jan and Dave such that their relationship continued. This suggested to me that a significant amount of trust had developed between them to contain these disruptions without either of them losing hope and falling into a sadomasochistic struggle. The dance of disruption and repair led them, eventually, to the inclusion of Jan's new experiences and desires into another chapter that retained a joint sense of being alive. In other words, over time, Jan and Dave generated a new narrative of their marriage – one that included the old stories as well as stories that portrayed new roles, rules, and desires.

The collapse of narrative potential space: culture, trauma, and therapy

A coherent, comprehensive, and satisfying narrative may signal the absence of neurosis (Schafer, 1983), but it does not mean that there is an attending sense of vitality. There are all kinds of examples of cultural stories, which are well organized, comprehensive, and unifying, where subjugation of and violence toward others are the rule. On a larger scale, nation-states promote master narratives and, at times, these national stories are created in relation to hated others, fostering communities of fear and survival and providing members with a shared sense of pseudo-aliveness. It is easy to point to Nazi Germany and the comprehensive or totalitarian narratives Nazis constructed in relation to Jews, homosexuals, and gypsies. It is a bit more difficult for those in the United States and Great Britain to acknowledge that the master narratives created by the Bush and Blair administrations before and during the second Iraq war paralleled less savory instances of domination, destruction, and hatred. Closer to home, comprehensive and complex psychoanalytic narratives can be used to sustain authoritarian interpretations in analysis. Or, an analysand's sadomasochistic narrative can be well organized and meaningful, yet represent the presence of subjugation, denial, distrust, pseudo repair, and ersatz aliveness (collapse of potential space).

I suspect that most therapists realize that the emptiness, numbness, and deadness patients express and experience are not easily divorced from cultural and familial stories that undergird their narration. Moreover, the absence of neurosis does not mean the person or community experiences a sense of aliveness. Persons and communities that experience real and imagined threats, along with intense anxiety, will close off potential space and the possibility of vitality to secure their survival, often confusing psychological-physical survival with the survival of cherished group stories.

Similarly, communities (and individuals) may rely on stories of hated others to safeguard the survival of shared agency and continuity. These narratives may act to contain anxiety, but the price is a loss of flexibility, openness, and the pleasure of creating new meaning with others.

Collapse or attenuation of potential space, then, is not simply linked to neurosis and psychopathology, nor is it only assigned to the narrative exchanges between two people. Indeed, my point here is that the collapse of potential space we normally associate with trauma and psychopathology is inextricably yoked to the larger potential space of the cultural narratives and discourse. For example, the female "hysteric" of the late nineteenth and early twentieth centuries was constructed by and linked to patriarchal, cultural narratives and discourse that rendered large segments of women's experiences and desires unthinkable, speechless, and meaningless. Narrative, community, and potential space are, in these situations, present, but for "hysterical women," it was (and is) a very circumscribed story and potential space. Their hysteria may be understood as a disruption of patriarchal narrative discourse and the search for new narratives.

While coherent and comprehensive narratives are not exempt from destructiveness, alienation, and the attenuation of potential space, the presence of disorganized, rigid, incomplete, and unsatisfying stories is joined, as Hesse and Main (2000) point out, to less than optimal attachments between parents and children. The prolonged collapse or attenuation of potential space between parents and children is characterized by the child's experience of being subjugated to the master narrative and totalitarian discourse of the parent. The parent's reliance on this master narrative leaves little or no room for the child's creative, narrative construction and representation of her experience. The parent(s) recognizes only his own narrative and, in so doing, disconfirms, minimizes, overlooks, or denies (negatively negates) the child's attempts to use cultural stories to construct and narrate her own story. The child, to maintain some level of attachment, passively accepts being constructed by totalitarian narration, which becomes linked to a false self. This false self represents her attempt to garner some sense of trust, loyalty and hope in the face of rejection and betrayal – albeit unconscious – while sacrificing and sequestering her desires. The false self signifies the loss or deflation of potential space and the loss of possible communal experiences of being alive.

Returning to Jan's struggle, we see the nexus of cultural stories and discourse that contributed to the attenuation of potential space. Jan's intrapsychic and interpersonal conflict became apparent when she grew aware of her desire to pursue dreams of becoming a lawyer and began to make this known to her husband and family. These hopes were not in line with the master narratives that Jan and her family had ascribed to. Uncertainty, confusion, hurt, disappointment, anger, and anxiety reduced the space for the development of shared meaning or the inclusion of new meaning between Jan and her husband (and both sides of the family). Previous dominant family and religious narratives, which were coherent, comprehensive, and initially satisfying, assigned specific meanings and expectations regarding women in their roles as wives and mothers. Jan's growing acceptance of cultural narratives that included more diverse meanings and desires with regard to women created tension within herself and between her and her family. Whereas earlier Jan felt content, she now bristled at the constriction of the stories that her family held. The increasing emotional tension in her family and marriage did not signify pathology. Rather, the conflict represented an attenuation of potential space and a reduction of individual and communal experiences of being alive.

Jan sought therapy because she did not feel supported by her husband and family and because she felt guilty for contradicting the dominant stories that she had identified with and used for most of her life. She noted that her husband and family also felt as if she was betraying them by seeking something outside their worldview. From my perspective, Jan was seeking a relationship where the dynamics of potential space would enable her to begin to "work through" the conflicts and to "play through" a narrative that housed her new sense of being – her newfound desires and hopes. Creative narrative construction does not necessarily mean that one must abandon previously held stories. Perhaps she would have left her husband and family if they had not eventually adjusted and accepted Jan's desires. Naturally, this took time and effort on everyone's part. In so doing, the potential space between Jan and her husband was, in the end, restored. To their credit, they discovered and recovered experiences of being alive together that required new stories to house them.

It is important to include my initial neglect of Jan's religious stories. When Jan confronted me about this, I realized that my own story, which is joined to the religious stories of my youth and adulthood, had served as a master narrative. I was not aware that my distaste for what I believed were oppressive religious narratives had served to keep me from being open to and curious about Jan's faith and how she was re-narrating this in light of new experiences. In other words, my "master" narrative foreclosed the potential space (in this one area) between us.[10] Jan's confrontation was an invitation to restore this potential space, which would require my letting go of my master narrative so that we could play, discover, and share new meanings and experiences of being alive.

In summary, the diminution of individual and communal experiences of being alive can be found in the consulting room and in the wider culture. Trauma is not the only source of deadness, alienation, and emptiness in human life. Human beings can find all sorts of ways to kill off desires and to subjugate themselves to or be subjugated by master narratives for the sake of real and imagined safety and survival. Likewise, we can form all kinds of associations and communities that lack openness, curiosity, creativity, and vitality. Psychoanalysis is one process and form of association that invites the co-creation of potential space where old stories can be told, shared, and worked through, while new stories are created. The courage needed to create new stories accompanies the shared capacity for communal experiences of being alive. In the final analysis, human beings are meant to be alive together for, as Eliot reminds us, "There is no life that is not in community." The hope and dread of psychoanalysis is found in the risk to narrate being alive together.

Chapter 6

Couch and culture

Trauma and cultural constrictions of vitality and the psychoanalytic process

> Life you may evade, but Death you shall not.
>
> (T. S. Eliot, 1999, p. 157)

> When all is said, what remains to be said is the disaster. Ruin of words, demise of writing . . . what remains without remains.
>
> (Blanchot, 1995, p. 33)

> We work in the dark – we do what we can – we give what we have. Our doubt is our passion and our passion is our task. The rest is the madness of art.
>
> (Phillip Roth, 1995, p. 77)

Any casual observer of life will note the plethora of ways human beings find to evade it. Wars, sexual abuse, physical violence, terrorism, oppression, and more subtle forms of homo-paranoia, racism, sexism, and ageism seem to be daily fare, sapping vitality from individuals and communities. Often, somatic symptoms, repetitive maladaptive behaviors, and rigid narratives mask the wounds that result from these very real actions. When it comes to *physical* wounds that drain life and energy, a medical doctor can easily observe, catalogue, and seek to repair a child's compound fracture, for instance. In six months, the child's resilient body will have sealed the break, leaving a scar and occasional discomfort. The physician of the psyche, however, struggles to explain and help heal the wounds that resulted from the parent's violent shove that led not only to the child's broken bone, but also to the withering of the child's spirit and sense of aliveness. The child, now an adult, comes to a therapist unsure of the source of his pain and sense of emptiness. The bone has long since healed, but a psychic fracture remains.

Added to the difficulties in identifying and understanding the developmental and familial sources of psychological injuries is the question of how culture constricts individual and communal experiences of being alive.

Could the father's violent shove be part of the patriarchal narratives that privilege male power and authority, rationalizing violence as discipline? Or perhaps the shove has tenuous links to cultural narratives that place little value on self-reflection and expression of male emotional vulnerability. To comprehend the complexity of human experiences of aliveness and the myriad of relational and cultural factors that drain human existence of vitality, our theories and models must take into account the intersection of couch and culture.

In the previous chapters, I argued that there are four organizations of experiences of being alive (and survival) – each with distinct signifying processes – that are contingent upon the dynamics of potential space. For the sake of clarity and simplicity, I described each mode as if it was separate, which belies the complexity not only of human experience, but also of human interactions. While each mode appears sequentially in development, the advent of new semiotic and relational capabilities depends on, alters, and interacts with previous modes. Imagine each mode as a neural web, with individual webs connected to and operating with the other nets as they come online. Activating the multifaceted layers of neural nets means that some parts of the webs are activated and work in concert, while other pieces of the web are slightly activated or deactivated altogether. This picture becomes more complex when we recognize that the organization of experience is in relation to an "other." The infant, for example, organizes experience in the C-C mode, yet the good enough parent is organizing experience using all four modes. An infant needs a parent who is capable of organizing experience in all four modes in order to experience being alive. The dynamic connections between the neural webs depend on the quality of interactions between human beings. Yet another layer of complication is that parent–child interactions take place within and depend on the particular ethos of the family and culture. Experience, then, is incredibly multifaceted because it represents the intersection of mind, body, social interaction, and culture.

The image of interconnected neural, semiotic webs that display different levels of activation and connectedness can include Freud's conflict model of the mind and more recent postmodern perspectives that emphasize relationality and multiplicity of self-states (Aron, 1996; Benjamin, 1998; Bromberg, 1998; Mitchell, 2000a). In addition, this model embraces the depth, breadth, and complexity of human beings' capacities to organize experiences of being alive (and survival) and how these experiences emerge and wane as a result of trauma or those cultural factors that obstruct vitality. This chapter comprises some concluding thoughts and questions, namely, how are we to understand the ideas of trauma and its relation to the repetition compulsion and regression, given the proposed model of human experience? How are we to account for experiences of survival, numbness, emptiness, and deadness that are not the result of trauma? In what ways, in other words, does culture play a role in the diminution of experiences of being alive? And how does this theory and model shape one's understanding of psychoanalytic goals and process?

Trauma, repetition, and regression

Trauma, derived from Greek, denotes wound and injury. Physical injuries are easy to see, but to witness, explain, and treat wounds of the psyche has confounded more than one physician of the soul. Freud, for instance, initially proposed that the hysteric's psychic wounds were the result of childhood sexual abuse, though he later opted for the idea that intolerable sexual fantasies were the cause of adult difficulties. If the adult hysteric's psychological trauma had been accompanied by physical scars, then Freud and many others may not have overemphasized the role of fantasy, suggestion, and hermeneutical, reconstructive imagination (e.g., *Nachträglichkeit* – deferred action) in the etiology of trauma.

During Freud's life, there were those who noted that psychological wounds resulted from real events, wherein persons felt absolutely helpless, overwhelmed, and terrified (see Breger, 2000, pp. 252–268). More recent studies of trauma (Terr, 1990; Herman, 1992; van der Kolk and McFarlane, 1996; Bremer and Marmar, 1998) confirm that, while there may be fantasy material that emerges from a traumatic event (Ulman and Brothers, 1988), real events such as profound betrayal by significant persons (Janoff-Bulman, 1992; Davies and Frawley, 1994; Freyd, 1996), physical and emotional abuse, and horrific violence evoke catastrophic experiences of powerlessness and helplessness (Krystal, 1968), shattering a person's core assumptions about self and the world (Janoff-Bulman, 1996). These very real events are psychologically disruptive and have long-term effects, depending on how caregivers respond to the traumatized person (Herman, 1992). In short, the wounds of the psyche are the result of real events (natural and human) that evoke a devastating sense of helplessness and powerlessness, leaving the person to strike a Faustian bargain – opting for a devitalized self and relationship to insure survival in a dangerous world.

Psychological wounds, from the perspective of this book, result from actions that lead to a calamitous collapse of potential space, a distortion of each of the four poles of the dialectical pairs, a loss of dynamic integration between the four modes of organizing experience, a hyperactivation of one or two of the four modes of organizing experience, an overwhelming sense of powerlessness and hopelessness, and a heightened drive for survival, motivated by real and imagined fears and anxieties. Defensive hyperactivation of one or more modes means there is a tear in the smooth operation of neural semiotic webs, which may be manifested in the form of fantasies,[1] hallucinations, maladaptive behaviors, and overly restrictive narratives. These various symptoms "share a common denominator – the inability to represent . . . they embody difficulties in psychic representation" (Kristeva, 1995, p. 9). A patient, Janet argued, suffers "an ensemble of maladies through representation" (Janet, quoted in Meares, 2000, p. 52). The psychic wound that results from trauma and the collapse of potential space, however, is not merely a psychological difficulty in semiotic representation; it is also a sundering of the relationship upon which discursive and non-discursive forms of semiosis depend. We limp away, licking this double wound by sacrificing freedom, spontaneity, and play, hiding in the thickets of the certainty of a desiccated life. Potential space, in other words, signifies psyches-in-relation and, thus, trauma manifests a wound in the psyche and in the relationship. This explains why the most devastating and long-lasting traumas are not necessarily natural disasters (unless the natural disaster is followed by the failure of other human beings to care), but disasters of profound human betrayal.

Trauma and the dynamics of potential space

In general, the eclipse of potential space and the hyper-attention on survival, which accompanies a draining of aliveness from the self and relationship, can be understood in terms of massive distrust, betrayal, and hopelessness and its relation to surrender, recognition, and disruption. Traumatic events lead to devitalized selves and relationships, because victims are too frightened to risk surrendering to experience and to the other (the object that evokes powerlessness). The victimizer's totalitarian construction of the victim's world is a betrayal and a form of subjugation – a perversion of surrender. To the victim, surrendering can mean only somatic-psychic-relational disintegration or annihilation. Evading life becomes a way of avoiding surrendering to death. Since it is difficult, if not impossible, to live in a world of distrust and betrayal, the victim ekes out a life by generating objects and situations that are trustworthy, though these are more likely to be fantasized. In addition, a victim of trauma has extreme difficulty surrendering to experience and the other, not only because of betrayal and distrust, but also because there is little hope of repair. There is a lack of hope that the "other" will recognize and negate me such that "I" will thrive and we will flourish together. Rather, recognition is accompanied by a distortion or denial of the victim's desires, needs, and hopes. What remains is the real possibility of disruption that is defended against by a rigid hyperactivation of semiotic process that constructs experience toward survival and fantasies of repair.

Before launching into a further explanation of this view of trauma, I offer two vignettes to illustrate these points as well as provide a way of reinterpreting the repetition compulsion and regression.

When John was a year old, his parents were killed in a car accident. Understandably, John does not have any memory of the crash and only hazy memories of the six months he spent in the hospital. Fully healed, at least physically, John went to live with his grandparents. They were nice enough folks, but their health problems often interfered with their ability to attend to John's needs and desires. As an adult, John has become an accomplished writer. He notes that he is content in his marriage and loves his two children, yet there is a ghostlike, emotional distance that haunts his relationships. At times, John is aware of an impending sense of disaster and he anxiously expects his successes to be taken away. Whenever he publishes a book or short story, he anticipates attacks by reviewers and this is a prelude to his impending sense of loss of his livelihood, his skills, and even his marriage. On other occasions, John watches his children in a detached sort of way, wondering how they would fare if he and his wife were to die.

For all practical purposes, Trudy's childhood was enjoyable. Like all families, there were times of stress and conflict, but they seemed to have the knack for navigating these rapids with little pain and turmoil. When Trudy married, she was fortunate to find a man whose family was equally supportive and affectionate. Eighteen months ago, when Trudy was 30 years old, a man emerged from a darkened corner of the city parking lot and raped her as she was leaving work. During the ensuing months, both families rallied around her as she struggled to deal with the aftermath of this horrible experience. At times, she was depressed and frightened, isolating herself from her husband, friends, and family. Throughout these periods, Trudy often stayed in bed, embracing a stuffed bear that her husband had bought her several years before. When she returned to work, every evening a friend or two walked Trudy to her car, which mitigated, but did not erase, her anxiety. During the daytime, Trudy, often without being aware, scanned the crowds, looking for places where someone could hide. Nowadays, there are moments Trudy begins to feel like her old self, which she describes as mostly happy, fun-loving, and carefree. Yet, a dark horizon always lurks in the distance.

Trauma, potential space, and modes of organizing experience

John's trauma occurred prior to his ability to symbolize or narrate experience. Apparently, though, his grandparents told John the story and so their memories are woven into his story. It would have been traumatic enough to lose his parents, but John also went to live with two people who had their own problems, which made it difficult for them to provide John with the attention, love, and emotional security he desperately needed. Initially, his parents had provided a relationship wherein John could safely surrender to experience and to them. The death of his parents not only robbed John of this matrix of potential space, but also left him feeling subjugated to the events of his parents' deaths, his hospitalization, and going to live with his grandparents. Put another way, powerlessness and helplessness meant that

John felt both constructed by the event and unable to construct meaning in relation to it. "It" (his parents' death) threatened to negate him; that is, the loss of his parents transformed negation into annihilation, leaving John struggling with a world and relationships that could not be relied on to be devoted to him or to help him construct experience. Moreover, while his grandparents stepped in to help, their own struggles with illness obstructed the kind of care needed to repair fully this breach in potential space. This further undermined his sense of hope with regard to recovering from the loss of loved ones.

At the time of his parents' death and John's hospitalization, John would have organized experience in the C-C and T-O modes. This means that he was unconsciously able to categorize what was happening as dangerous, which he extended to all relationships and contexts. Thus, the world and relationships were fraught with the threat of somatic-me-object annihilation. As he developed capacities connected to the S-S and N-C modes, the earlier semiotic processes would have significantly shaped these later modes, especially in situations that evoked anxiety. John carried forward in his psychosocial development not simply the unconscious memories of loss, but the anxiety-laden, hyperactivated semiotic processes that he relied on to survive in a world he understandably deemed to be dangerous (see Maldonado and Spiegel, 1998, p. 66).

As an adolescent and adult, the more significant a person, object, or activity (e.g., writing) became in his life, the more John experienced heightened anxiety related to his expectation of approaching disaster and loss. John defended against this by withdrawing or keeping his distance and, by and large, avoiding spontaneity and risk in relationships. It was too frightening to surrender to being alive with others. His writing, for example, was a solitary activity where he felt safe enough to play and be creative. John's anxiety and cautious stance toward friends and family represented the *hyperactivation* of the C-C and T-O modes in relation to and in concert with the S-S and N-C modes. His paranoia, then, represents the confluence of all the modes, though with the hyperactivated ones notably shaping and restricting symbolic and narrative constructions.

John: trauma and the repetition compulsion

If we were to consider John's plight in terms of the repetition compulsion, we would have a number of ways to interpret his behavior. We might say that his repeated behaviors toward people of importance signify his attempts to master the emotional distress of trauma (Russell, 1998). Or, perhaps John's behaviors were signs of some "daemonic power," force, or death drive that motivated him to repeat (Freud, 1920, p. 40). Or we could interpret his behavior to be motivated by a desire to seek an emotional and perceptual identity between present and past objects (Russell, 1998, p. 62).

Or knowing that John probably has unconscious, preverbal memories of the traumas (crash, deaths, and hospital), we could suggest that his expectation of disaster, regarding the reviews of his book and his tendency to maintain emotional distance, are connected to these early traumas. However, this would imply some concrete memory or content driving his behaviors and that he is unconsciously motivated to master this particular memory-experience or identify with his deceased, beloved parents.

While not denying the influence of conscious or unconscious memory systems and identification, it is more accurate to say that John's early responses to the traumas involved hyperactivation of two modes of organizing experience that established patterns of relating and organizing experience, securing his sense of identity, continuity, and affect regulation. Using the metaphor of neural webs, the interconnected C-C and T-O webs, which have numerous neural connections to the S-S and N-C webs, were repeatedly hyperactivated during times of heightened anxiety. This hyperactivation impeded a fuller, dynamic, and relatively smooth integration of the four modes. Thus, it is not strictly that he is trying to master the memory-experience, but that his "mastering" the losses in early childhood established patterns of hyperactivated neural connections that, in turn, shaped later neural webs (S-S and N-C semiotic processes), which together fostered rigid patterns of organizing experience and behavior. John, by repeating, carries forward emotionally salient patterns of constructing experience that help him regulate (via hyperactivation) emotional distress and ward off psychic-relational disruptions. This helps him maintain a secure identity, though at the cost of a sense of freedom and aliveness.

Typically, the repetition compulsion focuses on the individual and his/her memory, affect, and behavior. In my view, the repetition compulsion also signifies some lack in relational space. The death of John's parents represented the catastrophic loss of potential space, and his subsequent living arrangements with his grandparents were characterized by a significantly attenuated potential space. What John is also "repeating" is not simply the loss of his parents and patterns of hyperactivated modes of organizing experience, but also the attenuation of the potential space that had originally served as the medium for his risking being alive. He repeatedly brings to his relationships the unconscious belief and experience that "potential space" is dangerous. This attribution of danger keeps him safe from risking loss of experiences of being alive with significant others. It is safer, though not entirely satisfactory, to survive than to risk being alive. The compulsion to repeat, then, centers on avoiding catastrophic disruptions in potential-relational space by way of hyperactivation of semiotic processes, which in turn become characteristic patterns of organizing experience and relating to others.

For John to stop repeating would not only mean grieving past memories, letting go of shattered assumptions, and developing new schemata, but also require John's co-restoration of potential space with people who are emotionally important. In risking being alive with others, John would also have to contain, regulate, and learn to surrender to his fear and anxiety in relation to real and imagined losses such that fear and anxiety would not foreclose freedom and spontaneity and the possibilities of new meanings and novel intimacies. This is no easy assignment, because John attributes annihilation and loss to surrender. For John, surrender is equivalent to the powerlessness of subjugation. Having said this, ceasing the repetition compulsion is not John's task alone. Patient, devoted others need to support and invite John to begin to construct experience and narratives that are open to experiences of being alive with others. Given John's recurring patterns, we know that people like him can indeed survive and "master" trauma by way of repeating, but the end of the repetition compulsion and the recovery of a sense of aliveness requires the co-creation of the fourfold dynamics of potential space with other caring human beings.

Trudy: trauma and regression

Unlike John, Trudy was fortunate to have a childhood free of trauma and, for the most part, filled with adults who showed her love and affection. Her trauma is similar to John's, though it differs in important ways. The violence of the rape occurred long after childhood, which generally meant that, prior to the rape, Trudy used, non-defensively, all four modes of organizing experience. The violence, however, was similar in the sense that it represented a catastrophic collapse of potential space. The rapist absolutely constructed Trudy; she was violently forced to submit to his representations of women-objects. These projected representations were accompanied by negation marked by annihilation of her subjectivity, which were joined to Trudy's unspeakable humiliation and powerlessness. In the seeming eternal trauma of rape, there was certainly no paradoxical space of likeness in difference and difference in likeness between the rapist and Trudy.

This horror and trauma of the rape were connected to an experience of overwhelming distrust, betrayal, and hopelessness. By overwhelming, I mean the violence threatened Trudy's beliefs in and experience of embodied-global, object, and personal trust, devotion, and hope, crushing any sense of freedom and spontaneity. In the desolate landscape of rape, there is no realistic hope of repair, only disruption, annihilation, and the wish to survive.

Thankfully, Trudy was surrounded by people who cared deeply for her well-being and who were able to tolerate empathically her periods of disruption (see Eigen, 1996). After the initial shock, Trudy had moments of heightened distress, anxiety, and mood swings, which were understandable responses to trauma. In particular, Trudy would, at times, spend time cuddling a teddy bear her husband had given her and would anxiously scan people and places whenever she was out in public. One might interpret these behaviors as regressive. That is, Trudy, when she hugs her bear and stays in bed, regresses to an earlier period of development where she felt some measure of comfort and safety. In addition, Trudy's behavior of anxiously scanning the crowd and her unexplained wariness of her husband could be interpreted as a regression to the paranoid-schizoid position (Ogden, 1986).

One of the difficulties with the concept of regression, as it relates to trauma, is that it suggests that a person is actually returning to an earlier period of development – a period that either preceded or contained some deficit and struggle. This falling back is associated with a linear, hierarchical model of development, which tends to infantilize the patient's behavior and, more importantly, overlook the complexity of adult patterns of organizing experience. It is, for example, facile to interpret Trudy's paranoia or her hugging the teddy bear as a regression to early childhood, where she either was anxious about strangers or felt safe, secure, and alive. This belies her own experience and interpretation as well as overlooking Trudy's psychological capacities and achievements.

In the model proposed here, I interpret her understandable paranoia as a hyperactivation of the T-O mode, operating in concert with the other modes. There is, in this moment, not a paranoid-schizoid position, but a complex, anxiety-driven mode of organizing experience (T-O) that shapes the interplay between all modes. Trudy, during these moments, knows and can narrate what she is doing, which suggests the presence of all modes, though with the hyperactivation of the T-O mode. Similarly, when Trudy retreats to her bedroom and cuddles with her teddy bear, she is not regressing to some childhood state, per se. Rather, this illustrates the heightened presence of both the C-C and T-O modes and the under-activation of the S-S and N-C modes. In terms of the C-C mode, cuddling up to her bear (safe object – T-O mode) regulates her anxiety and depression; it is soothing in the face of a world that is dangerous and barren. Trudy is neither psychotic nor "regressing" to being a little girl. Rather, regression here means the presence of a hyperactivated mode(s) of organizing experience and the under-activation of other modes in an adaptive attempt to deal with the emotional vicissitudes of trauma. The hyperactivation of this mode may reverberate with memories relating to this period of development, but we need not conclude that she is returning to this period of development. Her adolescent and adult memories and capacities are present and intact, though underactivated.

There are two other aspects of regression with regard to potential space and being alive. First, Trudy's use of the teddy bear can be interpreted as an attempt to manifest and recover the potential space associated with the C-C and T-O modes of organizing experience. The somatic and object modes of regulating anxiety and more somatic and object related experiences of trust, loyalty, and hope are hyperactivated, which eclipses, but does not exclude, the other modes. Her "regression" to this potential space represents, in part, Trudy's omnipotent attempt to manage the anxiety and recover a sense of aliveness associated with more unconscious and basic somatic and object relation patterns of organizing experience. It is important to recall that the rape was a violent disruption of Trudy's body-psyche, which would have hit, in part, the corporeal-contiguous mode and related presentational organizations.

A second aspect of her regression is connected to an attenuation of potential space and the drive for survival. For instance, Trudy's paranoia is interpreted as a "regression" to a mode of organizing experience whereby she could omnipotently categorize objects and contexts in terms of safe and unsafe, giving her some sense of control and safety in the face of powerlessness and danger. Trudy, like other people, experienced and handled periods of anxiety (paranoia) by organizing experience in the mode that gave her some sense of control and offered the best opportunity for survival. This meant that, during these moments, potential space was attenuated, leaving only her need to survive. *Trudy's "paranoiac regression," then, signified those times when she could master the attenuation of potential space.* Put another way, the hyperactivation of the T-O mode of organizing experience points to her ability to handle and adapt to disruptions in potential space. Hyperactivation of the T-O mode, then, represents her attempt to master memories of the rape wherein potential space was violently disrupted, leaving her feeling powerless and helpless.

It would appear that Trudy's regression to the C-C and T-O modes is partially explained as first, a "return" to potential space and modes of organizing experience that offered secure sense of agency, continuity, and emotional regulation, and second, an attempt to garner some measure of omnipotent control in handling intense anxiety and powerlessness. Yet this perspective is not entirely satisfactory, because it raises a further question about why this or that mode is activated and not others (e.g., S-S and N-C modes), especially given Trudy's relatively happy and stable childhood and adulthood. An answer to this question may be found in recent perspectives and research on the brain, which can be used in conjunction with semiotic processes and potential space.

Decades ago, Hughlings Jackson proposed a hierarchical model of the human brain that depicted animal cognitive processes, which are present early in human development, overlaid by more specifically human ones (cf. Meares, 2000). Since then, research on the human brain has expanded exponentially with the rise of new methods and technologies for understanding how the brain works. While there are no definitive models, recent writers (Damasio, 1994; Greenspan, 1997; Siegel, 1999) have echoed Jackson's insights, suggesting a tripartite model of the brain. These "three" brains are interconnected by millions of neural connections, though some connections are stronger or more numerous, depending on the type of brain (genetic endowments) and whether these connections were developed by the interactions a person had growing up. For example, females generally have more neural connections between the two hemispheres than men do, which may be the result of different genes and/or different social interactions. Neural connections that are present at birth and those that come online very early in development appear to be hardwired – in the sense that they are activated unconsciously and automatically. When we face perceived danger or stress, for example, the "reptilian brain" is hyperactivated (fight-flight-freeze) without any conscious intent. As an adult, this hyperactivation of the reptilian brain does not exclude the prefrontal cortex, though it may not have the same level of activation. Indeed, the prefrontal cortex is implicated in our complex interpretations of contexts and objects that we deem dangerous, activating the reptilian brain. This suggests that those neural pathways, present or laid down early in development, are, in situations of real and imagined danger, unconsciously activated. Thus, we may, using the prefrontal cortex, interpret, consciously or unconsciously, a situation as dangerous, which is accompanied by the hyperactivation of the reptilian brain.

This perspective fits with the idea of regression as the hyperactivation of those neural pathways linked to semiotic processes that emerged first in development. In other words, regression represents the hyperactivation of neural connections that are both more numerous and more easily activated during periods of heightened anxiety. By "easily activated," I mean that they are unconsciously stimulated. A person does not "intend" to activate the neural pathways connected to the C-C and T-O modes. Neural pathways implicated in consciousness and associated modes (S-S and N-C) – prefrontal cortex – require more deliberate activation. In Trudy's situation, intense anxiety activates semiotic processes that developed first, though this hyperactivation of those neural webs does not exclude the prefrontal cortex, consciousness, and the S-S and N-C modes. Rather, the level of arousal means that the neural pathways associated with the C-C and T-O modes are lit up more, which in turn shape the S-S and N-C modes. This can be seen in Trudy's ability to speak about what she is doing, even during these periods of heightened distress.

By focusing on the brain, we can easily overlook the brain's inextricable connection to relationships. When Trudy "regresses," for example, the hyperactivation of neural pathways linked to semiotic processes of the T-O and C-C modes must include the presence and absence of potential space and its relation to survival and experiences of being alive. The violence of subjugation, the fear of physical-psychological annihilation, the violation of her body, the eclipse of subjectivity, the obliteration of trust, the presence of hopelessness, and the foreclosure of the possibility of repair left Trudy scrambling to survive, which involved the unconscious hyperactivation of those modes that offered help in handling powerlessness and helplessness. Developing these semiotic processes, especially in Trudy's case, depended, to a large degree, on the presence of good enough people. So, her "regression" to an "earlier" mode is also connected to experiences and memories that were good enough – times when she felt some measure of control, trust, loyalty, security, and hope.[2] Trudy's various behaviors, then, can be considered regressive as long as we also include the idea of potential space without simply locating it in an early or primitive stage of development.

I offer a final thought regarding regression. The idea that trauma violates a person's representational world, disrupts his/her structures of meaning, interrupts his/her personal theory of reality, and breaches his/her working models of attachment points to the fact that some events lie at the edge of human discourse and community. Trauma reflects a rift in discourse and community, leaving "a depleted and desymbolized subject who finds it extremely difficult to trust other human beings or the environment" (Walsh, 1996, p. 246). Even in our attempts to describe these disasters, they are, at their core, indescribable, evading the snares of symbol and language and, likewise, subjectivity and community (Davies and Frawley, 1994; Bar-on, 1999). As Blanchot (1995) wrote, "There is no reaching the disaster . . . When all is said, what remains to be said is the disaster. Ruin of words, demise of writing . . . what remains without remains" (pp. 1, 33). The helplessness and powerlessness associated with trauma include a person's use of words-in-relation. The profound sense of powerlessness in trauma is not only because of the shattering of subjectivity, but because of the inability and incapacity to use (and share) words to capture and convey the core of the experience. One reason for this ruin of words is that symbols, rituals, and attending subjectivity and intersubjectivity are *dependent* on the dynamics of care and the repair of disruption (LaMothe, 1999). Rape and other malicious acts are outside social norms and experiential bounds of routine experiences of distrust and betrayal, leaving persons without hope of speech. Indeed, in moments of violent coercion, speech and subjectivity are denied the victim, which only adds to the experience of powerlessness and aloneness.[3]

In the absence of being able to organize and describe experience using symbol and narrative, a person retreats to non-verbal means (C-C and T-O modes). *Trudy's "regressive" moments, then, can be further viewed as responses to the indescribable, leaving her to rely on the C-C and T-O modes to secure some semblance of self.*

In summary, some of Trudy's behaviors may be interpreted in terms of an emended concept of regression. The initiation of regression is through heightened anxiety and stress, which involves the hyperactivation of a mode(s) of organizing experience and associated semiotic processes. There are several ways to explain regression. First, Trudy "regresses" to a mode(s) whereby she possessed an unconscious sense of omnipotence, which provided some measure of somatic and object-related control and safety in the face of powerlessness. A similar type of regressive behavior involved an earlier mode that included the potential space wherein she experienced and omnipotently possessed a comforting sense of somatic and object-related trust. Regression, from this perspective, represents an activation of semiotic processes associated with somatic and object-related organizations of experience. Second, her regression represents an unconscious hyperarousal of neural pathways that are primary or more foundational with regard to the brain. This hyperactivation does not exclude the presence of other modes of organizing experience, though the hyperactivation of one or two modes significantly shapes the other modes (S-S and N-C). Finally, faced with the annihilation of subjectivity and intersubjectivity, Trudy was confronted with an experience that was, at its core, indescribable – a ruin of words. Regression, in this case, may be viewed as her reliance on nonsymbolic modes of organizing experiences in the face of powerlessness, desolation, and deadness.

Cultural constrictions of vitality

Trauma is not the only occasion when a sense of vitality is diminished. Maladies of representation and accompanying forms of deadness take their particular shape in the culture in which they reside.[4] The nexus of culture and psychoanalysis began with Freud's recognition that Victorian society contributed to the repression of sexual desires, which he believed was connected to hysterics' suffering (Gay, 1988; Sulloway, 1992). Later, Fromm (1941, 1973), Erikson (1952), Jung (1959), Laing (1959), Kovel (1970), Chodorow (1989), Sass (1992), and many others added their voices, using analytic tools to critique and understand culture and psychoanalysis. These writers recognize that it is a significant mistake to overlook the relation between couch and culture, because the various maladies of deadness that the analyst observes, day after day, do not all result from specific family traumas. Experiences of emptiness, ennui, numbness, and depression have roots in a particular culture, where persons struggle to join subjective desires to cultural, semiotic forms of meaning and value.

The goal of describing the connections between couch and culture is too ambitious for a chapter or a section of a chapter. My more modest and provisional aim is to provide, by way of two brief case illustrations, broad outlines of the dynamics of potential space as it pertains to the culture and the constriction of experiences of being alive.

Carmen's struggle illustrates the nexus of couch and culture. Carmen, a very bright 35-year-old African American woman, grew up in a working-class section of a large city. After months of feeling increasingly and inexplicably despondent, Carmen sought help. The first five sessions were filled with Carmen's tears, though she was unaware of their sources. Initially, she described her childhood as good and stated that she loved her mother dearly. Carmen's parents divorced when she was in her first year at college and, since then, Carmen has had only sporadic contact with her father. During the first few months of her work, Carmen remembered a time when she was 5 years old. She described, without affect, how she was playing with construction paper, sparkles, and glue. Like many young children, Carmen was enthralled by her work and, without thinking, brushed back her hair with her gluey hand. Shocked and scared, Carmen ran to her mother crying and her mother responded by slapping Carmen across the face, berating her for doing something "stupid." This type of discipline was characteristic of their relationship well into adolescence, though it did not entirely define their relationship. Carmen also said her mother was frequently affectionate and loving.

Carmen's parents, like most parents, wanted her to succeed and to have more opportunities than they had. They were delighted when Carmen was accepted at a prestigious university and very proud that she had received numerous scholarships. When Carmen went off to school, she was suddenly thrown into an almost completely different culture – mostly white, educated, upper-middle class. This culture shock and adjustment would have been difficult for any young woman, but Carmen also had the added burden of distrust. As a child, she was told to or had observed distrust of white people. You could be friendly with them, but you could never fully trust them. This was accompanied by the working-class distrust of the educated middle class. During her four years of college and long after, Carmen struggled between these two cultures. Most of her colleagues and friends were white and she herself was a successful professional woman, which increased the tension and distance between herself and her parents.

Dave is a handsome 44-year-old married man with two children (21, 20). Like his father, Dave is a flourishing executive in a Fortune 500 company. Dave says that he is close to both of his parents and his three siblings. Childhood seemed devoid of any notable trauma, but Dave does remark that he wished his father had spent less time focused on work and more time playing with his children. As a parent, Dave vowed he would be more involved in his children's lives and, for all practical purposes, seems to have done so.

What prompted Dave to seek therapy was a comment his wife made several months before. Driving home after their weekly "date" night, Marcia made the observation that Dave seemed preoccupied and appeared to be going through the motions at home and at work. Did he still love her, she asked. Dave was taken aback, quickly responding that, of course, he loved her. The following week, Dave told Marcia that he had thought a great deal about what she said and that he did feel a sort of lingering emptiness. It wasn't, he said, necessarily anything specific, though it seemed to be more connected to work. Dave went on to tell Marcia that this sense of emptiness had been present for a long time.

In both of these cases, the culture is an important factor in the attenuation of feelings of being alive. Carmen grew up against the background of racism and economic class system rooted in capitalism. Even her mother's discipline cannot be separated from a racist culture. That is, her mother, as I was later to learn, was preparing her child to withstand the blows and humiliations Carmen could expect to receive in a culture that silently (and loudly, at times) despised and feared black people. The message was, "You have to be strong and tough to survive in a world dominated by whites – a world where whites have economic and political power." Carmen also grew up being told, verbally and non-verbally, that white people could not be trusted. Because her parents valued education, this distrust was ambivalently joined to educated middle-class people.

Racism signifies, in its more hidden forms, a constriction of potential space and a corresponding eclipse of aliveness between whites and blacks. Cultural stories, dramas, and rituals in the United States contain representations of whites as educated and superior and blacks as lazy, stupid, ignorant, over-sexed, and dangerous. In US history, the aspirations of black persons were (and are) often negated whenever they conflicted with white constructions of black people. Whenever black people attempted to construct and represent their own experience, they were recognized by racists as disruptive and dangerous. Repair, in these situations, was corrupted because of the forms of violence that were used to force blacks into white constructions of reality. These white webs of significance were part of subtle and overt forms of degradation, humiliation, and depersonalization, which understandably gave rise to deep distrust, expectations of betrayal, and a sense of hopelessness. This history of racism may seem, at times, to be something of the past when we consider the achievements of the Civil Rights Movement, yet this history is very much part of today's society and present in therapy settings (Altman, 2000).

Racism, like other virulent examples of oppression, reduces potential space between blacks and whites, which, in Carmen's case, infected, to some degree, her relationships with whites and with her mother. Perhaps, her mother knew that the relationship between blacks and whites was marred by subjugation, distrust, fear, and hatred. To live in a white-dominated world, Carmen could expect little possibility of shared aliveness with whites. While I suggest that the diminished potential space that resulted from racism was part of her mother's discipline of Carmen, this was not the whole story.

People in oppressed groups find ways to survive in cultures of domination, and they also construct their own webs of significance and concomitant experiences of being alive. There was, then, a vital potential space manifested in Carmen's immediate and extended family. They had narratives that inspired survival, strength, and courage. She told stories that represented shared trust and experiences of being alive (e.g., trips to Mississippi, Thanksgivings, weekends at the city park). Even the tale of her mother's discipline was told in conjunction with vignettes of shared laughter and play, signifying a repair that restored potential space between child and mother. Carmen's depression and struggle, then, cannot be simply laid at the feet of her mother or her parents' divorce. Indeed, her depression and estrangement are partially linked to and the result of a racist constriction of potential space. Carmen struggled to be at home in two worlds, never quite feeling at ease in either.

The fact that a racist culture strangles potential space means that culture is not only on the couch; it is also in the relationship between therapist and patient (Leary, 2000). Carmen sought out a white, middle-class therapist who also grew up in a racist culture, though with a very different set of experiences and stories. Even a strong therapeutic alliance and attending dynamic potential space does not preclude moments when unconscious racist representations silently disrupt trust. Several months after Carmen told me about the incident with her mother, she came to a session and seemed to be more subdued and withdrawn. This lasted well into the next session before I told her what I had observed. Carmen said that she had read an article about discipline in African American families. The author had said that African American parents discipline their children with the aim of withstanding the humiliation and depersonalization they can expect in the white world. She thought that this was, in part, what her mother unwittingly did. Carmen went on to observe that my responses to her story (glue incident) tended to focus on the violence and the pain of humiliation. While never saying anything overtly negative about her mother, I had apparently let Carmen know that I had strong feelings about this behavior, in general, and her mother, in particular. This was a complicated exchange, but let me plainly note that, in my view, it represents how deeply intertwined culture, potential space, and interpersonal communication are. Carmen's revelation signified the strength of potential space between us. We had developed enough trust to handle disruptions that were linked to real and imagined betrayals. Yet, what took place also signified the presence of my unconscious racist and class representations and how they shaped potential space. In other words, Carmen was letting me know, and after some self-reflection I recognized that she was right on target, that my interpretations of her mother's discipline were tinged by unconscious, negative representations related to racist narratives. The fact that there may have been other interpretations of her mother's behavior, which had not occurred to me, points to my settling on a set of representations that excluded more positive perspectives.

Two other related comments are worth mentioning. First, Carmen's revelation was an attempt to repair the space and recover the possibility of a shared sense of aliveness. So, despite the fact that racism influenced the interaction, potential space was still present. Second, the question is not necessarily whether potential space exists or does not exist in a relationship. It may be quite strong overall, yet be diminished around certain self-states. The culture of racism shaped, but did not determine, the joint construction of potential space between Carmen and myself.

Dave grew up in quite different circumstances than Carmen, yet his struggle was likewise shaped by prevailing myths, rituals, and rules. As a young boy, Dave remembers his father going to work and taking many business trips, while his mother stayed at home to care for the kids. Now an adult, Dave remarked that his father loved him, though in the same breath he knew his father was ambitious. There was a curious mixture of pride and longing in Dave's story. He clearly admired and identified with his father's achievements, even to the extent of mirroring his success in business. But, Dave also ached for greater intimacy with his father, which was manifested in his vow regarding his own children.

Clearly, the ideologies, narratives, values, and expectations of a capitalistic system shaped Dave's family life. In this system, the father cares for his family by leaving home and making money. His father focused on being successful in the public sphere, where the values of competition, ambition, self-reliance, and independence reigned, while his mother strove to live up to the values of love, self-sacrifice, companionship, and self-denial in the private sphere of the home (Coontz, 1988; Mintz and Kellogg, 1988). Much of the meaning and sense of identity his parents obtained were derived from adhering to the precepts of the economic system.

While this may have been satisfactory for his parents, his father's devotion to the economic system diminished the potential space between father and son. This does not mean that the system itself was solely responsible for the constriction of potential space. Rather, his father's apparent devotion to the system contributed to Dave's unconscious belief that his father was not as emotionally devoted to him as he was to the ideals of the system. Dave's identification with his father (and capitalistic ego-ideals) may be understood as an attempt to keep the possibility of potential space alive and, in the process, Dave hoped for a shared sense of being alive with his father.

The constriction of potential space can be seen in Dave's current sense of emptiness. Now that his children have grown up, Dave has gradually discovered that he derives less meaning from his work. When his kids were young, Dave combined ambition-success with his paternal role as "breadwinner." Admittedly, he basked in the recognition following his promotions, feeling a sense of pseudo aliveness.[5] From the perspective of the dynamics of potential space, Dave initially "surrendered" to the values and expectations of the business system. This surrender cannot be separated from Dave's identification with and wish to surrender to his father, which accompanied the lack of recognition of his needs and assertions as a child. Success gave Dave a needed sense of recognition from others and, unconsciously, from his dad. It is fair to say that Dave started his career with a sense of passion and devotion to the company/system and this accompanied a wish for the blessings and loyalty of the company (dad) to him.

Dave's successes, however, were followed by the burdens of greater responsibility and more demands on his time and energy, trying to insure the company remained profitable. Dave increasingly felt confined and oppressed by the unceasing demands of his job. He also felt stuck, believing there were no other options. "This is the one thing I know I am good at." The system had bestowed recognition, meaning, and value and Dave feared giving this up because not only was he not sure anything would replace it (negation as annihilation), but also the loss would awaken childhood losses. Better to stay in the prison than risk the danger of a hostile world.

When Dave spoke to his wife, there was an emerging realization that his years of devotion would never be reciprocated – both in relation to the system and his father. My interpretation of this is that Dave recognized that the company-system was not loyal to him as a person, only as an object that performed (see Macmurray, 1949; Arendt, 1958). The loss of meaning and experience of emptiness, then, are connected to his recognition that the system he felt trapped by had no devotion to him and was inherently depersonalizing. This experience is well captured in movies and plays such as *Death of a Salesman*, *Glengarry Glen Ross*, and *About Schmidt*. Emptiness, despair, and desperation attend the realization that one is in bondage to a system that is merciless and incapable of loyalty to *persons*.

Of course, no system can be "loyal," but systems and their semiotic webs can value, support, encourage, and teach interpersonal (mutual) surrender, trust, devotion, and reconciliation, which enhance a sense of personhood and community (Macmurray, 1949). The capitalistic economic system qua system develops organizations and not communities of persons mutually devoted to each other. Rather, capitalistic organizations are geared toward production, efficiency, profit, competition, and the accumulation of capital. The rituals, myths, and values of capitalism reflect primarily I–it versus I–thou relations, which I associate primarily with the T-O mode of organizing experience. I am not condemning capitalism; I am simply recognizing its limits and noting that, as a system, it is not aimed toward developing a vitalizing potential space (*particularly with regard to the N-C mode*). It seems to me, then, that part of Dave's struggle is his realization that the company or the system is not devoted to him. Instead, Dave feels used and expendable, as if he is simply a cog that is easily replaced and this, not surprisingly, is connected to some of his experiences in relation to his father. His earlier surrender to the economic system had come to feel more like bondage. This revelation, which was joined to his hurt that his father seemed more devoted to the system than to his son, evoked a sense of emptiness and hopelessness that this situation/experience could be repaired.

Dave's and Carmen's struggles reflect the close connection between what is heard in the consulting room and the larger cultural webs of significance that shape experience and relationships. The dynamics of potential space are inextricably yoked to cultural, semiotic systems, which may promote or constrict this space and, correspondingly, experiences of personal and communal vitality. Our understanding of a person's lack of aliveness on the couch, then, can be expanded and deepened by identifying those cultural factors responsible for the constriction of potential space.

Psychoanalytic goals and process

Given the breadth and depth of the psychoanalytic traditions, it is daunting to consider how to articulate, briefly and in general terms, the aims of psychoanalysis and the process by which patient and analyst move toward achieving goals. Since any attempt will fall short, I would like to end this book by imagining a lively conversation that takes place after a sumptuous dinner at the home of a couple – the husband is an analyst and the wife is a professor of cultural anthropology at a nearby university.

Psychoanalytic goals

One of the guests, Gina, a linguistic anthropologist, has always been intrigued by psychoanalysis and is surprised to learn that she in the midst of a room filled with Freudians, Kleinians, Sullivanians, Winnicottians, Kohutians, Lacanians, Relationists, and Intersubjectivists.[6] Gina has, on occasion, toyed with going into analysis.

Sitting next to a steely-eyed Freudian, she asks for his thoughts about the goals of analysis. Harold avers with authority that we "'can express the aim of our efforts in a variety of formulae: making conscious what is unconscious, lifting repression, filling in gaps of the memory – all these amount to the same thing . . . the return of health of the neurotic patient'" (Freud, 1917b, p. 435). Taking a puff of his cigar, Harold continues, "or we can say the aim is to 'restore the ego, to free it from its restrictions, and to give it back the command over the id which it has lost owing to early repressions'" (Freud, 1927a, p. 205).

"But to what end?" Gina poses.

"Well," Harold pedantically responds,

> the restoration of the ego through "tedious labors of psychoanalysis" assists the person in becoming "another man, though, of course, he has

> remained the same; that is to say, he has become what he might have become at best under favorable circumstances" (Freud, 1917b, p. 435). I would add that, at the least, the patient, with "a mental life that has been restored to health,' is "better armed against unhappiness" (Breuer and Freud, 1895, p. 305). At best, [he continues] the patient begins or perhaps returns to "living a full life sexually" (Freud, 1917b, p. 432).

Harold pauses and looks for a moment at the ceiling as if trying to grasp some final answer. Sighing, he concludes, "'in the last resort we must begin to love in order not to fall ill'" (Freud, 1914, p. 85).

Winnie, an Englishwoman, pipes in:

> I agree with my friend, but "I like to think of my work this way, and to think that if I do this well enough the patient will find his or her own self, and will be able to exist and feel real. Feeling real is more than existing; it is finding a way to exist as oneself, and to relate to objects as oneself" (Winnicott, 1971, p. 117).

"Do you mean the aim is to cure people of feeling unreal?" Gina asks. Another English colleague chimes in:

> No, no, the "aim of psychoanalysis is not to cure people but to show them that there is nothing wrong with them." More positively, one of the aims of "psychoanalytic treatment may be to enable the patient to find, or be able to tolerate, more satisfying obstacles to contend with. Poor obstacles impoverish us" (Phillips, 1993, p. 86).

"Are you saying psychoanalysis helps people adapt to life?"

Sully, a brash American, replies:

> Not quite. The patient comes to us with a great deal of anxiety precisely because he has adapted by establishing a number of defensive security operations to protect his sense of self. We are simply "alleviating pain" (Strupp, 1982, p. 238) and thereby "increasing a patient's skill in living" (Sullivan, 1953, p. 175). So, you see, I agree, in part, with my Freudian friend, that the goal of psychoanalysis is "to help the patient develop into what he was meant to be" and, in so doing, the patient is better able to adapt to the vicissitudes of life (Mann, 1995, p. 561).

After a short pause, Karen adds, "When I work with patients, this reconciliation means that the patient's 'self will become stronger and more free, flexible and more resilient'" (Bacal, 1998a, p. 31).

A lanky man, sitting across from Gina, sets his glass down. Steve speaks softly with a New York accent:

> Many of my colleagues will say that, by re-structuring the ego or self, the patient is able to love and work more successfully. What I believe "the patient needs is a revitalization and expansion of his own capacity to generate experience that feels real, meaningful, and valuable" (Mitchell, 1993, p. 24). This means [he continues] "not a renunciation of infantile experience but a reconciliation of different organizations of experience throughout the life-cycle" (p. 35).

Julia, a Frenchwoman, jumps in, saying:

> Yes, yes, but I would put it this way: "all of suffering, all patients' symptoms share a common denominator – the inability to represent . . . they embody difficulties in psychic representation" (Kristeva, 1995, p. 9). As analysts, we are involved in a field of signification, helping the patient join her desires to symbol.

Julia can see that Gina is becoming confused, following the seemingly dissimilar strands of thought. "My dear," she chuckles, "We may say it differently, but the 'only possible metaphor one may conceive of for the life of the mind is the sensation of being alive'" (Arendt, in Kristeva, 2001, p. 89).

Masud, a kindly, older gentleman to Julia's right, says:

> I agree with Julia. I am not an analyst, but I have studied many cultures and religions, including [he smiles] psychoanalysis. You will find many analysts and philosophers saying that what "we are all seeking is the meaning for life. I don't think that's what we're really seeking. I think that what we're seeking is an experience of being alive, so that our life experiences on the purely physical plane will have resonances within our innermost being and reality, so that we actually feel the rapture of being alive" (Campbell, 1991, p. 3). All the arguments about the goals of psychoanalysis [Masud adds] are important, but they often remind me of a good friend's comment about philosophical and theological discourse that takes place in the academy. He once said to me, "Does God really exist? How does he exist? What is he? are so many irrelevant questions. Not God, but life, more life, a larger, richer, more satisfying life is, in the last analysis, the end of religion. The love of life, at any and every level of development, is the religious impulse" (James, 1958, p. 382). It seems to me, Gina, that the aim of analysis is the impulse and experience of being alive together.

Psychoanalytic process

Gina glances around the room and notices that no one seems to disagree. "Well, that seems to be a laudable goal, but what is the process through which one achieves these experiences?"

Tom, who had been listening, answers:

> There are, of course, many answers to this question, depending on one's language game and the needs and struggles of individual patients. For instance, George, my self-psychologist friend, who often uses vitality as a metaphor, speaks about self-object functions, optimal frustration, optimal responsiveness, and idealizing and twinship transferences. We both agree that free association and interpretation are key to the process, but I am inclined to attend to the patient's defenses and the associated modes of organizing experience – autistic contiguous, paranoid-schizoid, and depressive positions. Yet, even as I say this, I know that my self-psychologist colleague and I attend to the quality or sense of aliveness in the patient's free associations, in my interpretations, and in our non-verbal communications (Ogden, 1997). This sense of aliveness is dynamic, not static or some final state. It shifts and ebbs. In good-enough relationships, aliveness is both potential and actual.

Tom is quiet for a moment and, then, continues:

> This is the point where I struggle to articulate the process and its relation to vitality. In all our theorizing, we are trying to capture something ineffable, which Bion, Winnicott, and Lacan tried to include in their theories. Let me put it this way. The process of psychoanalysis is like poetry (Ogden, 2001). The poet uses words to convey and evoke some aspect of being alive, even when the poet speaks of death and suffering. Patient and analyst similarly are using language and silence to evoke and give shape to aliveness that is within and between them.

"I have some inkling about what you are saying, but I am in a muddle. Perhaps it is because I have never been in analysis, though I have read some of Freud's works and, as an anthropologist, recognize his influence on Malinowski, Lévi-Strauss and others," Gina responds.

June says:

> At the risk of frustrating or even angering my colleagues, we can liken psychoanalysis, its goals and process, to a dinner party such as this. Now George, before you interrupt, I am not saying there are not significant differences having to do with free association, regression,

asymmetrical relationships, etc. By the way, George, I did enjoy your book that describes what is unique about analysis. Because Gina is an anthropologist, I simply wish to suggest that psychoanalysis, while unique in many ways, is, above all else, a human activity.

"What, do you mean it's like a dinner party?"

This dinner party is an elaborate ritual. We have a time that we begin, moments of greeting, periods of conversation, numerous social rules and codes, and an unspoken, yet agreed-upon time to conclude the ritual – a liminal space, if you wish. Within this ritual, there are moments when we surrender to the conversation or to the sensual experiences of fine wine and succulent chicken cordon bleu. [June glances toward her hosts, nodding thankfully.] In surrendering to these moments, we are also generating experience, individually and intersubjectively. It would not be nearly as enjoyable if we were to eat and drink alone. Others are needed in order to have an experience of dining, of feeling alive with others – others who can handle the paradox of likeness in difference and difference in likeness. It seems to me that mutual trust makes it possible to surrender and handle the paradox. I have come to know and trust people here, because we have all demonstrated some loyalty to each other and not necessarily to systems of thought or particular schools of psychoanalysis. Now, I am not saying we don't have disagreements or tiffs that have their manifest origins in our ideological commitments and identifications. Even in our conversation tonight, there have been disagreements and possibly anxious moments of distrust. These disruptions are easily, I think, contained and repaired because of the trust we share and the hope that disruption will not be destructive. Or better, we all possess some hope that these small disruptions in conversation can be mended.

June glances affectionately at George:

Take George, for instance. I know him to be a passionate man and a strong advocate for his version of psychoanalysis. A few moments ago, I had the sense that George was going to challenge me and he may still do so. There may even be an intense disruption between us, but I have known and grown to love George over the last ten years. I know our differences can be disruptive, but they can be contained and repaired. This knowledge I have is part of the hope that we can handle these disruptions. Perhaps I am saying this too negatively. It is precisely these relatively "safe" disruptions that help the conversations take on a generative tenor. Speaking for myself, one of the reasons I love George is because our vigorous debates have moved me to alter my views. He is

> necessary to my creativity and I hope I am for his. This dinner party has certainly been enlivening for me, but I am sure we have attended social events that are stultifying. There are, of course, many reasons for this, but the sense of deadness or the lack of aliveness can usually be linked to some level of fear and anxiety related to distrust and hopelessness or futility and, at times, some sense of subjugation, bondage or onerous obligation.

June smiled at Gina, saying, "Like faculty parties."

Gina laughed and said:

> So, what you are saying is that potential and actual experiences of being alive are dependent on what is taking place between us and, since most of us have some history together, this makes it possible to surrender, as you say, to our own experiences vis-à-vis the other person, food, and the conversation. I can see, in part, how this fits, but you work with people who are suffering from psychological maladies.

"And we also do not," June chortles:

> You are quite right, though. I am much more cognizant of what is taking place between the analysand and myself and how each of us is organizing experience in the present and its relation to the past. I like to think that what I do is invite people to create potential space with me. Naturally, analysands, because of past betrayals and losses, are understandably cautious. They may equate surrender with bondage, negation with annihilation, and disruption with chaos, all of which makes it incredibly difficult for them to feel alive in their bodies, in relation to objects, or with other human beings. Anxiety and suffering may be so intense and prolonged that they are unable to possess a sense of spontaneity and freedom. Indeed, at times, their communications may evoke feelings and thoughts in me such that I collude in the collapse of potential space. In these moments, we often enact the kind of past and present relationships that close off the possibility of shared aliveness. Naturally, I, on my own, may reduce the space when my own personal struggles are silently shaping the interaction. In my view, it is not simply interpretation and insight into these enactments or transference–countertransference communications that move the analytic couple to potential space and vitality. Other verbal and non-verbal moments also engender trust, devotion, mutual recognition, forgiveness, shared spontaneity, such as laughing together, and shared playfulness, which are equally valuable in the process. So you see, I pay close attention to moments of feeling alive, however brief and slender they may be, and I also attend to the ways analysands organize experience.

"As an anthropologist, I could apply what you are saying to various cultures and rituals within these groups. My good friend and mentor," nodding toward the older man next to Julia, "has observed all kinds of rituals and belief systems that, one could argue, are part of the group's attempt to survive as well as the group's attempt to maintain potential space and experiences of being alive. Granted that psychoanalysis is a human activity, but is it unique in some way, or are there differences that distinguish it from other rituals aimed at helping people?"

"I believe George is best suited to address that question," June replies.

"Thanks, June. I was going to jump in a few minutes ago and disrupt you," he says with a wink:

> Gina, I would say that while psychoanalysis has many things in common with other human rituals, it is also distinct because of the method of free association. Free association "subverts the psychoanalyst's natural authoritarian tendencies as well as the patient's wish to be dominated by the other's knowledge." This method demands that the analyst "surrender to a form of listening that actively dispossesses the analyst of the ability to impart his or her own ideology" (Bollas, 2002, pp. 36–37). This dispossession creates a space for the patient's subjectivity, for the patient to express his or her own unique idiom – no matter how shameful or joyful – in the presence of a person who recognizes and honors him or her. There is something incredibly freeing and healing when the patient is able to say and show the analyst that which is most intolerable and hidden, and this only occurs when the patient, having been consistently recognized and understood, experiences the analyst as devoted and trustworthy (Casement, 1985). To use June's term, potential space, it is in this space the patient feels hope, even though there is suffering. My experience has been, personally and professionally, that even in these painful moments there is a sense of aliveness and freedom that had not previously existed because of shame and silence.

"I agree with George," June says,

> but I would add that when the patient truly is able to free associate and I am able to surrender to his or her associations and my experience, I know that we have created potential space. Likewise, when the patient is unable to free associate, there may be something taking place within the patient, me, or both of us that forecloses potential space. A patient free associates because she knows, at some level, she will not be subjugated to the analyst's knowledge and she knows that disruptions can be repaired and that they are necessary for the possibility of play. If an analysand is quick to free associate, I know that in the transference

> she has had many experiences of people who have been devoted to her and who have surrendered to her unique idiom. Of course, it is more likely that the person who comes to see me has not been so fortunate. The transference in these situations represents all kinds of experiences with others wherein the patient has felt the need to subjugate herself to remain attached. My hope is that she will come to believe, experience, and trust my willingness to surrender to her false self, as well as her unique idiom.

Gina says:

> I think I understand. I know it is getting late, but I have an observation and one, well maybe, two questions. This conversation and dinner party have been great fun. I can feel the sense of aliveness within myself and between us. So, to continue with June's analogy, when the patient feels alive or a sense of aliveness is present in the room, does that mean analysis is over? How does one let go of aliveness? It would seem to me that a person would try to hold onto it.

"Excellent questions," Tom notes:

> When I leave tonight, I will have fond memories of our time together, but as I drive away I may also be aware of a twinge of sadness that the vitality we have shared is fading into the past. The memory is not the same as the immediate experience. One way to think that analysis is over is when an analysand can grieve the loss of aliveness, even as she is open to generating it with others. Aliveness, it seems to me, must be approached obliquely. If we try to grasp it or hold onto it, then we are not open to surrendering to its loss, to its ineffableness. Instead, in those moments, we are interested in controlling it and, in that instant, there is no potential space. When the patient is able to be open to the possibility of being alive with others and to letting the experience fade, then I believe she has accomplished and surrendered to a great deal.

"Perhaps that is what makes human beings such tragic creatures," June adds:

> The very gift and work of aliveness become confused with survival. We clutch any real and imaginary fragment of aliveness, fearing that we will forever be deprived or that someone will steal the shards that we grasp. In the end, we end up with ashes. It is never an easy task for individuals or communities to handle the paradox of creating and giving up experiences of being alive.

"Thanks, June. What you have said seems right to me," Gina says, glancing at her watch. "I don't like to leave when I am in the presence of such a lively group, good conversation, and wonderful food, but I have a morning class. Thanks for giving me so much to ponder."

Conclusion

In the Midrash, there is a saying that all beginnings are difficult, but the same is true for endings. In life, as in analysis, endings are accompanied by unanswered questions, gaps in the story, regrets, unfinished lines of thought, unspoken desires and fears, unfulfilled longings, and uncertain futures or directions. This is no less true for ending a chapter or a book, despite one's attempts to cover the bases. This said, the foundational premise of this work is that vitality is inextricably a part of life from birth to death. Experiences of being alive are organized differently, depending on the stage of development, the individual person, and the community/culture. Human actions that contribute to experiences of deadness in individuals and communities are not always linked to trauma. Instead, there may be a slow and insidious foreclosure of potential space and draining away of vitality that is the result of the idolatrous use of the values and beliefs of any symbolic and ritual system, whether it be economic, political, religious, scientific, or social. I have tried to show that analysis, at its best, is an antidote for the poison of idolatry, restoring potential space and the possibility of vitality. Yet, analysis, too, can be absolutized, as Phillips noted (1993, p. 121). Perhaps openness to mystery, as well as a willingness to be moved by the "Other," will disrupt the certainty of our psychoanalytic knowing, our interpretations, and our theories and, in the process, give rise to the possibility of being alive with others.

Notes

1 Vitality in human life and psychoanalysis

1. In my view, the very plurality of definitions of psychoanalysis represents the vigor and vitality of its tradition. Philosophers Paul Ricoeur (1970) and Jürgen Habermas (1971) as well as analysts such as Donald Spence (1982) and Roy Schafer (1983, 1992) believed that psychoanalysis is primarily a study of meaning, while others (Ogden, 1986, 1989; Kumin, 1996; Fast, 1998; Mitchell, 2000a; Beebe and Lachmann, 2002) have extended this to include the importance of non-verbal aspects of the psychoanalytic process. Stolorow, Atwood, and Brandchaft (1994) argued that psychoanalysis is a historical and hermeneutic science of human experience. Gabbard (1990) proposed a more narrow definition, saying that psychoanalysis is "an approach to diagnosis and treatment characterized by a way of thinking about the patient and clinician that includes unconscious conflicts, deficits and distortions of intrapsychic structures and internal object relations" (p. 4).
2. Naturally, Freud (1912, 1913) said a great deal more about the technical aspects of the process of cure (e.g., neutrality, frustration, abstinence). Some of Freud's admonitions seemed to contradict (or to place in the background) the importance of love and tenderness in obtaining a measure of happiness and freedom.
3. Christopher Bollas (1987, 1992) has creatively extended Winnicott's views on true and false selves and their relation to vitality and deadness in child–parent interactions.
4. It is important to include Kohut (1984) and other self-psychologists (e.g., Bacal, 1998b) who also were concerned about vitality and its relation to development and the ritual of psychoanalysis.
5. As will become clear, the term "relational" encompasses theorists from different analytic schools and traditions (e.g., self-psychologists, intersubjectivists, interpersonal).
6. I believe Erikson struggled with the linear model of development, finding that it did not adequately fit the complexity of development. While maintaining a linear, hierarchical model, he argued that attributes of each stage "exist from the beginning in some form" (1952, p. 271) and the successive stages circle back on themselves (Friedman, 1999, p. 227).
7. Naturally, there are instances of disease or brain disorders namely, manic-depressive disorder or schizophrenia. Yet even in these cases, relationships, community, and interpretive frameworks are crucial to the person's achievement of some measure of well-being (see Szasz, 1970; Jamison, 1993).

8 Winnicott (1971) conceived of potential space primarily in terms of the vicissitudes of illusion and reality, which he argued not only pertained to a specific stage of infancy, but also to other venues of adult activity (e.g., art, science, and religion). Loosened from its ties to illusion and reality, potential space is depicted in terms of four interrelated, dialectical processes (surrender–generation, recognition–negation, Care, disruption–repair), which more adequately extends the concept to all aspects of human development.

9 My only quibble with Ghent's (1990) perspective is his view that surrender is not voluntary. "One cannot choose to surrender," he wrote, "though one can choose to submit" (p. 111). I would argue that one chooses to surrender and submission involves coercion and a distortion of reason and the will.

10 Ghent suggested that masochism reflects a "perversion of the wish for surrender" (p. 119), which screens the person's "longing to be reached and known, in an accepting and safe environment" (p. 118).

11 It is important to clarify that surrendering to and generating experience can include occasions of suffering and darkness, as Hidas (1981) argued. In surrendering to suffering, as Heidegger (1971) also suggested, meaning and even a sense of passion and aliveness are not *necessarily* annihilated. Thus, potential space may be present during intensely painful experiences, which we identify as powerful experiences in therapy when both patient and therapist are moved by shared suffering that does not obliterate self, relationship, meaning, or aliveness. Surrendering to suffering, then, is not necessarily a masochistic submission, though there are certainly times when the distortion of surrender becomes submission.

12 It is important to note that Stern (1985) and more recently Mitchell (2000) have identified stages of self-organization and modes of experience using concepts that do not denote or connote pathology.

13 Some of those who followed Freud (Laing, 1959; Winnicott, 1971; Fromm, 1973, Bollas, 1987; Chodorow, 1989) recognized that accommodation to "reality" was not necessarily something to be applauded. Poststructuralists such as Foucault (1965, 1972) and social constructionists (e.g., Berger and Luckman, 1966) awakened analysts (e.g., Donnel Stern, 1997; Hoffman, 1998) to the relation between power, authority, and the social construction of "truth" or "reality." Accommodation to "reality" may therefore represent coerced submission (versus surrender) and a corresponding sense of emptiness that accompanies the absence of social recognition of one's hopes and desires.

2 Embodied vitality

1 I am not saying that there is some external "reality" or "truth" to be discovered. Instead, I am suggesting that my perception of an object and concomitant organization of experience are not the object itself. The object is independent of my constructions in the sense that my perception of it is a representation of the object, although independence does not exclude the possibility of moving or transforming the object by my actions. The object "resists" my perceptions and actions because of its independence; that is, because it is not identical to me or my constructions of it. In psychoanalysis, for example, our theories and diagnoses shape how we perceive, understand, and experience patients, but it is an epistemological fallacy, however common, to believe that our theories, diagnoses, and experiences are the patient. Instead, these are simply ways we think about the patient and the interaction, which does not mean that the patient is not affected. Not surprisingly, a patient may agree with the analyst's diagnosis

and experience of the patient, but that does not mean that consent is reality. It may be shared experience, a shared reality, but not *the* reality. One's experience of something as real is quite distinct from believing it to be the reality (see Moore, 1999).

2 Winnicott (1971) believed that, after the initial phase of omnipotent merger with the mother, the infant is able to identify and *make use* of objects. This early use of objects demonstrates a budding intentionality that is pre-symbolic. I utilize quotation marks to indicate that the infant does indeed construct experience, but not intentionally. In other words, innate capacities are geared toward organizing experience long before the infant is conscious and intentional. Even adult experience is organized outside of conscious intentions. We cannot help but organize experience. Even unformulated experience (see Stern, 1997) possesses a "form."

3 While I do not address the complex and varied aspects of memory, it is important to define memory not solely in terms of what it is not. In the C-C mode, memory is visceral, presentational, global, proprioceptive, and unconscious. So, Carol's initial achy feelings are not organized or linked to autobiographical, episodic, or iconic memory systems. It was only later that Carol connected the bodily experiences to iconic, and then autobiographical, memory systems. The symptom (bodily aches) could be said to be a presentational, visceral memory that was disconnected from symbolic formulations.

4 Peirce (1991, 1998) and Charles Morris (1964) argued that signifying functions occur at the most primitive animal level, which suggests, contra Kumin (1996), that the pre-representational capacities possess rudimentary semiotic processes. I agree with Peirce. The infant is able to link, cross-modally (Stern, 1985), diverse sensory information, which is the most basic semiotic process – a somatic-sensory semiosis, which precedes primary semiosis (see Chapter 3).

5 Damasio (1994) remarked that "relative to the brain, the body proper provides more than mere support and modulation: it provides a basic topic for brain representations" (p. xvii). In brief, the body–mind is the foundation for pre-representational and representational organizations of experience and perception (see Trevarthen, 1998).

6 The idea that the infant is undifferentiated does not denote or connote disorganization or even lack of organization, as if the infant already begins life with a deficit.

7 McWilliams (1994) pointed out that primitive refers to primary or immature. "Primitive defenses operate in a global, undifferentiated way in a person's total sensorium, fusing cognitive, affective, and behavioral dimensions" (p. 98).

3 Living objects

1 A great deal has been written about semiotics and its relation to the mind–body problem (Olds, 2000), perception (Eco, 1997), language (Saussure, 1959), and knowledge (Peirce, 1998). In psychoanalysis, Lacan (1968), Kristeva (1980), Rapaport (1974), Barratt (1984), Shapiro (1991), Muller (1996), and Van Buren (1991) have explored the role of semiosis in relation to desire, fantasy, feeling, absence, the unconscious and other analytic interests. My concern is not to offer explanations of how semiosis appears or to repeat other works. Rather, I describe how semiosis is related to a particular mode of generating experiences and, in particular, an experience of being alive.

2 The most trenchant critique of the idea of a paranoid-schizoid mode of organizing experience is not that it tends to pathologize development, though this by

itself would be cause enough to search for other descriptors (Westen, 2002). Rather, my objection is that the paranoid-schizoid position does not portray fundamental mental processes that explicate pathological *and* healthy modes of organizing experience. Let me explain. A child, who is very anxious because she recognizes the object as dangerous and unconsciously *splits off* "bad" representations in order to remain attached (psychological survival), demonstrates complex and interrelated cognitive processes that are associated with recognition of the object, memory, judgment, valuation, semiosis, segmentation, and categorization. These processes are implicated in the child's ability to organize experience whether anxious, excited, or curious. The P-S position signifies a *type* of organization of experience that relies upon semiotic processes and the ability to categorize objects and experiences, both of which are dominated by anxiety. Clearly there are times when a child (or adult) may organize experience in a paranoid-schizoid fashion, but that signifies a category of experience that falls within the realm of the T-O mode of organizing experience and is itself not a phase of development. Klein, Fairbairn, and Ogden took the experience of anxiety and paranoia and created a developmental stage and human condition. What these theorists focused on was a child's (or adult's) anxious preoccupation with defending against real and imagined danger and interpreting this to be a normative aspect of human development and life. Thus, they did not attend to the processes upon which a child's paranoid-schizoid position depends. Instead, they attempted to understand and explain adult pathology by applying their hypotheses and models to a developmental stage. Although their views are merited, their notions do not adequately account for an adult's or child's healthy experiences. A healthy child or adult categorizes, associates, and segments experiences based on a variety of emotions and diverse valuations that provide a sense of freedom and aliveness. The P-S mode of organizing experience represents taxonomic, semiotic processes that are driven and dominated by anxiety and fear and are hardly occasions of aliveness.

3 Winnicott (Davis and Wallbridge, 1987) was known to extend a concept he liked to other stages and aspects of human life. The transitional object or phenomena of early childhood came to be associated also with adult activities (e.g., religion, science, art). Clearly the transitional object associated with early infancy is profoundly different from objects used and shared by adults, which is not to deny some similarities. I differentiate between primary, secondary, and tertiary transitional objects to highlight distinctive differences in what the object represents and differences with regard to a child's capacities and use of the object during later phases of development.

4 The primary transitional object represents a type of semiosis that is a precursor to an adult achievement of identification that entails the paradox of likeness in difference and difference in likeness in relation to other human beings. At this early stage, likeness and difference are joined to the object. The child does not yet possess the ability to recognize the other as a person or equivalent center of subjectivity.

5 This is an important point with regard to the psychoanalytic notion of splitting. Klein, Ogden, and others (e.g., McWilliams, 1994) associate the psychological defense of splitting with this early period of life. Splitting is a metaphor that refers to a person's unconscious ability to keep one affect-representation from another. The good mother is dissociated from the bad mother. The idea that a child's affect-representations are not yet unified suggests that distinct neural pathways are activated at different times. Splitting may then be understood in terms of the firing of neural pathways that are not consciously integrated or

perceived to be the same or similar. The hyperactivation of the good mother neural pathway may be defensive and accompanies a deactivation of the bad mother neural processes.

4 Vital subjects

1 Creativity and freedom with regard to representing experience can also be seen in the diverse cultural categories and ways of representing psychopathology (Gilman, 1982; Porter, 1989).

2 Of course, consciousness is closely related but not identical to subjectivity or I-ness. Freud (1923, 1940), for instance, depicted the ego in relation to the unconscious and the id, arguing that I-ness includes both conscious and unconscious knowing and desire.

3 Ogden (1986, p. 42), like Klein (1930), associates I-ness or subjectivity and symbolization with the transition from the paranoid-schizoid position to the depressive position.

4 Freud and Lacan had a less sanguine view regarding a child's appropriation of a civilization's ethos or entry into the symbolic order. There is an original unity that is initially disrupted in the infant's identification of self with the mirror image as reflected by the mother (Lacan, 1977). This primary identification and primitive alienation are compounded when the child appropriates language, believing that his desire is represented by the other's desire. The experience of alienation, though, is screened by jouissance – the pleasure and excitement of playing with language and desire. Put differently, the child's initial use of symbols enables him to master or handle the separation between himself and the mother, though mastery is accompanied by the ego's misrecognition of desire (Muller and Richardson, 1982). I believe what Lacan, Winnicott, and many other analysts are addressing is the paradoxical reality of human life. Entry into the symbolic order gives rise to the possibility of communion and alienation, freedom and bondage, desire and aversion, joy and suffering, temerity and timidity, and experiences of aliveness and deadness.

5 This is expressed in Charles Taylor's (1989) view of selfhood and human communication. "One cannot be a self on one's own. I am a self only in relation to certain interlocuters. A self exists only in what I call a web of interlocution" (p. 36).

6 Separation is necessary in the establishment of subjective reality. The independent other as subject resists my fantastic constructions even while I come to believe that my perceptions are correct. The symbolic web, which belongs to the social realm, also resists my omnipotent constructions, yet in the process of adopting the symbol system the subject makes it his own, altering the meanings of the symbol to come up with his own idiolect. Thus, there is an apparent paradox in the establishment and experience of reality.

7 The idea and experience of reality have long been bandied about in psychoanalysis (Moore, 1999; Fayek, 2002) and, of course, have been a topic of philosophical interest for several millennia. It is not necessary to explicate the various psychoanalytic views of reality to argue that there is a close relation between subjectivity, symbolization, and the experience and construction of reality.

8 Early subjective agency and the symbolic representation of needs and desires are not simply about words. In the S-S mode, gestures begin to take on symbolic character, which are the precursors for the complex rituals of adulthood. For example, the analyst and analysand's initial handshake – a seemingly common

gesture – has diachronic and synchronic signification in Western cultures and in psychosocial development. More particularly, this greeting is, ideally, a mutual confirmation of their subjectivity and a movement toward the ritual of analytic listening and talking. An analysand's nervous handshake may represent doubt about his own sense of agentic desires and hopes. A possible hypothesis is that this social symbol of salutation is related to the greetings that took place between the analysand and significant people in his childhood – meetings marred by disconfirmation of his subjectivity. Symbols and agentic subjectivity, then, include the movements of our bodies that have their roots in the playful and serious embodied language that takes place between parent and child.

9 As stated earlier (Chapter 3), I suggest that there are three types of transitional objects. Secondary transitional objects are symbols that represent the child's internal world and the social-cultural world, marking the transition from the taxonomic-object mode to symbolic-subjective mode of organizing experience (see LaMothe, 2001). The child, in other words, selects an object from the cultural field (e.g., stuffed animal) and makes it her own. Secondary transitional objects differ from primary transitional objects in two ways. First, STOs are symbols, while PTOs are signs. Second, the child imbues the STO with subjectivity. She plays as if the object is a subject. The PTO, to the child, is a functional object.

10 The birth of the historical subject includes some awareness that I will not be (Yalom, 1980). I and not-I is not only in relation to other objects and subjects, but in relation to oneself. The capacity for symbolic negation accompanies an awareness of the absence of an I and attending anxieties.

11 While cultural symbols can signify repair, they can also represent disruption. The Nazi symbol and Confederate flag can, for many people, signify disruption. Other symbols may join both the violence of disruption and the hope of repair (e.g., the cross for Christians).

12 The collapse into a symbolic equation is not equivalent to psychopathology, though it does represent the sacrifice of vitality for real and imagined protection of one's subjectivity. On the one hand, this collapse may preserve a person or a group's belief in reality and truth. On the other hand, a collapse into a symbolic equation (hyperactivation of the C-C or T-O modes) may be a person's attempt to defend against trauma, though the results are a false self, normotic self or experiences of de-realization, de-personalization, psychosis, etc. That is, in rigidly believing in some part of reality, there is a loss of a creative sense of symbolic reality and a concomitant constriction of subjectivity.

5 Enlivening stories

1 I wish to stress the claim that narratives are necessary for communal experiences of being alive, which does not mean narratives and narration are identical to experiences of being alive. Aliveness cannot be captured by narratives, but it can be represented, pointing to the possibility of aliveness with others.

2 Lacan (1977), Barratt (1993), and Muller (1996) argued, in different ways, that the semiotic web of language and narrative is fundamentally alienating, leaving desire unarticulated and unthinkable. While there is much I agree with, there seems to be a tendency to overemphasize the limiting and "alienating" aspects of language or the so-called totalitarian aspects of narrative discourse. There is a significant difference between the idea of separation, which is required for language and narrative, and the ideas of alienation and domination. The experience of alienation obliterates the paradox of separation and union that

Winnicott identified. Moreover, I would argue that language and narrative are not, in and of themselves, alienating. It is *the use* of language and narrative that contributes to dyscommunion.

3 Narrative competence is not simply the presence of semiotic processes that support a person's ability to organize and communicate his experience in temporally meaningful episodes. Nor does it refer only to "more complete, coherent, convincing, and adaptively useful" stories (Schafer, 1983, p. 240). Certainly, it is all of these, but I would also stress that narrative competence includes the capacity to communicate, understand, and share emotional meanings with others. A patient, for example, may tell a very coherent, useful, meaningful, and convincing narrative that lacks emotional intimacy or communion with others.

4 I am not addressing problems in narrative competence that result from brain disorders such as severe autism (see Palombo, 1993).

5 Within the history of psychoanalysis, there have been and continue to be discussions about the dyadic or triadic aspects of the analytic enterprise. Lacan's (1977) symbolic third, Green's (1975) analytic object as a third, and Ogden's (1994) analytic third, which refers to "the experience of being simultaneously within and outside of the intersubjectivity of the analyst-analysand" (p. 64), are examples of the attempt to take note of joint creations and outside forces and representations that are at play. When I use quadratic, I am referring to the meanings, values, expectations, roles, and representations relating to the cultural and family narratives that shape the patient–analyst interaction, as well as the past and present experiences of communion (or not) embedded in the stories that are told or that lie quietly in the background. Both analyst and patient are only part of larger stories and the communal lives of others.

6 Barratt (1993) distinguishes between psychoanalysis and other therapies, arguing that desire, which undergirds and undermines semiotic processes, cannot be captured by the stories we tell. Desire "represents" the otherwise other that is part of our capacity to represent, yet cannot be represented. Hence, there is always a remainder in all of our storytelling. This suggests that narrative constructions of agency, emotional regulation, continuity, and validation are always partial and dynamic. Put differently, narrative constructions of experiences of being alive are ephemeral and dynamic, leaving a remainder.

7 Tertiary simply refers to the kind of transitional object that attends new semiotic capacities (narration and self-reflection) of the child that appear after symbolization and the child's use of an STO.

8 In the history of psychoanalysis, this struggle is apparent. In earlier psychoanalytic discourse, the larger story of civilization and religion was viewed as repressive, though necessary for banding together to survive against the threat of Nature (or useful in soothing one's anxiety in the face of extinction). "Surrender" to civilization's story may provide safety and security, but at the cost of repressing one's desires and needs. Lacan (1977), Barratt (1993), and other analysts argued that subjectivity is fundamentally alienated because of the seemingly inescapable, developmental subjugation to more dominant and powerful cultural-family narratives. Psychoanalysis as a process was an attempt to free people from subjugating discourse of religion or civilization.

9 The idea of personhood is distinct from the idea of subjectivity. I can recognize the other as a subject, while treating him impersonally (in terms of a functional role). To recognize the other as a person requires acceptance of them as a unique individual agent, a thou, who is more than any function or role. As Macmurray (1961) stated, "The unity of the personal is, then, to be sought in the community

of the 'You and I', and since persons are agents, this community is not merely a matter of fact, but also a matter of intention" (p. 27).

10 Postmodern perspectives question the notion of a unitary self – except as a necessary illusion – and instead point to the reality of multiple self-states (e.g., Pizer, 1992; Mitchell, 1993; Bromberg, 1998). Reformulating potential space in terms of these fourfold pairs captures the complexity and paradox of the presence and absence of self-states in successful and failed developmental and psychoanalytic interactions. Put differently, from a clinical perspective, this means attending to the interpersonal dynamics and shifting self-states of the analyst and patient. There is, then, a paradox of the presence and absence of self-states vis-à-vis self-states in successful and failed psychoanalytic interactions.

6 Couch and culture

1 Ulman and Brothers (1988) argued that real traumatic events shatter central, pre-existing organizing fantasies (e.g., merger fantasies, grandiosity and exhibitionist fantasies). There is one problem with this perspective. It suggests that what is shattered is a fantasy rather than "real" experiences a child or an adult has in relation to significant others. In my view, it would be more accurate to say that the fantasy is the defense a person uses that points to his/her experience of real trauma, rather than positing some ontological or core fantasies in human development. As Walsh (1996) pointed out, the child's illusion of omnipotence is related to real experiences of maternal care. Thus, trauma "is not a pathology of falsehood or displacement of meaning, but history itself" (Caruth, 1996, p. 5).

2 With regard to regression, John's situation is similar, though different. His defensive response to the traumas of numerous losses in childhood resulted in patterns of hyperactivation of semiotic processes and relational patterns associated with the T-O mode, which shaped later modes. The concept of regression does not fit with his day-to-day way of relating to others. John, then, is not "returning" to a previous mode and potential space.

3 I wonder if analytic attempts to explain trauma in terms of imagination, displacement of meaning, or fantasy represent a countertransference response to the indescribable horror of violence. It is certainly safer for the analyst to believe the patient's trauma resides in fantasy than to gaze into and experience the abyss of the horror and speechlessness of traumatic violence. Perhaps the attribution of fantasy to trauma reflects a type of dissociation.

4 Geertz (1973) posited that the "concept of culture . . . is essentially a semiotic one. Believing, with Max Weber, that man is an animal suspended in webs of significance he himself has spun, I take culture to be those webs" (p. 5). Semiotic processes, as the basis of culture, are usually taken to mean symbols and symbolic actions such as rituals, dramas, and social discourse (Turner, 1974). A Peircean interpretation of Geertz's definition would include non-symbolic semiotic forms that are shared – somatic, iconic, and taxonomic. Culture, then, is a term used to denote the web of signs, symbols, stories, and rituals and their attending stated and unstated rules, roles, meanings, desires, and values that a group uses in representing and communicating experience. Culture gives shape and definition to persons' use of objects and to the structures of experience, whether the experience is one of aliveness or deadness.

5 The sense of aliveness I am referring to here is best understood in terms of Dave's need for being mirrored by his father. It is a pseudo sense of aliveness in two ways. First, it is based on Dave's lack of being mirrored (deprivation) and

his corresponding wish to be valued by his father. Granted, he felt a sense of aliveness, but it was not lasting because it did not address the fundamental losses that fueled it. Second, the kind of recognition Dave received was for how well he performed in relation to achieving the goals of the company. This form of recognition, which parallels his father's, did not take into account Dave's aspirations, except to the extent they might conform (subjugation) to the company's.

6 Since this is fiction, we can imagine a diverse group of analysts representing numerous analytic schools.

References

Abrams, S. and Neubauer, P. (1978). Transitional objects: Animate and inanimate. In S. Grolnick and L. Barkin (eds.), *Between reality and fantasy* (pp. 3–14). Northvale, NJ: Jason Aronson.

Ackerman, D. (1999). *Deep play*. New York: Vintage.

Albom, M. (1997). *Tuesdays with Morrie*. New York: Doubleday.

Altman, N. (2000). Black and white thinking: A psychoanalyst reconsiders race. *Psychoanalytic Dialogues*, 10(4), pp. 589–606.

Amery, J. (1995). Torture. In L. Langer (ed.), *Art from the ashes*. Oxford: Oxford University Press.

Angyal, A. (1965). *Neurosis and treatment*. New York: De Capo Press, 1982.

Anzieu, D. (1990). Formal signifiers and the ego-skin. In D. Anzieu (ed.), *Psychic Envelopes* (pp. 1–25). London: Karnac.

Applegate, J. (1989). The transitional object reconsidered: Some sociocultural variations and their implications. *Child and Adolescent Social Work*, 6(1), pp. 38–51.

Arendt, H. (1958). *The human condition*. Chicago: University of Chicago Press.

Aron, L. (1996). *A meeting of minds: Mutuality in psychoanalysis*. Hillsdale, NJ: Analytic Press.

Auerbach, J. and Blatt, S. (2002). The concept of mind. In R. Lasky (ed.), *Symbolization and Desymbolization* (pp. 75–118). New York: Other Press.

Bacal, H. (1998a). Optimal responsiveness and the therapeutic process. In H. Bacal (ed.), *Optimal responsiveness* (pp. 3–34). Northvale, NJ: Jason Aronson.

Bacal, H. (1998b). Optimal responsiveness and the specificity of selfobject experience. In H. Bacal (ed.), *Optimal responsiveness* (pp. 141–172). Northvale, NJ: Jason Aronson.

Bakhtin, M. (1981). *The dialogic imagination*. Austin, TX: University of Texas Press.

Balamuth, R. (1998). Re-membering the body: A psychoanalytic study. In L. Aron and F. Anderson (eds.), *Relational perspectives on the body* (pp. 263–286). Hillsdale, NJ: Analytic Press.

Balint, E. (1993). *Before I was I*. London: Guilford Press.

Bar-on, D. (1999). *The indescribable and the undiscussable*. Budapest: Central University Press.

Barratt, B. (1984). *Psychic reality and psychoanalytic knowing*. Hillsdale, NJ: Analytic Press.

Barratt, B. (1993). *Psychoanalysis and the postmodern impulse*. Baltimore, MD: Johns Hopkins University Press.

Bass, A. (2002). Desymbolization in the third area. In R. Lasky (ed.), *Symbolization and desymbolization* (pp. 142–163). New York: Other Press.

Beebe, B. and Lachmann, F. (1994). Representation and internalization in infancy: Three principles of salience. *Psychoanalytic Psychology*, 11, pp. 127–165.

Beebe, B. and Lachmann, F. (1998). Optimal responsiveness in a systems approach to representational and selfobject transferences. In H. Bacal (ed.), *Optimal responsiveness* (pp. 305–328). Northvale, NJ: Jason Aronson.

Beebe, B. and Lachmann, F. (2002). *Infant research and adult treatment*. Hillsdale, NJ: Analytic Press.

Beebe, B., Lachmann, F., and Jaffe, J. (1997). Mother–infant interactions: Structures and presymbolic self and object representations. *Psychoanalytic Dialogues*, 7(2), pp. 133–182.

Benjamin, J. (1988). *The bonds of love*. New York: Pantheon.

Benjamin, J. (1990). Recognition and destruction: An outline of intersubjectivity. In S. Mitchell and L. Aron (eds.), *Relational psychoanalysis* (pp. 181–210). London: Analytic Press.

Benjamin, J. (1995). *Like subjects, love objects*. New Haven, CT: Yale University Press.

Benjamin, J. (1998). *The shadow of the other*. London: Routledge.

Berger, P. and Luckmann, T. (1966). *The social construction of reality*. New York: Anchor.

Bick, E. (1968). The experience of the skin in early object relations. *International Journal of Psychoanalysis*, 49, pp. 484–486.

Binswanger, L. (1963). *Selected papers of Ludwig Binswanger*. London: Souvenir Press.

Black, M. (2003). Enactment: Analytic musings on energy, language, and personal growth. *Psychoanalytic Dialogues*, 13(5), pp. 633–655.

Blanchot, M. (1995). *The writing of the disaster*. Lincoln, NE: University of Nebraska Press.

Bollas, C. (1987). *The shadow of the object*. New York: Columbia University Press.

Bollas, C. (1991). *Forces of destiny*. London: Free Association Books.

Bollas, C. (1992). *Being a character*. New York: Hill and Wang.

Bollas, C. (2000). *Hysteria*. London: Routledge.

Bollas, C. (2002). *Free association*. London: Icon.

Brazelton, T., Koslowski, B., and Main, M. (1974). The origin of reciprocity. In M. Lewis and L. Rosenblum (eds.), *The effect of the infant on its caregivers* (pp. 49–75). New York: Wiley.

Breger, L. (2000). *Freud: Darkness in the midst of vision*. New York: John Wiley and Sons.

Bremer, J. and Marmar, C. (eds.) (1998). *Trauma, memory, and dissociation*. Washington, DC: American Psychiatric Press.

Brenner, I. (2001). *Dissociation of trauma: Theory, phenomenology, and technique*. Madison, CT: International Universities Press.

Breuer, J. and Freud, S. (1895). Studies in hysteria. *Standard Edition*, 2, pp. 1–306. London: Hogarth Press.

Brody, S. (1980). Transitional objects: Idealization of a phenomenon. *Psychoanalytic Quarterly*, 59, pp. 561–605.
Bromberg, P. (1998). *Standing in spaces: Essays on clinical process, trauma, and dissociation*. Hillsdale, NJ: Analytic Press.
Brown, N. (1959). *Life against death*. Middletown, CT: Wesleyan University Press.
Bruner, J. (1990). *Acts of meaning*. Cambridge, MA: Harvard University Press.
Buber, M. (1958). *I and thou*. New York: Charles Scribner.
Bucci, W. (1997). Symptoms and symbols: A multiple code theory of somatization. *Psychoanalytic Inquiry*, 17, pp. 151–172.
Bucci, W. (2001). Pathways of emotional communication. *Psychoanalytic Inquiry*, 20, pp. 40–70.
Bucci, W. (2002). From subsymbolic to symbolic – and back. In R. Lasky (ed.), *Symbolization and Desymbolization* (pp. 50–74). New York: Other Press.
Burrell, D. (1977). From systems to story. In S. Hauerwas, R. Bond, and D. Burrell (eds.), *Truthfulness and tragedy* (pp. 15–39). Notre Dame, IN: University of Notre Dame Press.
Busch, F., Nagera, H., McKnight, J., and Pezzarossi, G. (1973). Primary transitional objects. *Journal of the American Academy of Child Psychiatry*, 12, 193–214.
Campbell, J. (1991). *The power of myth*. New York: Doubleday.
Caruth, C. (1996). *Unclaimed experience: Trauma, narrative, and history*. Baltimore, MD: Johns Hopkins University Press.
Casement, P. (1985). *On learning from the patient*. London: Routledge.
Chesterton, G. K. (1959). *Orthodoxy*. New York: Image.
Chodorow, N. (1989). *Feminism and psychoanalytic theory*. New Haven, CT: Yale University Press.
Chodorow, N. (1999). *The power of feelings*. New Haven, CT: Yale University Press.
Chused, J. (2003). The role of enactments. *Psychoanalytic Dialogues*, 13(5), pp. 677–687.
Clavell, M. (2000). Self reflections. *Psychoanalytic dialogues*, 10(3), pp. 513–529.
Colapietro, V. (1989). *Peirce's approach to the self*. Albany, NY: SUNY Press.
Coontz, S. (1988). *The social origins of private life*. London: Verso.
Coontz, S. (1992). *The way we never were*. New York: Basic Books.
Corrigan, G. and Gordon, P. (1995). The mind as an object. In E. Corrigan and P. Gordon (eds.), *The mind object* (pp. 1–22). Northvale, NJ: Jason Aronson.
Costello, J. (2002). *John Macmurray: A biography*. Edinburgh: Floris Press.
Crites, S. (1986). Story-time: Recollecting the past and projecting the future. In T. Sarbin (ed.), *Narrative psychology* (pp. 152–173). New York: Praeger Special Studies.
Cushman, P. (1995). *Constructing the self, constructing America*. New York: Addison Wesley.
Damasio, A. (1994). *Descartes' error: Emotion, reason, and the human brain*. New York: Avon.
Davies, J. and Frawley, M. (1994). *Treating the adult survivor of sexual abuse*. New York: Basic Books.
Davis, M. and Wallbridge, D. (1987). *Boundary and space*. New York: Brunner/Mazel.
DeCasper, A. and Fifer, W. (1980). Of human bonding: Newborns prefer their mothers' voices. *Science*, 208, pp. 1174–76.

DeCasper, A. and Spence, M. (1986). Prenatal maternal speech influences newborns' perception of speech sounds. *Infant Behavior and Development*, 4, pp. 19–36.

Deri, S. (1978). Transitional phenomena: Vicissitudes of symbolization and creativity. In S. Grolnick and L. Barkin (eds.), *Between reality and fantasy* (pp. 43–60). Northvale, NJ: Jason Aronson.

Dilthey, W. (1989). *Introduction to the human sciences*, volume 1, Makkreel, R., and Frithjof, R. (eds.). Princeton, NJ: Princeton University Press.

Eagle, M. (1984). Psychoanalysis and "narrative truth." *Psychoanalysis and Contemporary Thought*, 7(4), pp. 629–640.

Eco, U. (1997). *Kant and the platypus: Essays on language and cognition*. New York: Harcourt Press.

Edelman, G. and Tononi, G. (2000). *A universe of consciousness*. New York: Basic Books.

Eigen, M. (1995). Psychic deadness: Freud. *Contemporary Psychoanalysis*, 31, pp. 277–299.

Eigen, M. (1996). *Psychic deadness*. Northvale, NJ: Jason Aronson.

Eisold, B. (1998). Dissociation and physical difference. In L. Aron and F. Anderson (eds.), *Relational perspectives on the body* (pp. 173–190). Hillsdale, NJ: Analytic Press.

Eliot, T. S. (1999). *Collected poems*. New York: Harcourt Brace.

Emde, R. (1980). Toward a psychoanalytic theory of affect. In A. Greenspan and G. Pollock (eds.), *The course of life: Psychoanalytic contributions toward understanding personality development* (pp. 85–112). Atlanta, GA: National Institute of Mental Health.

Erikson, E. (1952). *Childhood and society*. New York: W. W. Norton.

Farley, E. (1990). *Good and evil: Interpreting a human condition*. Minneapolis, MN: Fortress Press.

Fast, I. (1992). The embodied mind: Toward a relational perspective. *Psychoanalytic Dialogues*, 2(3), pp. 389–409.

Fast, I. (1998). *Selving: A relational theory of self-organization*. Hillsdale, NJ: Analytic Press.

Fayek, A. (2002). Psychic reality and mental representation. *Psychoanalytic Psychology*, 19, pp. 475–500.

Ferenczi, S. (1931). Child analysis in the analysis of adults. *International Journal of Psychoanalysis*, 12, pp. 468–482.

Ferenczi, S. (1988). *The clinical diary of Sándor Ferenczi*, Dupont, J. (ed.). Cambridge, MA: Harvard University Press.

Fink, B. (1995). *The Lacanian subject*. Princeton, NJ: Princeton University Press.

Fonagy, P. (2001). *Attachment theory and psychoanalysis*. New York: Other Press.

Fonagy, P. and Target, M. (1996). Playing with reality: Theory of mind and the normal development of psychic reality. *International Journal of Psychoanalysis*, 77, pp. 217–233.

Fonagy, P. and Target, M. (1997). Attachment and reflective function: Their role in self-organization. *Development and Psychopathology*, 9, pp. 679–700.

Fonagy, P., Gergely, G., Jurist, E., and Target, M. (2002). *Affect regulation, mentalization, and the development of the self*. New York: Other Press.

Fosshage, J. (1998). Optimal responsiveness and listening/experiencing perspectives.

In H. Bacal (ed.), *Optimal responsiveness* (pp. 117–140). Northvale, NJ: Jason Aronson.
Foucault, M. (1965). *Madness and civilization*. New York: Vintage.
Foucault, M. (1972). *Power and knowledge*. New York: Pantheon.
Freeman, M. (1985). Psychoanalytic narration and the problem of historical knowledge. *Psychoanalysis and Contemporary Thought*, 8(2), pp. 133–182.
Freud, S. (1895). The psychotherapy of hysteria. *Standard Edition*, 2, pp. 253–305. London: Hogarth Press.
Freud, S. (1907). Obsessive actions and religious practice. *Standard Edition*, 9, pp. 115–128. London: Hogarth Press.
Freud, S. (1911). Formulations on the two principles of mental functioning. *Standard Edition*, 12, pp. 215–226. London: Hogarth Press.
Freud, S. (1912). Recommendations to physicians practicing psychoanalysis. *Standard Edition*, 12, pp. 110–120. London: Hogarth Press.
Freud, S. (1913). On beginning treatment. *Standard Edition*, 12, pp. 122–144. London: Hogarth Press.
Freud, S. (1914). On narcissism: An introduction. *Standard Edition*, 14, pp. 69–102. London: Hogarth Press.
Freud, S. (1915). The unconscious. *Standard Edition*, 14, pp. 166–213. London: Hogarth Press.
Freud, S. (1917a). Mourning and melancholia. *Standard Edition*, 14, pp. 237–259. London: Hogarth Press.
Freud, S. (1917b). Introductory lectures. *Standard Edition*, 16, pp. 243–463. London: Hogarth Press.
Freud, S. (1920). Beyond the pleasure principle. *Standard Edition*, 18, pp. 7–64. London: Hogarth Press.
Freud, S. (1923). The ego and the id. *Standard Edition*, 19, pp. 3–59. London: Hogarth Press.
Freud, S. (1924a). The economic problem of masochism. *Standard Edition*, 19, pp. 155–170. London: Hogarth Press.
Freud, S. (1924b). The dissolution of the Oedipus complex. *Standard Edition*, 19, pp. 172–179.
Freud, S. (1925). Negation. *Standard Edition*, 19, pp. 235–243. London: Hogarth Press.
Freud, S. (1926). Inhibition, symptoms and anxiety. *Standard Edition*, 22, pp. 87–178. London: Hogarth Press.
Freud, S. (1927a). The problem of lay analysis. *Standard Edition*, 20, pp. 182–258. London: Hogarth Press.
Freud, S. (1927b). The future of an illusion. *Standard Edition*, 21, pp. 5–58. London: Hogarth Press.
Freud, S. (1930). Civilization and its discontents. *Standard Edition*, 21, pp. 64–148. London: Hogarth Press.
Freud, S. (1940). The splitting of the ego in the process of defense. *Standard Edition*, 23, pp. 273–278. London: Hogarth Press.
Freud, S. (1950). *Totem and taboo*. New York: W. W. Norton.
Freyd, J. (1996). *Betrayal trauma*. Cambridge, MA: Harvard University Press.
Friedman, L. (1999). *Identity's architect*. Cambridge, MA: Harvard University Press.

Fromm, E. (1941). *Escape from freedom*. New York: Avon Books.

Fromm, E. (1966). *You shall be as gods: A radical interpretation of the Old Testament and its traditions*. New York: Holt, Rinehart and Winston.

Fromm, E. (1973). *Anatomy of human destructiveness*. New York: Holt, Rinehart and Winston.

Gabbard, G. (1990). *Psychodynamic psychiatry in clinical practice*. Washington, DC: American Psychiatric Press.

Gay, P. (1988). *Freud: A life for our time*. New York: W. W. Norton.

Geertz, C. (1973). *The interpretation of cultures*. New York: Basic Books.

Ghent, E. (1990). Masochism, submission, surrender. *Contemporary Psychoanalysis*, 26, pp. 108–136.

Gilman, S. (1982). *Seeing the insane*. Lincoln, NE: University of Nebraska Press.

Goldberg, P. (1995). "Successful" dissociation, pseudovitality, and inauthentic use of the senses. *Psychoanalytic Dialogues*, 5, pp. 493–510.

Grand, S. (2000). *The reproduction of evil*. Hillsdale, NJ: Psychoanalytic Press.

Green, A. (1972). *On private madness*. London: Rebus Press.

Green, A. (1975). The analysts, symbolization and absence in the analytic setting. *International Journal of Psychoanalysis*, 56, pp. 1–22.

Green, A. (1978). Potential space in psychoanalysis. In S. Grolnick and L. Barkin (eds.), *Between reality and fantasy* (pp. 167–190). Northvale, NJ: Aronson.

Green, A. (1999). *The dead mother: The work of André Green*. London: Routledge.

Greenberg, J. and Mitchell, S. (1983). *Object relations in psychoanalytic theory*. Cambridge, MA: Harvard University Press.

Greenspan, S. (1997). *The growth of the mind*. Cambridge, MA: Perseus.

Grotstein, J. (1979). Demoniacal possession, splitting and the torment of joy. *Contemporary Psychoanalysis*, 15: 407–445.

Grotstein, J. (2000). Notes on Fairbairn's metapsychology. In J. Grotstein and D. Rinsley (eds.), *Fairbairn and the origin of object relations* (pp. 112–150). New York: Other Press.

Grotstein, J. and Rinsley, D. (2000). Editors' introduction. In J. Grotstein and D. Rinsley (eds.), *Fairbairn and the origin of object relations* (pp. 3–16). New York: Other Press.

Gunsberg, L. and Tylim, I. (1998). The body-mind: Psychopathology of its ownership. In L. Aron and F. Anderson (eds.), *Relational perspectives on the body* (pp. 117–138). Hillsdale, NJ: Analytic Press.

Guntrip, H. (1969). *Schizoid phenomena, therapy, and the self*. New York: Basic Books.

Habermas, J. (1971). *Knowledge and human interests*. Boston, MA: Beacon.

Heidegger, M. (1971). *On the way to language*. San Francisco, CA: HarperCollins.

Heimann, P. (1956). Dynamics of transference interpretations. *International Journal of Psychoanalysis*, 37, pp. 303–310.

Herman, J. (1992) *Trauma and recovery*. New York: Basic Books.

Hesse, E. and Main, M. (2000). Disorganized infant, child, and adult attachment. *Journal of the American Psychoanalytic Association*, 48(4), pp. 1097–1126.

Hidas, A. (1981). Psychotherapy and surrender: A psychospiritual perspective. *Journal of Transpersonal Psychology*, 13(1), pp. 27–32.

Hinshelwood, R. (1994). *Clinical Klein*. London: Free Association Books.

Hoffman, I. (1998). *Ritual and spontaneity in psychoanalysis*. Hillsdale, NJ: Analytic Press.

Holmes, J. (1996). *Attachment, intimacy, and autonomy*. Northvale, NJ: Jason Aronson.

Houzel, D. (1990). The concept of psychic envelope. In D. Anzieu (ed.), *Psychic Envelopes* (pp. 27–58). London: Karnac.

Jacobs, T. (1991). *The use of the self*. Madison, CT: International Universities Press.

James, W. (1958). *The varieties of religious experience*. New York: Signet.

Jamison, K. (1993). *Touched by fire*. New York: Free Press.

Janoff-Bulman, R. (1992). *Shattered assumptions: Towards a new psychology of trauma*. New York: Free Press.

Johnson, M. (1987). *The body in the mind*. Chicago: University of Chicago Press.

Jung, C. G. (1959). The archetypes and the collective unconscious. *Collected Works*, 9, pp. 3–41. Princeton, NJ: Princeton University Press.

Kahr, B. (1996). *D. W. Winnicott: A biographical portrait*. Madison, CT: International Universities Press.

Keller, H. (1954). *The story of my life*. London: Hodder and Stoughton.

Kennedy, R. (1997). Aspects of consciousness: One voice or many? *Psychoanalytic Dialogues*, 6(1), pp. 73–96.

Kernberg, O. (1984). *Severe personality disorders*. New Haven, CT: Yale University Press.

Kernberg, O. (2000). Fairbairn's theory and challenge. In J. Grotstein and D. Rinsley (eds.), *Fairbairn and the origin of object relations* (pp. 41–65). New York: Other Press.

Kestenberg, J. and Weinstein, J. (1978). Transitional objects and body image formation. In S. Grolnick and L. Barkin (eds.), *Between reality and fantasy* (pp. 75–96). Northvale, NJ: Jason Aronson.

Keylor, R. (2003). Subjectivity, infantile Oedipus, and symbolization in Melanie Klein and Jacques Lacan. *Psychoanalytic Dialogues*, 13(2), pp. 211–242.

Khan, M. (1963). *The concept of cumulative trauma*. In *Privacy of the self* (pp. 42–58). New York: International Universities Press, 1974.

Kierkegaard, S. (1980). *The sickness unto death*, H. Hong and E. Hong (eds. and trans.). Princeton, NJ: Princeton University Press.

Kirkpatrick, F. (1986). *Community: A trinity of models*. Washington, DC: Georgetown University Press.

Kirsner, D. (2001). The future of psychoanalytic institutes. *Psychoanalytic Psychology*, 18(2), pp. 195–212.

Klein, M. (1928). Early stages of the Oedipus complex. In *Envy and gratitude and other works, 1946–1963*. New York: Delacorte Press, 1975.

Klein, M. (1930). The importance of symbol formation in the development of the ego. In J. Mitchell (ed.), *The selected Melanie Klein* (pp. 95–111). New York: Free Press, 1986.

Klein, M. (1946). Notes on some schizoid mechanisms. *International Journal of Psychoanalysis*, 27, pp. 99–110.

Klein, M. (1949a). *Contributions to psychoanalysis*. London: Hogarth Press.

Klein, M. (1949b). *The psychoanalysis of children*. London: Hogarth Press.

Klein, M. (1952). Some theoretical considerations regarding the emotional life of the

infant. In *Envy and gratitude and other works, 1946–1963* (pp. 61–93). New York: Delacorte Press, 1975.
Klein, M. (1957). Envy and gratitude. In *Envy and gratitude and other works, 1946–1963* (pp. 176–235). New York: Delacorte Press, 1975.
Klein, M. (1964). Love, guilt, and reparation. In M. Klein and J. Riviere, *Love, hate, and reparation* (pp. 57–119). New York: W. W. Norton.
Kohut, H. (1984). *How does analysis cure*? Chicago: University of Chicago Press.
Kovel, J. (1970). *White racism: A psychohistory*. New York: Pantheon.
Kristeva, J. (1969). Word, dialogue and novel. In R. Moi (ed.), *The Kristeva Reader* (pp. 34–61). New York: Columbia University Press, 1986.
Kristeva, J. (1973). The system and the speaking subject. In *Times Literary Supplement*, 12 October.
Kristeva, J. (1980). *Desire in language*. New York: Columbia University Press.
Kristeva, J. (1995). *New maladies of the soul*. New York: Columbia University Press.
Kristeva, J. (2001). *Hannah Arendt: Life is a narrative*. Toronto: University of Toronto Press.
Krystal, H. (1968). *Massive psychic trauma*. New York: International Universities Press.
Krystal, H. (1997). Desomatization and the consequences of infantile psychic trauma. *Psychoanalytic Inquiry*, 17, pp. 126–150.
Kumin, I. (1996). *Pre-object relatedness*. London: Guilford Press.
Lacan, J. (1968). *Speech and language in psychoanalysis*. Baltimore, MD: Johns Hopkins University Press.
Lacan, J. (1977). *Ecrits*. New York: W. W. Norton.
Laing, R. D. (1959). *The divided self*. New York: Penguin.
Lakoff, G. and Johnson, M. (1999). *Philosophy in the flesh: Embodied mind and its challenge to Western thought*. New York: Basic Books.
LaMothe, R. (1999). The absence of cure: The core of malignant trauma and symbolization. *Journal of Interpersonal Violence*, 14(11), pp. 1193–1210.
LaMothe, R. (2001). Vitalizing objects and psychoanalytic psychotherapy. *Psychoanalytic Psychology*, 18(2), pp. 1–21.
LaMothe, R. (2004). Freud's envy of religious experience. *International Journal for the Psychology of Religion*, 14(3), pp. 159–174.
LaMothe, R., Arnold, J., and Crane, J. (1998). The penumbra of religious discourse in psychoanalytic psychotherapy. *Psychoanalytic Psychology*, 15(1), pp. 1–11.
Lamott, A. (1994). *Bird by bird*. New York: Anchor.
Langer, S. (1942). *Philosophy in a new key*. Cambridge, MA: Harvard University Press.
LaPlanche, J. (1999). *Essays on otherness*. London: Routledge.
Lawrence, D. H. (1980). *Apocalypse and the writings on revelation*, M. Kalnins (ed.). Cambridge: Cambridge University Press.
Lear, J. (1998). *Open-minded*. Cambridge, MA: Harvard University Press.
Leary, K. (2000). Racial enactments in dynamic tension. *Psychoanalytic Dialogues*, 10(4), pp. 639–654.
Levi, P. (1960). *Survival in Auschwitz*. New York: Collier.
Lewis, T., Amini, F., and Lannon, R. (2000). *A general theory of love*. New York: Vintage.

Lichtenberg, J., Lachmann, F., and Fosshage, J. (1992). *Self and motivational systems*. Hillsdale, NJ: Analytic Press.

Lifton, R. (1993). *The protean self*. New York: Basic Books.

Litowitz, B. (1998). An expanded developmental line for negation: Rejection, refusal, denial. *Journal of the American Psychoanalytic Association*, 46(1), pp. 121–148.

Loewald, H. (1978). Primary process, secondary process, and language. In *The Essential Loewald* (pp. 178–206). Hagerstown, MS: University Publishing Group, 2000.

Loewald, H. (1987). Sublimation: Inquiries into theoretical psychoanalysis. In *The Essential Loewald* (pp. 439–525). Hagerstown, MS: University Publishing Group, 2000.

Looker, T. (1998). "Mama, why don't your feet touch the ground?" Staying with the body and the healing moment. In L. Aron and F. Anderson (eds.), *Relational perspectives on the body* (pp. 237–262). Hillsdale, NJ: Analytic Press.

Luria, A. (1980). *Higher critical functions in man*, 2nd edn. New York: Basic Books.

Lyotard, J. F. (1999). *The postmodern condition: A report on knowledge*. Minneapolis, MN: University of Minneapolis Press.

MacIntyre, A. (1983). *After virtue*. Notre Dame, IN: University of Notre Dame Press.

Macmurray, J. (1949). *Conditions of freedom*. London: Humanities Press International.

Macmurray, J. (1957). *The self as agent*. London: Humanities Press International.

Macmurray, J. (1961). *Person in relation*. London: Humanities Press International.

McGuire, W. (1974). *The Freud/Jung letters*. Princeton, NJ: Princeton University Press.

McWilliams, N. (1994). *Psychoanalytic diagnosis*. London: Guilford Press.

Mahler, M. (1968). *On human symbiosis and the vicissitudes of individuation: Volume 1. Infantile psychosis*. New York: International Universities Press.

Main, M. (2000). The organized categories of infant, child and adult attachment. *Journal of the American Psychoanalytic Association*, 48(4), pp. 1055–1096.

Maldonado, J. and Spiegel, D. (1998). Trauma, dissociation, and hypnotizability. In J. Bremer and C. Marmar (eds.), *Trauma, memory, and dissociation* (pp. 57–106). Washington, DC: American Psychiatric Press.

Mann, C. (1995). The goals of interpersonal psychoanalysis. In M. Lionells, J. Fiscalini, C. Mann, and D. B. Stern (eds.), *The handbook of interpersonal psychoanalysis* (pp. 555–567). Hillsdale, NJ: Analytic Press.

Marcus, R. and Rosenberg, A. (1998). *Psychoanalytic version of the human condition*. New York: New York University Press.

Maroda, K. (1999). *Seduction, surrender, and transformation: Emotional engagement in the analytic process*. Hillsdale, NJ: Analytic Press.

Maroda, K. (2004). *The power of countertransference*. Hillsdale, NJ: Analytic Press.

Meares, R. (2000). *Intimacy and alienation: Memory trauma and personal being*. London: Routledge.

Meissner, W. (1978). *The paranoid process*. New York: Jason Aronson.

Meltzoff, A. and Moore, M. (1998). Infant intersubjectivity: Broadening the dialogue to include imitation, identity, and intention. In S. Braten (ed.),

Intersubjective communication and emotion in early ontogeny (pp. 47–62). Cambridge: Cambridge University Press.

Merleau-Ponty, M. (1964). *The primacy of perception.* Chicago: Northwestern University Press.

Messer, S., Sass, L., and Woolfolk, R. (1988). *Hermeneutics and psychological theory.* New Brunswick, NJ: Rutgers University Press.

Milner, M. (1952). Aspects of symbolization in comprehension of the not-self. *International Journal of Psychoanalysis*, 33, pp. 181–195.

Mintz, S. and Kellogg, S. (1988). *Domestic revolutions.* New York: Free Press.

Mitchell, J. (1986). *The selected Melanie Klein.* New York: Free Press.

Mitchell, S. (1988). *Relational concepts in psychoanalysis.* Cambridge, MA: Harvard University Press.

Mitchell, S. (1993). *Hope and dread in psychoanalysis.* New York: Basic Books.

Mitchell, S. (2000a). *Relationality.* Northvale, NJ: Jason Aronson.

Mitchell, S. (2000b). The origin of the object in the theories of Klein and Fairbairn. In J. Grotstein and D. Rinsley (eds.), *Fairbairn and the origin of object relations* (pp. 66–87). New York: Other Press.

Mitchell, S. and Greenberg, J. (1983). *Object relations in psychoanalytic theory.* Cambridge, MA: Harvard University Press.

Mittelmann, B. (1954). Motility in infants, children, and adults. *Psychoanalytic Study of the Child*, 9, pp. 142–177.

Moore, R. (1999). *The creation of reality in psychoanalysis.* Hillsdale, NJ: Analytic Press.

Morris, C. (1964). *Signification and significance.* Cambridge, MA: MIT Press.

Morris, H. (1993). Narrative representation, enactment, and psychoanalytic construction of history. *International Journal of Psychoanalysis*, 74, pp. 33–54.

Muller, J. (1996). *Beyond the psychoanalytic dyad.* London: Routledge.

Muller, J. and Richardson, W. (1982). *Lacan and language.* New York: International Universities Press.

Ogden, T. (1980). On the nature of schizophrenic conflict. *International Journal of Psychoanalysis*, 61, pp. 513–533.

Ogden, T. (1982a). *Projective identification and psychotherapeutic technique.* New York: Jason Aronson.

Ogden, T. (1982b). The schizophrenic state of non-experience. In L. Boyer and P. Giovacchini (eds.), *Technical factors in the treatment of the severely disturbed patient* (pp. 217–260). Northvale, NJ: Jason Aronson.

Ogden, T. (1985). On potential space. *International Journal of Psychoanalysis*, 66, pp. 129–141.

Ogden, T. (1986). *The matrix of the mind.* Northvale, NJ: Jason Aronson.

Ogden, T. (1989). *The primitive edge of experience.* Northvale, NJ: Jason Aronson.

Ogden, T. (1994). *Subjects of analysis.* Northvale, NJ: Jason Aronson.

Ogden, T. (1997). *Reverie and interpretation.* Northvale, NJ: Jason Aronson.

Ogden, T. (1999). Analysing the forms of aliveness and deadness of the transference-countertransference. In G. Kohon (ed.), *The dead mother* (pp. 128–148). London: Routledge.

Ogden, T. (2001). *Conversations at the frontier of dreaming.* Northvale, NJ: Jason Aronson.

Olds, D. (2000). A semiotic model of mind. *Journal of the American Psychoanalytic Association*, 48(2), pp. 497–529.

Ornstein, A. (1997). A developmental perspective on the sense of power, self-esteem, and destructive aggression. *The Annual of Psychoanalysis*, 25, pp. 145–154.

Palombo, J. (1993). Neurocognitive deficits, developmental distortions, and incoherent narratives. *Psychoanalytic Inquiry*, 13, pp. 85–102.

Parsons, M. (1999). Psychic reality, negation, and the analytic setting. In G. Kohon (ed.), *The dead mother* (pp. 59–75). London: Routledge.

Peirce, C. (1991). *Peirce on signs: Writings on semiotic by Charles Sanders Peirce*. J. Hoopes (ed.). Chapel Hill, NC: North Carolina University Press.

Peirce, C. (1998). *The essential Peirce: Selected philosophical writings, 1893–1913*. Edited by the Peirce Edition Project. Bloomington, IN: Indiana University Press.

Peterfreund, E. (1983). *The process of psychoanalytic therapy*. Hillsdale, NJ: Analytic Press.

Phillips, A. (1993). *On kissing, tickling, and being bored*. Cambridge, MA: Harvard University Press.

Pinkard, T. (2000). *Hegel: A biography*. Cambridge: Cambridge University Press.

Pizer, S. (1992). Negotiating potential space. *Psychoanalytic Dialogues*, 6(5), pp. 689–712.

Pizer, S. (1998). *Building bridges: The negotiation of paradox in psychoanalysis*. Hillsdale, NJ: Analytic Press.

Polkinghorne, D. (1988). *Narrative knowing and the human sciences*. Albany, NY: SUNY Press.

Porter, R. (1989). *A social history of madness*. London: Weidenfeld and Nicolson.

Rapaport, D. (1974). *The history of the concept of association of ideas*. New York: International Universities Press.

Ricoeur, P. (1970). *Freud and philosophy*. New Haven, CT: Yale University Press.

Ricoeur, P. (1984). *Time and narrative, vol. 1*. Chicago: University of Chicago Press.

Ringstrom, P. (2003). "Crunches," "(k)nots," and double binds – When what isn't happening is the most important. *Psychoanalytic Dialogues*, 13(2), pp. 193–205.

Rizzuto, A. M. (1998). *Why did Freud reject God?* New Haven, CT: Yale University Press.

Rizzuto, A. M. (2004). Paradoxical words and hope in psychoanalysis. *Psychoanalytic Psychology*, 21(2), pp. 203–213.

Rocha Leite Haudenschild, T. (1997). Towards symbolisation: 6-year-old from adhesive identification. *International Journal of Psychoanalysis*, 78, pp. 733–754.

Roth, P. (1995). *Zuckerman unbound*. New York: Vintage.

Russell, P. (1998). *Trauma, repetition, and affect: The works of Paul Russell*. J. Teicholz and D. Kriegman (eds.). New York: Other Press.

Rustin, J. (1997). Infancy, agency, and intersubjectivity. *Psychoanalytic Dialogues*, 7(1), 43–62.

Safran, J. and Muran, J. (1996). The resolution of ruptures in the therapeutic alliance. *Journal of Consulting and Clinical Psychology*, 64, pp. 447–458.

Safran, J. and Muran, J. (2000). *Negotiating the therapeutic alliance*. London: Guilford Press.

Sander, L. (1977). The regulation of exchange in infant–caretaker system and some aspects of the context–content relationship. In M. Lewis and L. Rosenblum (eds.), *Interaction, conversation, and the development of language* (pp. 133–156). New York: Wiley.

Sander, L. (1995). Identity and the experience of specificity in a process of recognition: Commentary on Seligman and Shanok. *Psychoanalytic Dialogues*, 5(4), pp. 579–592.

Sandler, J. and Sandler, A. (1998). *Internal objects revisited.* London: Karnac.

Sarbin, T. (1986). The narrative as a root metaphor for psychology. In T. Sarbin (ed.), *Narrative Psychology* (pp. 3–21). New York: Praeger Special Studies.

Sass, L. (1992). *Madness and modernism.* Cambridge, MA: Harvard University Press.

Sass, L. and Woolfolk, R. (1988). Psychoanalysis and the hermeneutic turn: A critique of narrative truth and historical truth. *Journal of the American Psychoanalytic Association*, 36(2), pp. 429–453.

Saussure, F. de (1959). *Course in general linguistics.* New York: McGraw-Hill.

Schafer, R. (1976). *A new language for psychoanalysis.* New Haven, CT: Yale University Press.

Schafer, R. (1983). *The analytic attitude.* New York: Basic Books.

Schafer, R. (1992). *Retelling a life: Narration and dialogue in psychoanalysis.* New York: Basic Books.

Scharfstein, B. (1980). *The philosophers: Their lives and the nature of their thought.* New York: Oxford University Press.

Schecter, D. (1973). On the emergence of human relatedness. In E. Witenberg (ed.), *Interpersonal exploration in psychoanalysis* (pp. 17–39). New York: Basic Books.

Segal, H. (1957). Notes on symbol formation. *International Journal of Psychoanalysis*, 38, pp. 391–397.

Shane, M., Shane, E., and Gales, M. (1997). *Intimate attachments.* New York: Guilford Press.

Shapiro, T. (1991). Words and feelings in the psychoanalytic dialogue. *Journal of the American Psychoanalytic Association*, 39, pp. 321–348.

Siegel, D. (1999). *The developing mind.* London: Guilford Press.

Silverman, D. (2003). Theorizing in the shadow of Foucault. *Psychoanalytic Dialogues*, 13(2), pp. 243–258.

Solomon, A. (2001). *The noonday demon.* New York: Scribner.

Sorenson, R. (2004). *Minding spirituality.* Hillsdale, NJ: Analytic Press.

Spence, D. (1982). *Narrative truth, historical truth.* Hillsdale, NJ: Analytic Press.

Spence, D. (1987). *The Freudian metaphor: Toward a paradigm change in psychoanalysis.* New York: W. W. Norton.

Spence, D. (1989). Narrative appeal versus historical validity. *Contemporary Psychoanalysis*, 25(3), pp. 517–524.

Spitz, R. (1957). *No and yes: On genesis of human communication.* New York: International Universities Press.

Spitz, R. (1965). *The first year of life: A psychoanalytic study of normal and deviant developmental object relations.* New York: International Universities Press.

Sroufe, A. (1995). *Emotional development.* Cambridge: Cambridge University Press.

Stern, D. B. (1997). *Unformulated experience: From dissociation to imagination in psychoanalysis.* Hillsdale, NJ: Analytic Press.

Stern, D. N. (1985). *The interpersonal world of the infant.* New York: Basic Books.

Stern, D. N. (1995). *The motherhood constellation: A unified view of parent–infant psychotherapy*. New York: Basic Books.

Stolorow, D., Atwood, G., and Brandchaft, B. (1994). *The intersubjective perspective*. Northvale, NJ: Jason Aronson.

Stolorow, D., Brandchaft, B., and Atwood, G. (1987). *Psychoanalytic treatment: An intersubjective approach*. Hillsdale, NJ: Analytic Press.

Strenger, C. (1998). The desire for self-creation. *Psychoanalytic Dialogues*, 8(5), pp. 625–655.

Strupp, H. (1982). Psychoanalytic failure: Reflections on an autobiographical account. *Contemporary Psychoanalysis*, 18, pp. 235–250.

Sullivan, H. (1953). *The interpersonal theory of psychiatry*. New York: W. W. Norton.

Sulloway, F. (1992). *Freud: Biologist of the mind*. Cambridge, MA: Harvard University Press.

Szasz, T. (1970). *The manufacture of madness*. New York: Harper Torchbooks.

Taylor, C. (1989). *Sources of the self: The making of the modern identity*. Cambridge, MA: Harvard University Press.

Terr, L. (1990). *Too scared to cry*. New York: Harper and Row.

Trevarthen, C. (1998). The concept and foundations of infant intersubjectivity. In S. Braten (ed.), *Intersubjective communication and emotion in early ontogeny* (pp. 15–46). Cambridge: Cambridge University Press.

Tronick, E. (1989). Emotion and emotional communication in infants. *American Psychologist*, 44, pp. 112–119.

Tronick, E. and Cohn, J. (1989). Infant–mother face-to-face interaction: Age and gender differences in coordination and the occurrence of miscoordination. *Child Development*, 60, pp. 85–92.

Tronick, E. and Gianino, A. (1986). Interactive mismatch and repair: Challenges to the coping infant. *Zero to Three Bulletin of the National Center Clinical Infant Program*, 5, pp. 1–6.

Turner, V. (1974). *Dramas, fields, and metaphors*. Ithaca, NY: Cornell University Press.

Tustin, F. (1984). Autistic shapes. *International Review of Psychoanalysis*, 11, pp. 279–290.

Ulman, R. and Brothers, D. (1988). *The shattered self: A psychoanalytic study of trauma*. Hillsdale, NJ: Analytic Press.

Van Buren, J. (1991). The psychoanalytic semiosis of absence or, the semiotic murder of the mother. *International Review of Psychoanalysis*, 18, pp. 249–263.

Van der Kolk, B. and McFarlane, A. (1996). The black hole of trauma. In B. van der Kolk, A. McFarlane, and L. Weisaeth (eds.), *Traumatic stress* (pp. 3–23). New York: Guilford Press.

Ver Eecke, W. (1984). *Saying "no."* Pittsburgh, PA: Duquesne University Press.

Verhaeghe, P. (1999). *Does the woman exist: From Freud's hysteric to Lacan's feminine*. New York: Other Press.

Volf, M. (1996). *Exclusion and embrace*. Nashville, TN: Abingdon Press.

Vygotsky, L. (1978). *Mind in society*. Cambridge, MA: Harvard University Press.

Walsh, N. (1996). Life in death. In C. Strozier and M. Flynn (eds.), *Trauma and self* (pp. 245–254). Lanham, MD: Rowman and Littlefield.

West, C. and Hewlett, S. (1998). *War against parents*. Boston, MA: Houghton Mifflin.

Westen, D. (2002). The language of psychoanalytic discourse. *Psychoanalytic Dialogues*, 12(6), pp. 857–898.

White, G. (1994). Affecting culture: Emotion and morality in everyday life. In S. Kitayama and H. Markus (eds.), *Emotion and culture: Empirical studies of mental influence* (pp. 219–239). Washington, DC: American Psychological Association.

Winnicott, D. (1945). Primitive emotional development. *International Journal of Psychoanalysis*, 26, pp. 137–143.

Winnicott, D. (1956). Primary maternal preoccupation. In *Collected Papers* (pp. 300–305). London: Tavistock, 1958.

Winnicott, D. (1964). Book review: Memories, dreams, reflections by C. G. Jung. *International Journal of Psychoanalysis*, 45, pp. 450–455.

Winnicott, D. (1965). Ego distortion in terms of true and false self. In *The maturational process and the facilitating environment* (pp. 140–152). New York: International Universities Press.

Winnicott, D. (1971). *Playing and reality*. London: Routledge.

Winnicott, D. (1986). *Home is where we start*. New York: W. W. Norton.

Winnicott, D. (1989). *Psychoanalytic explorations*. Cambridge, MA: Harvard University Press.

Winnicott, D. (1990). *Delinquency and deprivation*. London: Routledge.

Wolf, E. (1998). Optimal responsiveness and disruption-restorations. In H. Bacal (ed.), *Optimal responsiveness* (pp. 237–248). Northvale, NJ: Jason Aronson.

Wright, K. (1991). *Vision and separation: Between mother and baby*. Northvale, NJ: Jason Aronson.

Yalom, I. (1980). *Existential psychotherapy*. New York: Basic Books.

Young-Bruehl, E. (2000). Beyond the female homosexual. *Studies in Gender and Sexuality*, 1, pp. 97–124.

Index